E-Z RULES®

For

The Bankruptcy Code

With Selected Provisions From
The Uniform Fraudulent Conveyances Act
and Article 9 of the Uniform Commercial Code

BY:

Jack S. Ezon, Esq.
and
Jeffrey S. Dweck, Esq.

Consulting Editor:
Professor Wayne Greenwald

LAW REVIEW PUBLISHING
Old Tappan, New Jersey
(800) 371-1231

Library of Congress Catalog Card Number: 98-

ISBN # 1-887-426-31-0

LAW RULES PUBLISHING CORPORATION
River Vale, New Jersey

Printed in the United States of America

NOTE: E-Z Rules is not a substitute for the actual text of the official Federal Bankruptcy Code, and should not be quoted or cited to. E-Z Rules is meant to be used as a quick reference and guide to understanding The Bankruptcy Code, and cannot completely replace them. In addition, the "overview" for each section of the Bankruptcy Code is not meant to be a comprehensive teaching tool, as it does not consider case law. It is merely meant to provide the general scheme and remind the reader of certain key points of the Code.

E-Z RULES FOR BANKRUPTCY

To Robin

IMPORTANT NOTE

All rules follow the format of the Federal Bankruptcy Code. Where the actual subsection letter or number of the rule is used, it is enclosed between parenthesis "( )." <u>All other numbers and letters are produced by E-Z Rules</u> and therefore, should not be cited to when discussing a rule. "E-Z Rules bullets" have been added in addition to the official sub-sections found in the actual code in order to make the substance more comprehensive.

For Example, in §362 there are eight sections, referred to in E-Z Rules as (a) - (h). These are actual sections used in the Code and may be called, for example, "subsection (a)." Under §362(a), however, there are items labeled "i.", "1.", and so forth. Since these are not enclosed in parenthesis, they are not the letters or numbers used by the Code.

USING E-Z RULES FOR
THE BANKRUPTCY CODE

Welcome to E-Z Rules, a new way of presenting rules and laws, designed to put the "ease" into legalese!

E-Z Rules translates the confusing statutory language of the Bankruptcy Code into plain and simple English. E-Z Rules are designed to give you quick access to important information you often need, without the unnecessary strain of dissecting long, monotonous, statutory texts. And remember, E-Z Rules does this WITHOUT EXCLUDING ANY KEY POINTS OF THE ACTUAL RULE OR STATUTE!

E-Z Rules is easy to use. It has been carefully tailored to meet the needs of both the law student and today's active law firm. In order to take full advantage of the E-Z Rules system, it would be beneficial to review some of its features:

- E-Z Rules is laid out so that the entire substance of a rule or statute could be grasped at a single glance.

- The rules are boldly titled for quick spotting.

- All rules follow the format of the Bankruptcy Code. Where the actual subsection letter or number of the rule is used, it is enclosed between parenthesis "( )." All other numbers and letters are produced by E-Z Rules and therefore, should not be cited to when discussing a rule. "E-Z Rules bullets" have been added in addition to the official sub-sections found in the actual code in order to make the substance more comprehensive.

  For Example, in §362 there are eight sections, referred to in E-Z Rules as (a) - (h). These are actual sections used in the Code and may be called, for example, "subsection (a)." Under §362(a), however, there are items labeled "i.", "1.", and so forth. Since these are not enclosed in parenthesis, they are not the letters or numbers used by the Code.

- Key words and phrases are emphasized with either bold, italic, or underline. All defined terms begin with Capital Letters so as to alert the reader that the term has a definition provided by the rules. This not only helps in making the rules easier to understand, but has been proven to help the user focus in on pivotal words or phrases, which may otherwise go unnoticed. In addition, certain words have been abbreviated in order to facilitate quick referencing and easier reading.

<u>Note</u>: E-Z Rules is not a substitute for the actual text of the Bankruptcy Code, and should not be quoted or cited to. E-Z Rules is meant to be used as a quick reference and guide to understanding the Bankruptcy Code, and cannot completely replace it. In addition, the "overview" for each section of the "Roadmap to the Bankruptcy Code" is not meant to be a comprehensive teaching tool. It is merely meant to remind the reader of certain key points.

SUMMARY TABLE OF CONTENTS

SECTION	PAGE
ROADMAP TO THE BANKRUPTCY CODE	1
OVERVIEW	3
TABLE OF CONTENTS FOR THE BANKRUPTCY CODE	147
THE BANKRUPTCY CODE IN E-Z RULES FORMAT	158
INDEX	321

THE E-Z RULES ROADMAP

One of the most beneficial features of E-Z Rules is its Roadmap to the Bankruptcy Code. This section consists of an overview of the key topics of the Code and the relevant rules or sections alongside. The "Roadmap" places all sections needed for a given topic at your fingertips. Please note that the overview appears in a different typeface than the text of the rule and is surrounded by a border. Also note that at times, only a portion of a rule is included in the overview (its title is not bolded).

The Roadmap will be most beneficial to readers who are looking to analyze problems. By using the roadmap as a checklist, it will help the reader breakdown a problem and "attack" it in a comprehensive and organized fashion and in accordance with the Code sections.

Studying the Roadmap will also help the reader grasp the concepts behind the Bankruptcy Code and get an overall picture of the relevant law.

The use of the Roadmap is one of the most beneficial features of E-Z Rules, and we strongly recommend it.

BANKRUPTCY

I. Administration and Commencement of the Case
   A) General Overview
   B) Commencement of the Case
   C) Appointment of the Trustee or DIP (§321, §322, §1104, §1107)
   D) Application of State Law

II. Bankruptcy

   A) The Bankruptcy Estate
      1. Inclusions (§541)
      2. Exclusions (§541)
      3. Exemptions (§522)

   B) The Automatic Stay (§362; §361)
      1. Introduction
      2. Damages
      3. Grounds for Lifting the Stay
      4. Subjects of the Automatic Stay

   C) Claims in Bankruptcy
      1. The Proof of Claim (§501) - Late Claims
      2. Allowance of Claims (§502)
      3. Valuation of Collateral (§502; §507)
      4. Bifurcation (§506)

   D) Rights to Setoff (§553; §506(a))

   E) Liquidation and Priority of Distribution of Estate (§507; §503; §509; §510; §724; §726; §727)

III. Powers of the Trustee:
   A) Turnover Orders (§542)
   B) Trustee's Use of Secured Collateral (§363)
   C) Rights over Executory Contracts or Leases (§365)
   D) Strong –Arm Power to Avoid Liens (§544, §545, §565)
   E) Right to Avoid Voidable Preferences(§547)
      1. The Voidable Preference
      2. Special Timing Rules
      3. The Savings Clauses

4. <u>Who Trustee May Recover Voidable Preferences From</u>
   (§550)
F) Right to Avoid Fraudulent Conveyances (§548)

IV. <u>Other Rights:</u>
   A. Chapter 13 Proceedings
   B. Redemption Rights (§554)
   C. Discharge (§523; §524; §727)
   D. Chapter 11 Proceedings: The Reorganization Plan

I. ADMINISTRATION AND COMMENCEMENT OF THE CASE

A) GENERAL OVERVIEW:

OVERVIEW ───────────────────────────────

- The Bankruptcy Code was created to help parties in financial distress get a "fresh start." The goals are to:
  - 1) Pay Creditors some "compromised" payment so that all "similarly situated" Creditors get equal treatment, and
  - 2) Work out a payment plan so that an Insolvent Debtor can emerge solvent.

- There are various forms of Bankruptcy relief.
  - ☞ Liquidations - Chapter 7 of the Code, which focuses on proper liquidation and distribution of the Debtor's assets.
  - ☞ Reorganizations - Chapters 9, 11, 12, and 13, oriented to helping the Debtor restructuring its finances and getting a "fresh start." Creditors get paid pursuant to a "plan" (which is subject to the Bankruptcy Court's approval).

B) COMMENCEMENT OF THE CASE:

OVERVIEW ───────────────────────────────

1) The Petition Date

- The Petition Date is probably the most significant date in any bankruptcy proceeding. It is this date which starts the clock ticking for many deadlines and, most significantly, ends the "Preference Period," which begins 90 days before the Petition is filed (1 Year for "Insiders" as will be discussed later).

- Most Transfers made during this "Preference Period" may be "voided" by the Bankruptcy Estate, forcing the Person who received the Transfer to return the property to the Estate.

- The Petition Date is used to calculate various other statutes of limitation.

2) Automatic Stay on All Property:

- On the Petition Date, the Bankruptcy Court freezes all assets of the Debtor as well as all claims or proceedings against the Debtor. This freeze is known as an "Automatic Stay." The "Stay" is created for various reasons, which include the following:

    ☞ It gives the Debtor time to assess its assets and, liabilities and develop a strategy for maximizing its opportunities in Bankruptcy.

    ☞ It allows the Bankruptcy Court time to determine what property belongs to the Bankruptcy Estate and what belongs to the Debtor.

    ☞ It allows the Bankruptcy Court to distribute property in an orderly fashion, rather than having mass chaos result from Creditors grabbing whatever assets they can get their hands on, possibly leaving "aggressive Creditors" with more than they are entitled.

3) Property of the Estate:

- The Bankruptcy Code divides all of the Debtor's property into two categories:
    1. Property of the Estate: Most of the Debtor's property will be deemed "Estate Property." This property belongs to the "Bankruptcy Estate" and will be used to satisfy Debtor's Debts.
    2. Debtor's Property: Other property of the Debtor, such as "Exempt Property" or "Post-Petition Property," will not belong to the Estate, and may not be subject to certain of the Bankruptcy Court's powers (such as the Automatic Stay). For Personal Debtors, this property will not be used to pay Creditors. Instead, it will be used to help the Debtor get his "fresh start."
- Think of the Bankruptcy Estate and the Debtor as two separate entities.

- Once the Debtor files his Petition, all property deemed "Property of the Estate" flows into a new Entity known as the "Bankruptcy Estate." The property of the Bankruptcy Estate will be used to satisfy the claims of the Debtor's Creditors. Meanwhile, the Debtor may use his own assets on a "going-forward basis" without being subject to the Bankruptcy Court's control.

C) APPOINTMENT OF THE TRUSTEE AND THE DIP:

OVERVIEW

- The Bankruptcy Court, the United States Trustee or the Creditors may appoint someone to manage the assets of the Bankruptcy Estate. This Person is known either as a "Trustee" or a "Debtor-in-Possession."
  - ☞ Trustee – the Person is known as a Trustee if the Person appointed is an Outside Party.
  - ☞ Debtor-in-Possession ("DIP") – the Person is known as a "DIP" if the appointed Person is the Debtor himself or an "Insider" of the Debtor company under Chapters 11 and 12.

- Note: On most occasions in the Bankruptcy Code (and in this book) when the term "Trustee" is used, it includes a DIP. The powers of a Trustee under the Code also apply to a DIP (see §1107, §1203, and §1304).

D) APPLICATION OF STATE LAW:

OVERVIEW

- State law plays an important role in Federal Bankruptcy law. There are many occasions when the Code defers to State law.

- The Uniform Commercial Code ("UCC") is a state-adopted body of law. Article 9 of the UCC deals with secured parties and Security Interests in collateral. Even under Bankruptcy, the UCC usually dictates when a Creditor is secured or unsecured, and what priority a Creditor will have. Article 9 of the UCC is an integral body of law in Bankruptcy.

7

- **Fraudulent Conveyance Law**: The UFCA (Uniform Fraudulent Conveyance Act) and the UFTA (Uniform Fraudulent Transfer Act) are State laws governing fraudulent Transfer claims beyond the powers given to a Trustee in bankruptcy.

- **Other State Law Applications**: State law will come into play in various other areas, including:
  - ☞ Exemptions – Certain property may be exempt from the Bankruptcy Estate according to State laws.
  - ☞ Many contract claims and rights of payment are governed by State law.
  - ☞ Property and ownership rights are governed by State law.

II. BANKRUPTCY

A) THE BANKRUPTCY ESTATE:

1. Inclusions (§541):

OVERVIEW ————————————————————————————

- One of the first and most important steps in working through a bankruptcy problem is determining what is considered part of the "Bankruptcy Estate." This is because property of the Bankruptcy Estate is subject to the Bankruptcy laws. Property owned by a Creditor which is not property of the Bankruptcy Estate may be retrieved by a Creditor without restriction (ex: A Trade Creditor delivers goods to the Debtor on consignment. These goods are still owned by the Creditor. Since they are owned by the Creditor and are not part of the Bankruptcy Estate, the Creditor may retrieve them).

- If such property were part of the Bankruptcy Estate, however, the Creditor would have to ask the Bankruptcy Court's permission before taking the property.

- There are other reasons why determining what is in the Estate is important:

  ☞ Property Subject to the Automatic Stay: Property which is part of the estate will be subject to the Automatic Stay placed on all of the Debtor's property (subject to exceptions in §362, §522 and §541) (see "Automatic Stay " below).

  ☞ Evaluating the Estate: The Value of the property in the estate will ultimately determine how much parties receive from the Bankruptcy Estate and may determine what property can be sold or distributed.

  ☞ Validity of Claims: In order for a Creditor to get money from the estate it must file a "proof of claim" with the Bankruptcy Court. The court will only consider "admissible claims" (usually property in which the Debtor had an interest before the Bankruptcy Petition was filed) (See "PROOF OF CLAIMS" below).

- Property of the Estate:

  ☞ All Legal or Equitable interests that the Debtor has in property at the time the Bankruptcy Petition is filed will be considered Property of the Estate.

  ☞ Only property owned by or entitled to the Debtor before the Petition for Bankruptcy is filed may be property of the Bankruptcy Estate (subject to certain exceptions in §541(b) and (c)).

  ☞ Note: After the Petition is filed, any property acquired by the Estate or proceeds from the Estate's property (such as insurance proceeds on Estate Property) will belong to the Estate and not the Debtor.

  ☞ Note: Estate Property may be in the possession of a third party during or prior to Bankruptcy. The third party is required to "turn over" such property to the Bankruptcy Trustee (ex: Debtor gives Joe $1,000 as payment for an old bill, 10 days before Debtor files its Petition. The $1,000 is considered part of the Bankruptcy Estate because it is considered a "Preference" (see "PREFERENCES" below). Joe is obligated to return ("turn over") the $1,000 payment to the bankruptcy Trustee. He must then file a "claim" with the court. After filing the claim (pursuant to §502), he will be put on equal ground with all other Creditors of his class when trying to get his money back).

  ☞ Classifying Pre- and Post-Petition Property is therefore one of the most basic elements in determining what is Property of the Estate.
      - ➤ §522 describes property exempt from the estate
      - ➤ §541 describes Property of the Estate (note the difference between §541 and §502 -- §502 deals with admissible claims and not Property of the Estate).

  Understanding these sections will help one get a strong grasp on one of the most fundamental bankruptcy questions.

- **Applications:** Examples of property as Property of the Estate:

1) **Amortized Loans, Interest Payments** (for interest owed to Debtor): Interest on amortized loans is partially pre-Petition interest. Only interest which has actually accrued will be Property of the Estate, even if it is not due before the Petition date (§502(b) acts as an acceleration clause for these purposes. Ex: If a note for $5 million would be due in three more years, a bankruptcy would cause the note to be due immediately.).

2) **Abandoned Property:**
   a) Abandoned property is not considered Property of the Estate (See §554).
   b) Property cannot be abandoned if it is valuable or if there is an Environmental Claim on it, unless significant tax burdens will arise with a capital gain from the sale.

3) **Dissolved Partnership Interests:** "Winding-down" interests are considered Estate Property, even though some of the income being earned by such interests may accrue after the Petition date.

4) **Spendthrift Trusts:**
   - A Spendthrift Trust is usually not Property of the Estate (though this is very much determined by State law).
   - Most courts apply State law -- if State law enforces and allows such Spendthrift Trusts, it will not be considered part of the Estate.
   - A Creditor cannot garnish a Spendthrift Trust (§541(c)(2)).
   - If Debtor is also the Settler of the Spendthrift trust (i.e. the Person who created it), this restriction will usually not apply (i.e. Creditors can garnish the trust).
   - Control - Debtor's lack of control over the Trust is an important factor in finding whether or not it is part of the Estate.

5) **Pensions** (ERISA's) :
   - Money put into a pension plan is not considered income; money coming out of a pension is deemed income.

- Creditors cannot garnish ERISA funds since "non-bankruptcy law" (i.e. the ERISA Statute), which §541(c)(2) directs us to look at, prohibits garnishment of pension plans.
- Some courts hold that ERISA plans are Property of the Estate because the Debtor has control over Transfers.

6) Executory Contracts for Personal Services:
- Income of an Individual Debtor from a contingent or executory contract must be pro-rated (§541(a)(6))
- Pre-Petition income =

> Total Income (from Contract) x "Performance Ratio"

- Performance Ratio:

> Amount of work done before the Petition
> ---
> Amount of work to be done after Petition

- The remainder of the contract income is post-Petition property (ex: Debtor receives $5,000 to paint Robin's house. Debtor files a Petition for Bankruptcy on April 1. By April 1, Debtor only painted ¾ of Robin's house. Pre-Petition income = ¾(5,000) = $3,750.00 (as pre-Petition property) (unless exempt under State law). The remaining $1,250 would not be Property of the Estate.).

7) Tax Refunds:
- Income from Tax Refunds must be pro-rated.
- Pre-Petition income =

> Total Tax Refund x "Tax Ratio"

- "Tax Ratio" =

> Number of Months in Bankruptcy refund year
> ---
> Number of Months not in Bankruptcy refund year

- A Tax refund may be considered a "General Intangible" (under §9-106 of the UCC). Therefore, a secured party with a Security Interest in general intangibles would have a secured claim over a tax refund.

•   Special Note: If the refund arises from work for "Personal Services" by an individual Debtor then it would not be included as part of Estate Property (§541(a)(6)) (since income from post-Petition Personal services is not Property of the Estate).

8)   Royalties: Royalties are considered proceeds of Intellectual Property; thus, it all depends on who owns the rights to the Intellectual Property (ex: who is the copyright owner). If the Debtor owns the Intellectual Property then royalty payments would be Property of the Estate for periods in which the royalties accrued before the Petition was filed.

9)   Tenancy by Entirety:
•   Property owned jointly by spouses may (in most states) be classified as a Tenancy by the Entirety ("TBE").
  ☞   Whether or not a TBE is included in the estate depends on how each State treats the TBE:
   ➢   Some states create a "separate Entity" which owns the TBE, thus excluding it from Debtor's property. This type of TBE will therefore not be part of the Estate.
   ➢   Some states consider the Debtor a "joint owner," thus making the property part of the Estate. The Debtor's spouse will become a Secured Creditor with a right to the monetary Value of her portion of the property.
   ➢   Some states give the Debtor a co-tenancy + a right of survivorship, which becomes the Property of the Estate; thus, the estate will have the right of survivorship, but not the present right to possession (the Debtor's spouse and family can still remain on TBE property).
   ➢   Living in Estate Home: Even though the Debtor remains in his home (which becomes Property of the Estate), many courts have ruled that he does not have to pay rent, since such rent is considered "post-Petition" rent.
10)   Tenancy in Common: The portion belonging to the Debtor becomes part of the estate (and may be sold if not apportionable (under §363)).
•   Rental income: If the entire property becomes part of the estate then post-Petition rents should also be a part of estate.

11) <u>Post-Petition Rents/Proceeds:</u> (§541(a)(6))
- Rents and Proceeds from Estate Property are considered Property of the Estate, even if they are realized after the bankruptcy Petition was filed (§541(a)(6)) (ex: A building is deemed Property of the Estate. Any rents or sale proceeds on that building will be Property of the Estate).
- Rents from Estate Property which are normally Property of the Estate and considered proceeds of collateral (for Secured Creditors).
- Proceeds from Personal services by an <u>Individual Debtor</u> are <u>not</u> Property of the Estate, even if earned before the Petition. (<u>Note</u>: We attribute only the Value of the service to the Debtor. The Estate will get the proceeds from the use of the Estate's property, tools, goodwill, office property, work of employees, etc. used to produce the income.).

12) <u>Recovered Property</u>: Any property which the Trustee recovers under §542 (ex: "Voidable Preference" property (§541(a)(5)) is Property of the Estate.

13) <u>Property of Converted Cases</u>: In a case converted from Chapter 13, the estate will include property of the Debtor before the Chapter 13 Petition was filed, but will <u>not</u> include property/wages obtained between the Chapter 13 Petition and the conversion Petition.

14) <u>Tort Claims</u>: A Debtor's claims for injuries arising before the Petition will become part of the estate, even if they are unliquidated.

15) <u>Constructive Trusts</u>: Property over which the Debtor is a constructive Trustee will usually not become part of the estate (ex: loans given for school; Note, however, that many jurisdictions are split on this issue).

16) <u>Property Foreclosed but not Sold</u>:
- A Debtor has the following rights in the property belonging to the estate:
  - ☞ The right to redeem the property
  - ☞ The right to the excess proceeds of the sale
- Relief from the Automatic Stay is therefore necessary in order to proceed with a foreclosure sale, even if the property has already been foreclosed upon (since the Debtor still has a property interest at stake).

17) <u>Property Purchased by the Estate</u> after Bankruptcy is Estate
Property (§541(a)(7)). (Rationale: Since it is the Estate and not the
Debtor purchasing the property, the purchased property remains
Estate Property).

2. Exclusions:

OVERVIEW ─────────────────────────────────

The following property is <u>never</u> part of the bankruptcy estate:

* <u>Post-Petition Income from Personal Services</u>: Income earned by an
individual Debtor for his Personal services.
* <u>Post-Petition income from Personal Services with Estate Property</u>:
Profits, proceeds, or rents earned from Estate Property in
conjunction with an individual Debtor in rendering Personal
services after the Petition. (ex: Debtor mows lawn with a
lawnmower which is Estate Property) (§541(a)(6)).
* <u>Rights of Others</u>: Any power which the Debtor may exercise solely
for the benefit of another Person is <u>not</u> Estate Property
(§541(b)(1)).
* <u>Interest as a Lessee</u>: A lease interest on an expired non-residential
real property lease (ex: interest on a Security deposit) (§541(b)(2)).
* <u>Cash Proceeds from a Money Order</u>: Certain proceeds of any
interest in cash which are proceeds from a money order
(§541(b)(5)).
* <u>Higher Education</u> participations (§541(b)(3)).
* Certain Interests in liquid gases (§541(b)(4)).

RELEVANT SECTIONS: §541

§541: Property of the Estate:

(a)   The Estate: The Bankruptcy Estate (created by the
commencement of the case under §301, §302 or §303) is
comprised of all of the following property (regardless of where it
is located or who holds it):

(1) All <u>Legal</u> or <u>Equitable</u> interests in property of the Debtor as of the commencement of the Petition (subject to §541(b) and (c)(2) below).

(2) All interests of the Debtor and his spouse in Community Property that is:
   (A) Under the Debtor's control (sole or joint); or
   (B) Liable for a claim against the Debtor or for both a claim against the Debtor and the Debtor's spouse

(3) Any interest in property which the Trustee recovers (under §329(b), §363(n), §543, §550, §553 or §723)

(4) Any Interest in property which is either:
   a) Preserved for the benefit of the estate (under §510(c)); or
   b) Ordered Transferred to the Estate under §551

(5) Any interest that would have been Property of the Estate if:
   a) The Debtor would have had an interest in it on the date of filing; or
   b) The Debtor acquired/became entitled to the property within <u>6 months</u> after the filing, <u>and</u> the property was acquired:
     1) By devise, bequest, or inheritance; or
     2) As a result of a Property Settlement Agreement (with the Debtor's spouse); or
     3) As a Beneficiary of a Life Insurance plan

(6) Proceeds, Product, Offspring, Rents, or Profits from Estate property, unless earned by an <u>individual debtor</u> after the Petition (Personal Services).

(7) Any interest in property acquired by the <u>Estate</u> (<u>not</u> the Debtor) <u>after</u> the Petition was filed.

(b) Exclusions from Estate:

(1) Any Power which the Debtor may exercise solely for the benefit of another Person or entity.

(2) Any interest as a lessee under an expired non-residential real property lease, where the lease has terminated by its terms before the Petition date (or interest in a lease that terminated during the case – that ceases to be included)

(3) Any eligibility for Debtor to participate in higher Education Act of 1965.

(4) Any Interest of Debtor in liquid or gaseous hydrocarbons. * * *

(5) Cash Proceeds - Any interest in Cash or cash equivalents
which are proceeds from the sale of a Money Order that is
made:
   (A) On or after the date 14 days before the Petition date;
       and
   (B) Under an agreement with a money order issuer that
       prohibits commingling such proceeds with the Debtor's
       property (even if the proceeds were commingled
       anyway, contrary to the agreement)

(c) Superceding Contract Clauses:
   (1) This section applies (subject to §541(c)(2)) regardless of
        contractual restrictions that:
        (A) Restrict or condition the Transfer of the Debtor's
            interest by the Debtor; or
        (B) Require the Debtor to return property or terminate its
            interest in its property in the case of bankruptcy or
            insolvency, before giving it to the Bankruptcy Estate.
   (2) Pension Plans/Spendthrift Trust: A restriction on a Transfer
        of a trust for the benefit of the Debtor is enforceable under
        the Bankruptcy Code, if the Spendthrift Trust/ERISA Plan
        is enforceable under non-Bankruptcy law.

(d) Debtor's Legal Title in Trust Property:
   (1) If the Debtor only holds the legal title to property and no
        equitable interest (ex: he is the Trustee of a trust), only the
        legal interest will become Property of the Estate (and not the
        equitable interest).
   (2) Note: This section does not apply to Real Property held in
        Trust (because §541(a)(3) makes property recoverable under
        §544(a)(3): REAL PROPERTY OF THE ESTATE)

3. Exemptions (§522):

OVERVIEW ─────────────────────────────────
• Section 522 exempts property which would otherwise become
  Property of the Estate under §541.
• Available to Individuals: The exemptions under §522 are only
  available to Individual Debtors.
• Choice of Exemptions: The Bankruptcy Code gives the Debtor a

---

choice of two exemption "plans," but 40 of 50 states have disallowed (i.e. "opted out of") exemptions under §522(b)(1) (i.e. §522(d) exemptions are not available) and only allow State law and other federal exemptions to apply.

- State Law Exemptions: Each State may exempt additional Debtor property from the estate (§522(b)).
- Creditor's Objection Required: §522 requires the Debtor to file a list of all property which the Debtor wants exempt from the Estate. Even if that property is not exempt under any law, it will become exempt if a Creditor does not object to it in a timely manner (§522(l)).
- Partially Exempt Property: When property is partially exempt, the property becomes part of the estate, and the Debtor retains the equivalent of a Security Interest in the property for the monetary Value of the exempt portion.
- Avoiding Liens: Liens which "impair an exemption" under §522 may sometimes be avoided (§522(f)). If the Lien impairs certain exempt property, it may be avoided.

RELEVANT SECTIONS: §522

---

§522: Exemptions:

(a) Definitions:
  (1) "Dependent" includes spouse (whether or not actually dependent)
  (2) "Value" = Fair Market Value as of:
    a. The date of the Petition; or
    b. The date property became part of the estate if after the Petition is filed

(b) Available Exemptions:
  i) An Individual Debtor may choose to exempt property either under §522(b)(1) or §522(b)(2).
  ii) In cases where the proceeding is for Joint Debtors (filed under §302) or Husband and Wife (filed under §301 or §303), both Debtors must choose to exempt property under the same subsection. If they cannot agree, they are deemed to have chosen §522(b)(1) (unless not permitted by local law)
  iii) Exemptions Choices: A Debtor may choose to exempt the following property under either of the two sections:

18

(1) Property specified in §522(d), unless applicable State law specifically does not authorize the exemption

(2) Other Exempt Property:

  (A) Any property exempt under both:

    1. State or <u>Local</u> law where the Debtor was domiciled in the <u>180 days</u> (or for most of the 180 days) immediately preceding the Petition date (the law applicable on the Petition date governs); OR

    2. <u>Federal</u> Law (other than §522(d)); and

  (B) Any property where the Debtor has an interest as a Tenant by the Entirety or Joint Tenant exempt from process under non-bankruptcy law

(c) Effect of Exemption: Exempt property will not be subject to any Pre-Petition Debt (including "Relation Back" Claims under §502) unless:

(1) The Debt falls under §523(a)(1) or §523(a)(5) and is <u>not</u> discharged; or

(2) The Debt is secured by:

  (A) A Lien that is not void:

    (i) Under Voidable Preference Law (§544, §545, §547, §548, §549, or §724(a))

    (ii) After Bifurcation Lien (not void under §506(d)); or

  (B) A <u>Tax Lien</u> or

(3) The Debt is non-dischargeable under §523(a)(4) or §523(a)(6) because it is owed by an institution-affiliated party of an insured depository institution to a regulatory agency (for Federal depository institutions) acting as a conservator, receiver or liquidating agent for the institution; or

(4) The case is dismissed.

(d) §522(b)(1) Exemptions: The following property will be exempt from the Bankruptcy Estate if the Debtor elects the §522(b)(1) exemption:

(1) <u>Homestead</u>: The Debtor's aggregate interest in Real or Personal Property used as a Residence (including co-op stock) or the Debtor's interest in a Burial Plot (for the Debtor or a dependent) up to $15,000[1]

(2) The Debtor's interest in a <u>motor vehicle</u> up to $2,400[2]

---

[1] $16,150 as of April 1, 1998.
[2] $2,575 as of April 1, 1998.

(3) Personal Goods - up to $8,000[3] total (and no more than $400,[4] per item), in goods which are used primarily for the personal, family, or household use of the Debtor (or a dependent), which includes:
   a. Household Furniture/Household Goods
   b. Clothing
   c. Appliances
   d. Books
   e. Animals
   f. Crops
   g. Musical Instruments

(4) Jewelry - the Debtor's aggregate interest in personal jewelry, up to $1,000[5]

(5) Miscellaneous Exemption:
   a) $800[6] in any other property; and
   b) $7,500[7] of any unused Homestead exemption amount (exempt under §522(d)(1))

(6) Debtor's interest in his Tools of Trade up to $1,500[8] (i.e. professional books, tools)

(7) Unmatured Life Insurance contracts (unless it is a credit Life Insurance Contract)

(8) Debtor's interest in a dividend from an Unmatured Insurance Interest up to $8,000[9] - Value of Turnover Property Recovered

(9) Medically Prescribed Medicine or Health Aids

(10) The Debtor's Right to Receive:
   (A) Social Security Benefits, Unemployment, and other Government Assistance
   (B) Veteran's Benefits
   (C) Disability or Unemployment Benefits
   (D) Alimony, Child Support reasonably necessary for the Debtor's support

(11) Payment under a Stock Pension/Profit-sharing plan, unless:
* * * *

(12) The Debtor's Right to Receive property traceable to:
   (A) An Award under a Crime Victim's reparation Law

---

[3] $8,625 as of April 1, 1998.
[4] $425 as of April 1, 1998.
[5] $1,075 as of April 1, 1998.
[6] $850 as of April 1, 1998.
[7] $8,075 as of April 1, 1998.
[8] $1,625 as of April 1, 1998.
[9] $8,625 as of April 1, 1998.

   (B) Payment on account for Wrongful Death Action
   (C) Payment under a Life Insurance Contract from
        deceased family member
   (D) Up to $\underline{\$15,000}^{10}$ of a personal injury claim (not
        including Pain, Suffering, or Pecuniary Loss)
   (E) Compensation for Loss of Future Earnings from a
        dependent
(e) Waivers Unenforceable: The following actions will be
     unenforceable:
   1) The Debtor waives an exemption of §522(d) property in
       order to satisfy an <u>unsecured Creditor's</u> claim (because the
       unsecured Creditor would be better off than others. In such a
       case, the property will be a Debt to the Estate.)
   2) The Debtor waived the right to avoid a Transfer of exempt
       property (under §522(g) and (i)).
   3) The Debtor waived the right to recover property (under
       §522(g) and (i)).
(f) Avoiding Liens on Exempt Property:
   (1) The Debtor may avoid fixing a Lien on property he has an
        interest in to the extent the Lien will impair his right to a
        §522(b) exemption, if the Lien is:
        (A) An unassigned <u>Judicial Lien</u> that:
             1. Was not made to secure a debt
             2. Was based on Alimony or Child Support
                 * * *

        (B) <u>Property Subject to §522(f)</u>: A non-possessory, non-
             Purchase Money Security Interest in any:
             (i) Household/personal consumer goods (under
                  §522(d)(3) and (4))
             (ii) Professional books/ tools of the trade (under
                  §522(d)(6))
             (iii) Health aids/medicines (under §522(d)(9))

   (2) When Lien Impairs Exemption:
        (A) A Lien "<u>impairs an exemption</u>" to the extent the
             Debtor's interest in the property plus all Liens on the
             property is less than the sum of:
             (i) The Lien, plus
             (ii) All other Liens on the Property; plus

---

[10] $16,150 as of April 1, 1998.

21

         (iii) The amount of the exemption the Debtor could
           claim (as per §522(b))
    (B) Calculations when more than 1 Lien exists: Any
       avoided Liens are not considered in calculating the
       above equation.
    (C) §522(f) shall not apply with respect to a judgement
       arising out of a Mortgage Foreclosure.

(3) Cases Where State Law Applies to Debtor:
    i)   The Debtor may not avoid fixing a Lien (i.e. the Lien
       will survive) on property exempt under State law if:
      (A) State law either permits a Person to voluntarily
         waive a right to claim exemptions under §522(d) or
         prohibits the Debtor to claim exemptions under
         §522(d); and
      (B) Either:
         1.   State law permits the Debtor to claim
            exemptions under without monetary
            limitations (except to the extent the Debtor has
            allowed the property to be encumbered by a
            consensual Lien). or
         2.   State law prohibits the Debtor to avoid a
            consensual Lien on property which would
            otherwise be exempt; and
      (C) The Lien is a non-possessory, non-purchase money
         Security Interest in §522(d)(3) or (6) property.
    ii) The Trustee may recover $5,000 from the Lien Value.

(g) Exempting Recovered Property: The Trustee may exempt
    property recovered (under §510(c)(2), §542, §543, §550, §551,
    §553, etc.) to the extent it would have been exempt if the
    Transfer were never made if either:
    (1) Both:
        (A) The Transfer was not a voluntary Transfer by the
          Debtor (ex: a Judicial Lien); and
        (B) The Debtor did not conceal the property; or
    (2) The Debtor could have avoided the Transfer under
        §522(f)(2) (WHEN LIEN IMPAIRS EXEMPTION).

(h) Avoiding Exempted Property: The Debtor may avoid a Transfer
    or recover a setoff to the extent they would have been exempt
    under §522(g)(1) had the Trustee avoided the Transfer , so long
    as:

    (1) The Transfer is avoidable by the Trustee (under Voidable Preference Law).

    (2) The Trustee does not attempt to avoid the Transfer .

(i) Exempting Property Recovered From Setoffs:
    (1) The Debtor may recover voidable preferences and setoffs (under §522(f) or (h)) and exempt such property.
    (2) An avoided Transfer may be preserved for the benefit of the Debtor to the extent it would have been exempt under §522(g) or §522(i)(1).

(j) Exempting Other Property: The Debtor may exempt a particular type of property under §522(g) or (i), but only to the extent the Debtor has exempted less property (in Value) than the type of property that the Debtor is allowed under §522(b)(AVAILABLE EXEMPTIONS).

(k) Administrative Expenses: Property exempt under this section is not subject to payment of any Administrative Expenses, except:

    (1) The proportional share of unpaid costs and expenses of:

        a. Avoiding a Transfer of property that the Debtor exempts under §522(g); or
        b. Recovering property that the Debtor exempts under §522(g); and
    (2) Any unpaid costs and expenses of:
        a. Avoiding a Transfer under §522(f) or (h); or
        b. Recovering property under §522(i)(1)

(l) Debtor's Filing:
    1. The Debtor (or dependent) shall file a list of property it claims as exempt under §522(b).
    2. Unless a Party in Interest objects, any property claimed as exempt on the list will be exempt (regardless of its allowance under law).

(m) Joint Exemptions: In a joint case, this section shall apply separately with respect to each Debtor (subject to the limitation in §522(b)(2)).

B) The Automatic Stay (§362):

1. Introduction:

OVERVIEW ——————————————————

• The Automatic Stay puts a "freeze" on estate interests. The stay is automatically placed on all Estate Property the moment the Petition is filed.
• The freeze prohibits anyone (other than the Bankruptcy Trustee) from touching, taking, encumbering, or disposing of any Estate Property.
• The Automatic Stay is placed on Estate Property in order to prevent the mass chaos which might occur if all Creditors of the Debtor were able to jump on the Debtor's assets in place of payment by the Debtor. The Automatic Stay ensures that Creditors will get paid in an orderly and fair manner – the court decides who gets what, at what time, and under what conditions.
• The Automatic Stay continues on the Estate Property until:
   ☞ Discharge; or
   ☞ The Stay is lifted; or
   ☞ The Case is closed; or
   ☞ The property no longer becomes part of the Estate (§362(c)(2)).

2. Damages from Automatic Stay:

A Creditor will have to pay the Debtor (usually only Individual Debtors) for any damages which the Estate suffers from a violation by the Creditor of the Automatic Stay (§362(h)).

3. Grounds for Lifting the Stay (§362(d)):

OVERVIEW ——————————————————
• Certain property can be "unfrozen" if the Bankruptcy Court grants the Creditor's request to "lift the stay" off of certain property.
• Grounds for Lifting the Stay:
         1)   Lack of Adequate Protection (as per §361; See ADEQUATE

PROTECTION under SALE/USE)
2) Lack of Good Faith in filing the bankruptcy Petition
3) Judicial Discretion
4) Relief for Property:
☞ The Debtor has no equity in the property (§362(d)(2)(A))
(i.e. Liens are greater than the property Value); and
☞ The Property is not necessary for a reorganization (in a
Chapter 11 proceeding)(§362(d)(2)(B)), which can be
implemented in a reasonable time.

RELEVANT SECTIONS: §362(d), (e)

---

§362(d): Relief From Automatic Stay:

i. When Relief is Granted - The court must grant relief from the
Automatic Stay (by terminating, annulling, modifying or
conditioning the stay) if:
(1) Cause if Shown - including lack of Adequate Protection of a
party's interest (as per §361). or
(2) For stays affecting actions against property:
(A) Equity Test: The Debtor does not have an Equity in the
property; AND
(B) Necessity Test: The property is not necessary for an
effective reorganization ; OR
(3) For stays of acts affecting Single Asset Real Estate: If the
creditor's Claim is secured by the real estate, he may be
given relief from the Stay, unless:
(A) The Debtor has filed a Reorganization plan within 90
days of the Order for Relief (this can be changed by the
Court within the 90 day period) that will probably be
confirmed within a reasonable time; or
(B) Within 90 days the Debtor begins paying the secured
creditors monthly payments equal to the interest (at a
Fair Market Rate) of the creditor's property interest.

ii. Additional Requirements:
1. A Party in Interest requests the relief; and
2. There is notice and a hearing

§362(e): Lifting the Stay:

1) The Automatic Stay will be terminated (i.e. "lifted") 30 days after the Creditor makes the request for relief, unless the court orders otherwise (after notice and hearing).
2) The hearing may either be a preliminary hearing, or a final hearing (as required under (d)).
3) If the hearing is a preliminary hearing, the final hearing must take place within 30 days, unless the parties in interest consent or the court has an otherwise compelling reason.
4) The court shall order the Stay to continue until the court makes a final determination that there is a reasonable likelihood that the party opposing the stay will prevail at the final hearing.

4. Subjects of the Automatic Stay:

OVERVIEW ─────────────────────────────
- The following are subject to the Automatic Stay:

  1) Guarantors – A Guarantor of a Debtor's Debt is not protected by the Debtor's Automatic Stay. Thus, a Creditor may go after the guarantor to obtain payment for the Debtor's Debt (without being subject to the Automatic Stay), unless the Debtor is in a Chapter 13 proceeding.
  2) Goods – goods not yet shipped by the Debtor
  3) Benefactor of an Letter of Credit - is usually not subject to the Automatic Stay (the bank is like a guarantor, though some courts disagree).
  4) Government Injunctions (such as a CRCLA injunction) are not effected by the Automatic Stay since they are considered a "Policing Power" under §362(b)(4) and (5).
  5) Judgment Claimants – cannot levy, place a Lien, or otherwise enforce a pre-Petition judgment on Property of the Estate (§362(a)(2)).
  6) Lawsuits: - lawsuits cannot be commenced nor continued unless
- They will benefit the estate; or
- They relate to post-Petition claims; or
- They relate to Criminal or Alimony/Child Support proceedings
  7) Tax Court Proceedings

- The IRS cannot assess a pre-Petition claim unless the Bankruptcy Court so allows.
- The IRS may give the Debtor notice of a tax deficiency (see §362(b)(9)).
- IRS may not continue or commence a tax court proceeding.

8) Liens - Liens cannot be Attached (i.e. created), Perfected, improved, or enforced in any way (subject to certain relation-back provisions and allowances in §542(e) and also §362).

9) Setoffs: are not allowed (§362(a)(7)), but banks can usually put a freeze on Debtors' Accounts.

10) Presenting Negotiable Instruments (ex: cashing a check) or giving a Notice of Dishonor on a check is not barred by the Automatic Stay (§362(b)(11)).

11) Wages

- If pre-Petition wages are not paid, Inventory can be claimed by the employees to secure their claim, even while the Automatic Stay is in place (§362(b)(5)/ FLSA).
- The cost of freeing up the inventory and selling it for purposes of paying wages will be considered to be a §503(b) Administrative Expense, which has a high priority (§507(a)(1)).
- Pre-Petition wages may not be made available to the employees, however, until the bankruptcy proceeding is over.
- Some Courts allow immediate payment under the Doctrine of Necessity.
- Other Courts allow immediate payment under §506(c), since it is for the Creditor's benefit to free up their inventory to be sold.

12) At-will Contract: An at-will contract cannot be canceled after the Petition is filed; it is acceptable, however, if the contract was canceled before the Petition was filed but the actual termination did not take effect until after the Petition was filed (ex: 6 month notice is needed to terminate the contract).

13) Acts Against Estate Property – including lawsuits and other proceedings (§362(a)(3)).

RELEVANT SECTIONS: §361, §362

§361: Adequate Protection

A.   Adequate Protection may be provided by:

(1) Cash Payments: Requiring the trustee to make Cash
     Payments to the extent that the actions by the Trustee (under
     §362, §363, and §364) result in a decrease in Value of the
     Creditor's interest in the property; or
(2) Extra Liens: Providing the Creditor with an Additional or
     Substituted Security Interest to the extent that actions by the
     Trustee (under §362, §363, and §364) result in a decrease in
     Value of the Creditor's interest in the property; or
(3) Other Relief: an "indubitable equivalent" of the Creditor's
     interest (other than giving the Creditor payment as a
     §503(b)(1) Administrative Expense).

B.   Sections 362 (AUTOMATIC STAY), §363 (USE, SALE, AND LEASE
     OF PROPERTY), or §364 (OBTAINING CREDIT) may require
     "Adequate Protection" of a Person's interest in property.

§362: Automatic Stay:

(a) The Automatic Stay:

i)   Creation: Except as provided in §362(b), filing one of the
     following Petitions will create an Automatic Stay:
     1)   §301 (VOLUNTARY PETITIONS)
     2)   §302 (JOINT PETITIONS)
     3)   §303 (INVOLUNTARY PETITIONS)
     4)   §5(a)(3) of the Securities Investor Protection Act of
          1970
ii) Applicability: The Automatic Stay applies to and affects all
     entities involved in any of the following:
     (1) The Commencement or Continuation of an Action
          against the Debtor, including the issuance or
          employment of Process of either a
          a)   Judicial Action; or
          b)   Administrative Action; or
          c)   Other action or proceeding against the Debtor
               which was (or could have been) brought before the
               Bankruptcy Petition was filed; or

28

    d)   An Action to recover from the Debtor a Claim arising before the Bankruptcy Petition was filed

(2)   The Enforcement of a Judgment against the Debtor or the Estate if the judgement was obtained before the Petition was filed.

(3)   Any Act to Obtain Possession or Control of property belonging to the estate

(4)   Any Lien Against the Estate: Any Act to Create, Perfect, or Enforce a Lien against any Property of the Estate

(5)   Any Liens Against the Debtor: Any Act to Create, Perfect, or Enforce a Lien against any property of the Debtor to the extent that the Lien secures a Claim arising before the Petition was filed.

(6)   Any Act to Collect, Assess, or Recover from the Debtor a Claim which arose before the Petition was filed

(7)   A Setoff of a Debt to the Debtor for any Claim against the Debtor for any obligation to the Debtor which arose before the Petition was filed.

(8)   A Tax Proceedings: The Commencement or Continuation of a proceeding concerning the Debtor, before the U.S. Tax Court.

(b) Exceptions To The Automatic Stay - The following are not subject to the Automatic Stay in §362(a):

    (1) Criminal Actions: The Commencement or Continuation of a Criminal Action

    (2) Family Actions:
      (A) The Commencement or Continuation of an Action to:
         (i) Establish Paternity; or
         (ii) Establish or Modify an order for Alimony, Maintenance, or Support
      (B) The Commencement or Continuation of an action for the Collection of Alimony, Maintenance or Support, from property that is not Property of the Estate

    (3) Perfecting, Maintaining, or Continuing Liens: An act to Perfect, Maintain or Continue the perfection of an interest in property will be exempt from the Automatic Stay to the extent that:
      a)   The Trustee is subject to such perfection under §546(b) (EXCEPTIONS TO TRUSTEE'S AVOIDING POWERS); or

b) The act to perfect or maintain or continue the perfection takes place within 10 days after property is Transferred (under §547(e)(2)(A))

(4) Government Actions: against the Debtor are exempt from the Automatic Stay under §362(a)(1)

(5) Government Judgements: against the Debtor are exempt from the Automatic Stay under §362(a)(2) if obtained in an action by a government unit, and the action is brought to enforce the government agency's regulatory or police power.

(6) Securities Setoffs: Debts will not be subject to the Automatic Stay for purposes of Setoff if the obligor is a:
a) Commodity Broker
b) Forward Contract Merchant
c) Stock Broker
d) Financial Institutions
e) Security Clearinghouse Agency * * * *

(7) Setoffs by Repo Participants: (repurchase agreements, margin, or settlement payment)
* * * *

(8) Foreclosure Action by Secretary of Housing and Urban Development * * * *

(9) Tax Matters: The following tax matters will not be subject to the Automatic Stay:
(A) An audit by a Governmental Unit to determine Tax Liability; or
(B) The issuance to the Debtor of a Notice of Tax Deficiency (by a Government Unit); or
(C) A demand for tax returns; or
(D) A tax assessment Tax Liens that would attach to Estate Property because of the assessment shall only be effective if:
i) The tax liability will not be discharged; and
ii) The property/proceeds are Transferred out of the Bankrupt Estate to the Debtor, itself.

(10) Non-Residential Leases: Acts by the Lessor to obtain possession of his property will not be subject to the Automatic Stay if:
a. The lease is for non-residential property
b. The lease term expires before or during the Bankruptcy Petition

(11) Negotiable Instruments - The Automatic Stay will not effect:

a) Presentment of the instrument
b) Giving Notice of Dishonor of the instrument
c) Protesting the Dishonor of the instrument

(12) Chapter 11 Foreclosures on Ships by the Secretary of Transportation (for Bankruptcy Petitions filed on or before 12/31/89)

(13) Chapter 11 Foreclosures on Ships by the Secretary of Commerce (for Bankruptcy Petitions filed on or before 12/31/89)* * *

(14) Actions by an Accrediting Agency: An agency accrediting the Debtor as an education institution may continue to do so, without being subject to the Automatic Stay

(15) Actions by State Licensing Division for Education – regarding licensing of the Debtor as an educational institution.

(16) Action by a Guaranty Agency for Higher Education - regarding the Debtor's eligibility to participate in Higher Education programs.

(17) Swap Agreement Setoffs: * * * *

(18) Tax Liens: The Creation or Perfection of a statutory tax if:
   a. The tax becomes due after the filing of the Petition; and
   b. The tax is an ad valorum property tax; and
   c. The tax is imposed by a State or domicile.

(c) Duration of Automatic Stay:

(1) Stay on Actions: The Automatic Stay (under §362(a)) of actions against property will continue until the property is no longer Property of the Estate.

(2) Stay on Other Acts: The stay of other acts in §362(a) remains until the earlier of:
   (A) The time the bankruptcy case is closed
   (B) The time the case is dismissed
   (C) The time discharge is granted or denied (in a Chapter 7 case concerning an individual or a case under Chapters 9, 11, 12 or 13)

(d) Relief From The Automatic Stay:

   i. When Relief is Granted - The court must grant relief from the Automatic Stay (by terminating, annulling, modifying or conditioning the stay) if:
      (1) Cause if Shown - including lack of Adequate Protection of a party's interest (as per §361). or

(2) For stays affecting actions against property:
  (A) Equity Test: The Debtor does not have an Equity in the property; and
  (B) Necessity Test: The property is not necessary for an effective reorganization ; or
(3) For stays of acts affecting Single Asset Real Estate: If the creditor's Claim is secured by the real estate, he may be given relief from the Stay, unless:
  (A) The Debtor has filed a Reorganization plan within 90 days of the Order for Relief (this can be changed by the Court within the 90 day period) that will probably be confirmed within a reasonable time; or
  (B) Within 90 days the Debtor begins paying the secured creditors monthly payments equal to the interest (at a Fair Market Rate) of the creditor's property interest.

  ii. Additional Requirements:
    1. A Party in Interest requests the relief; and
    2. There is notice and a hearing

(e) Lifting the Stay:
  1) The Automatic Stay will be terminated (i.e. "lifted") 30 days after the Creditor makes the request for relief, unless the court orders otherwise (after notice and hearing).
  2) The hearing may either be a preliminary hearing, or a final hearing (as required under (d)).
  3) If the hearing is a preliminary hearing, the final hearing must take place within 30 days, unless the parties in interest consent or the court has an otherwise compelling reason.
  4) The court shall order the Stay to continue until the court makes a final determination that there is a reasonable likelihood that the party opposing the stay will prevail at the final hearing.

(f) Irreparable Damage: The court may lift the Stay (with or without a hearing) if an interest in property would suffer irreparable damage before there is an opportunity for notice and a hearing.

(g) Burden of Proof - In hearings under (d) and (e):

(1) <u>Party Requesting Relief</u>: Burden on issues of Debtor's equity in property

(2) <u>Party Opposing Relief:</u> Burden on all other issues

(h) Recovery of Actual Damages: An individual injured by any willful violation of the Stay shall recover:
1. Actual Damages; and
2. Costs and Attorney Fees; and
3. Punitive Damages (in appropriate circumstances)

C) <u>CLAIMS</u>:

1. The Proof of Claim:

OVERVIEW ───────────────────────────────

- Since the Automatic Stay inhibits a Creditor from taking its property or payment from the Debtor, an Unsecured Creditor must "apply" for its payment or property by filing a "<u>Proof of Claim</u>" with the Bankruptcy Court.
  - ☞ A Secured Creditor may file a claim (§506(d)(2)). If it does not file, most courts hold that although it will not get a distribution from the Estate, its secured Lien will survive the bankruptcy.
- If an unsecured Creditor does not file a proof of claim it will not be able to recover payments from the Estate, since all Debts are <u>discharged</u> once the Bankruptcy proceeding is over ((§542(a)(2)) -- - proof that Bankruptcy notice was sent "is proof" that it was received), (unless it was a non-dischargeable claim, such as a Tax Lien (§507(a)(8) or a Lien for Alimony/Child Support).
- <u>Timing</u>: An Unsecured Creditor must file a proof of claim within <u>90 days</u> after the first Creditor's meeting (exceptions in Chapter. 11) (BR §3002).
  - ☞ Under §726(a)(3), "late" Creditors will lose part of their priority to those who submitted timely claims
  - ☞ "<u>Excusable Neglect</u>" - The <u>90 day</u> Statute of Limitations may be extended for "excusable neglect," but only in <u>Chapter 11</u> cases.
- Unless a claim is objected to by the Trustee, all claims filed will entitle the claimant to its share of the Estate distribution.

2. Allowance of Claims

OVERVIEW ───────────────────────────────

- Not all claims will be considered by the court. The claim must represent a <u>pre-Petition</u> Debt unless it is one of the "Relation Back" exceptions in §502.
- "<u>Relation Back</u>" Exceptions under §502: The following post-Petition

claims will be admitted for consideration by the Bankruptcy Court:
- ☞ Claims for Reimbursement by a Surety
- ☞ Claims for Payments made in the Ordinary Course of the Debtor's business if:
  1) The Bankruptcy Petition was <u>involuntarily</u> filed
  2) The claim arose before the <u>earlier</u> of:
     a. The Order for Relief; and
     b. Appointment of the Trustee
- Claims arising from Contracts/Leases rejected (under §363)
- Claims from Recovered Property
- Claims from §507(a)(8) Tax Liens
- <u>Non-allowable Claims</u>: (§502(b)) The following claims will not be admitted for consideration:
- <u>Unenforceable claims</u> against the Debtor (i.e. claims in which the Debtor has a valid defense)
- Claims for <u>Unmatured Interests</u> – on an Unsecured or Under-secured Claim
- <u>Property Taxes</u> exceeding the property Value
- <u>Services of an Insider or Debtor's Attorney</u> - if fees exceed reasonable Value
- <u>Unmatured Debt</u> which may mature (i.e. Debt which will remain after the Debtor emerges from bankruptcy).
- Certain Damages from a <u>Debtor who broke its lease</u> (see VALUATION below)
- <u>Surety's Contingent right to reimbursement</u> (i.e. if the Surety never paid the Creditor (see §502(e)))
- <u>Certain Damages for Employer's Breach of Contract</u> (up to 1 Year's compensation)

3. Valuation of Collateral:

OVERVIEW ———————————————————

- The Value of the Debtor's property is very important in a Bankruptcy proceeding because it determines:
  ☞ How much an unsecured Creditor gets
  ☞ How much secured Creditors are entitled to
  ☞ The Equity Cushion - for purposes of post-Petition interest on secured property, Adequate Protection issues, etc.
  ☞ The type of Adequate Protection required
  ☞ The Amount of the Debtor's exemptions
  ☞ The Redemption Value of certain property Confirmation of a repayment plan under Chapters 11, 12, or 13.

Applications:
Debtor Terminates Lease: (i.e.- the tenant leaves before the lease is up):
  ☞ A Landlord of the Debtor may recover the greater of (§502(b)(6)(A)) :
    ➢ 1 year's rent; or
    ➢ 15% of rent due until the remainder of the term (not to exceed 3 years)
Tort Claims:
  ☞ The Court shall estimate the Value of the claim (ex: 51% chance of winning a tort claim worth $100,000 is Valued at approx. $51,000) (§502(c))
  ☞ Estimation is mandatory for liquidation of the tort claims if:
    ➢ It is before a trial in a non-Bankruptcy forum; AND
    ➢ It would unduly delay the Bankruptcy case
Suretyships:
  ☞ If Debtor is the Principal Obligor - the surety will have a contingent claim against the Debtor if the Surety pays the Creditor. It will then obtain the status of the Creditor (viz. The Debtor).
    ➢ §502(e)(1) disallows claims before the Surety actually pays on the guaranty.
    ➢ If the Surety paid the Creditor part of the Debtor's Debt, the Surety will have a partial claim against the Estate (as per

§502(e)(2)).
> The Surety-Creditor will get paid for the Value of the partial claim once the Creditor is paid the remaining balance (§509(c))
> The Surety's priority of payment is only subordinated to the Creditor (to whom it is a Surety/Guarantor). The Surety's portion is paid to the Creditor, and once the Creditor is fully paid, the surety can take the surplus (i.e.- The Surety's "portion" doesn't get re-distributed via the Estate after the Creditor gets paid (because it is for the benefit of the Surety's credit and not for the benefit of the Creditor's themselves. One should consider this transaction as if the Surety assigns its Bankruptcy dividend ("portion") to the Creditor).
☞ Capital Gains Tax – The Court must subtract potential Capital Gains Tax from Value of property, even if it does not think the estate will sell the property.

RELEVANT SECTIONS: §501, §502, §503, §509, §510

§501: Filing Proofs of Claims and Interests:

(a) Who May File:
    1. The following may file a Proof of Claim:
       a. A Creditor
       b. An Indenture Trustee
    2. A Proof of Interest may be filed by an Equity Security Holder.
(b) Alternate Filers: If a Creditor does not timely file a Proof of Claim, the following may file a Proof of Claim in his place:
    1. An Entity liable to the Creditor with the Debtor (i.e. a Guarantor); or
    2. An Entity that has Secured the Creditor
(c) Debtor's Filing: The Debtor or Trustee may file a Proof of Claim for the Creditor if the Creditor does not timely file.
(d) Special "Relation Back" Claims: The following Claims may be filed under this section, as if they were Claims against the Debtor arising before the Petition is filed:
    1. Claims for Reimbursement or Contribution (§502(e)(2))

2. Claims for Ordinary Course Payments in an Involuntary Case (§502(f))
3. Claims for Damages from Rejected Contracts/Leases (§502(g))
4. Claims for Damages resulting from Recovered Property (§502(h))
5. Claims for §507(a)(8) Priority Tax Claims (§502(i))

§502: Allowance of Claims or Interests:

(a) Presumption that Claim is Allowed:
1. A Claim filed under §501 will be presumed allowed unless a Party in Interest objects.
2. A Party in Interest includes the Creditor of a general partner, where the partnership is a Debtor in a Chapter 7 case.

(b) Procedure Upon Objection:
  i) Valuation by Hearing:
    a) The Court shall determine the admissible dollar Value of the Claim (if any).
    b) There must be notice and a hearing.
  ii) Inadmissible Claims: The Court shall not allow the Claim to the extent the Claim is:
    (1) Unenforceable against the Debtor under any agreement or applicable law (ex: State law exemptions) (for reasons other than the fact that the Claim is contingent or unmatured)
    (2) For Unmatured Interest
    (3) For Property Taxes which exceed the Estate's interest in the property
    (4) For Services of an Insider or Attorney which exceed the reasonable Value of the services
    (5) For Unmatured Debts (as of filing date) which are exempt from discharge under §523(a)(5).
    (6) For a Lessor's Damages from early termination of a real property lease, which exceeds:
      (A) The greater of the following:
        1. 1 years' rent, after the earlier of:
          (i) The Petition Date; or
          (ii) The Date the Lessee surrendered the property; or

    2. 15% of Rent for the remaining term of the lease (up to 3 years' rent), after the earlier of:
      (i) The Petition Date; or
      (ii) The Date the Lessee surrendered the property; PLUS

  (B) Any Unpaid Rent (without acceleration) due on the earlier of:
    1. The Petition Date; or
    2. The Date the Lessee surrendered the property

(7) For Damages of employee resulting from termination of an employment contract which exceed:

  (A) 1 Year's Compensation provided for under the contract (without acceleration), from the earlier of the following:
      (i) The Petition Date; or
      (ii) The date the employee was terminated; PLUS

  (B) Any Unpaid Compensation due under the contract by the earlier of:
    1. The Petition Date; or
    2. The date the employee was terminated

(8) Resulting from a reduction of a federal employment tax credit caused by late payment of tax

(9) Proof of Claim Untimely:

  a. Claims where the Proof of Claim is not timely filed, unless:
    1. Excused under §726(a)
    2. Excused under Federal Rules of Bankruptcy Procedure

  b. For Governmental Units – filed within 180 days after the Order for Relief (that is considered "timely")

iii) Exceptions: This section is subject to the "Relation Back" provisions of §502:

1. Claims for Reimbursement or Contribution (§502(e)(2))
2. Claims for Ordinary Course Payments in an Involuntary Case (§502(f))
3. Claims for Damages from Rejected Contracts/Leases (§502(g))
4. Claims for Damages resulting from Recovered Property (§502(h))
5. Claims for §507(a)(8) Priority Tax Claims (§502(I))

(c) Estimations: For purposes of this section, the court shall estimate the Value of:
   (1) Any Contingent or Unliquidated Claim - if the fixing of the amount would cause undue delay to the administration of the case.
   (2) Any Right to Payment arising from a right to an equitable remedy for breach of performance.

(d) Other Disallowed Claims: The Court shall disallow the following Claims unless the Claimant returns the property or pays the Value of the property:
   1. Property recoverable under a Turnover Order (under §542 and §543).
   2. Property recoverable for a Voidable Preference (under §544, §545, §547, §548, §549, and §550).
   3. Property recoverable due to a Setoff (under §553).
   4. The Transfer is exempt (under §522(i)).
   5. The Property is subject to a Tax Lien (under §724(a)).

(e) Claims for Contribution or Reimbursement:

   (1) Disallowed Claims: The Court shall disallow Claims for Reimbursement or Contribution to an Entity that is a co-Debtor, surety or guarantor, to the extent that:
   (A) The Principal Creditor's Claim is disallowed; or
   (B) The Claim for Reimbursement is contingent as of the time of allowance or disallowance of the Claim (i.e. the surety has not paid the Creditor); or
   (C) The Surety chooses Subrogation to the rights of the Creditor (under §509) (i.e. the Creditor can either Claim Reimbursement for a Claim paid or a Right of Subrogation).

   (2) Relation Back for Fixed Claims: If the Claim for Reimbursement or Contribution was fixed after the Petition was filed, the Claim is considered to have been fixed as of the Petition date for purposes of allowing or disallowing the Claim (i.e. it becomes a pre-Petition Claim).

(f) Claims Arising Out of the Ordinary Course:

1. <u>Relation Back</u>: Claims arising out of the <u>Ordinary Course</u> of the Debtor's Business Affairs are considered pre-Petition Claims if:
   a) The Claim arises out of the <u>Ordinary Course</u> of the Debtor's Business Affairs; and
   b) The case is an <u>Involuntary Proceeding</u>; and
   c) The Claim arose:
      1) After the filing, but before the <u>earlier</u> of:
         a) A Trustee's appointment; and
         b) An Order for Relief; and
      2) The Claim shall be determined as of the date the Claim arose, as if it arose before the Petition date
2. Although the Claim will "date back" to Petition date, the Value of the Claim will be determined as of the date the Claim actually arose.

(g) Claims Resulting From Rejected Contracts and Leases: A Claim arising from the Trustee's Rejection of an executory contract or unexpired lease (under §365 or pursuant to a Reorganization Plan) is considered a pre-Petition Claim.

(h) Claims Resulting From Recovered Property: A Claim arising out of the following recovered property shall be considered to have arisen before the Petition was filed for purposes of allowing or disallowing the Claim:
   a) Exempt Property (as per §522) ; or
   b) Voidable Preference Property (as per §550); or
   c) Setoff Property (as per §553)

(i) Claims Arising From Post-Petition Tax Assessment: A Claim for a tax entitled to §507(a)(8) priority which arises after the commencement of the case is considered a pre-Petition Claim.

(j) Reconsideration of Allowed/Disallowed Claims:
   1. A Claim that has been allowed/disallowed may be reconsidered <u>for cause</u>.
   2. <u>Grounds for Changing Decision</u>: A reconsidered Claim may be allowed/disallowed based on the <u>equities of the case</u>.
   3. <u>Treatment of Priority to Distribution</u>: If an allowed Claim is reconsidered, the validity of any <u>payment</u> or <u>Transfer</u> from the estate made to the Claim holder (of the allowed Claim) will not be affected.

4. Creditors will also not be entitled to further payments until the Creditor with the newly allowed Claim is paid in the same proportion that the other Creditors of the class are paid.
5. This subsection does not change the Trustee's right to recover any excess payment or Transfer made to the Creditor.

§503: Allowance Of Administrative Expenses:

(a) Filing for Administrative Expenses:[11]
    1. Timely Claims: Entities holding Claims for Administrative Expenses may timely file a request for payment.
    2. Untimely Claims: An Entity may only file a late Claim if:
        a) It shows cause; and
        b) The court grants permission to do so.
(b) Kinds of Administrative Expenses Allowed:
    i) The following are various Administrative Expenses (in addition to those under §502(f)) allowed after notice and a hearing:
        (1) Expenses:
            (A) Costs of Preserving the Estate: The actual and necessary costs of preserving the estate, including:
                1. wages; and
                2. salaries; and
                3. commissions for services rendered after the commencement of the case (e.g. Attorney's fees); and
                4. Payment to an individual Debtor for services rendered to the estate (ex: When the individual was a sole proprietor and was employed by the estate to run the business after the commencement of the case. (Local Loan v. Hunt, 292 U.S. 234, 243 (1943)).

            (B) Taxes - Either:
                (i) Post-Petition taxes - incurred by the estate, except those specified in §507(a)(8)

---

11 Note: The Rules of Bankruptcy Procedure will specify the time, the form, and the method of the filing

34(Note: This includes taxes on capital gains from sales of property by the trustee and taxes on income earned by the estate during the case).

or (ii) Taxes due as a result of an excessive carryover allowance - which the Estate benefited from, regardless of whether the taxes related to a year ending before or after the Petition was filed.[12]

(C) Fines & Penalties (or reduction in credit) - relating to a tax specified in §503(B) (including interest on tax liabilities and certain tax penalties incurred by the trustee.)

(2) Compensation and Reimbursement - awarded under §330(a) (to a trustee, examiner, Debtor's Attorney, and other professionals)

(3) The actual and necessary expenses – incurred by any of the following (other than compensation and reimbursement specified in (4)) :
(A) A creditor that files an involuntary Petition (§303).

or (B) A creditor who (with the court's approval) recovers property for the benefit of the estate that the Debtor Transferred or concealed.

or (C) A creditor who incurred expenses in a criminal prosecution related to the bankruptcy case or the Debtor's business or property.

or (D) Any of the following who incur expenses in making a substantial contribution to a Chapter 9 or 11 case:
1.   A creditor

---

12 Background: The tax code allows the trustee of an estate which suffers a net operating loss to carry back the loss against an earlier profit year of the estate/Debtor and to get a tentative refund for the earlier year. This is subject, however, to a later full audit of the loss which led to the refund. The IRS is required to issue a tentative refund to the trustee (whether the refund was applied for by the Debtor or by the trustee), but if the refund amount later proves to have been wrong, the IRS can request that the tax due because of the error be payable by the estate as an Administrative Expense.

or 2. An Indenture trustee

or 3. An equity Security holder

or 4. A committee representing creditors or equity
        Security holders (other than an "official
        committee" appointed under §1102)

or (E) A <u>Custodian</u> superseded under §543 (and in
        addition to actual and necessary expenses,
        compensation for the Custodian's services which
        benefit the estate)

or (F) A <u>member of a committee</u> appointed under §1102,
        if the expenses are incurred in the performance of
        the committee's duties.

(4) Compensation for Professionals – allowed if:

    1. <u>Compensation is reasonable, based on the:</u>

        a. Time of the services

  and b. Nature of the services

  and c. Extent of the services

  and d. Value of the services

  and e. Cost of comparable services in a non-
        bankruptcy case

and 2. Services are of an <u>Attorney</u> or an <u>accountant</u>.

and 3. The Entity incurring the Professional expenses is
        one listed in paragraph (3) above (i.e. an Entity for
        which necessary and actual expenses are allowed)

and 4. Compensation represents reimbursement for <u>actual,
        necessary expenses</u> incurred by the Attorney or
        accountant

(5) Indenture Trustees:

    1. <u>Reasonable Compensation</u> for the service of an
        Indenture trustee making a substantial contribution
        in a Chapter 9 or 11 case

    2. The reasonableness of the compensation shall be
        based on the :

        a. Time of the services

  and b. Nature of the services

  and c. Extent of the services

  and d. Value of the services

  and e. Cost of comparable services in a non-
        bankruptcy case

(6) Fees and Mileage are payable pursuant to Title 28, Ch.
     119 (§2041 et seq.).

ii)   None of the above Claims will be allowed if they are Claims or expenses allowed under §502(f), which include:
    a)   Claims that arise in the <u>ordinary course</u> of the Debtor's business
and b)   Claims that arise between the <u>commencement</u> of an involuntary case and
      1.   The <u>appointment</u> of a Trustee
or 2.   The <u>Order for Relief</u>

§509: Claims of Co-Debtors:

(a)   Right of Subrogation:[13] A surety or co-Debtor is subrogated to the rights of a creditor (except as provided in (b) and (c)) to the extent that:
    1.   Any payments are made by the surety or co-Debtor to the creditor; or
    2.   The Surety or co-Debtor secured any Claim of the creditor

(b)   Exceptions to Subrogation: A co-Debtor may <u>not</u> be subrogated to the extent that:
    (1)   The co-Debtor's Claim for reimbursement or contribution (already paid to the primary creditor) is:
      (A)   allowed under §502; or
      (B)   disallowed other than under §502(e); or
      (C)   subordinated under §510; or
    (2)   The co-Debtor, rather than the Debtor, actually received the consideration for the Claim held by the creditor (i.e. a Debtor that is ultimately liable on the Debt cannot recover from a surety or co-Debtor).

(c)   Subordination Allowed Claims of Co-Debtor:
    1.   A co-Debtor's allowed Claims will be subordinated to the principal creditor's Claim until that Claim is paid in full.
    2.   The principal creditor's Claim may be paid in full either:
      a.   Through payments under the Bankruptcy Code; or
      b.   Otherwise
    3.   <u>The co-Debtor's Claim which are subordinated under this section may arise either:</u>
      a.   By way of subrogation under §509; or

---

13 Note: Whether the creditor's Claim was filed under § 501(a) or 501(b) is irrelevant. The right of subrogation will exist even if the primary creditor's Claim is allowed by being listed under proposed 11 U.S.C. 924 or 1111, and not by reason of a proof of Claim.

b.   For reimbursement or contribution

§510: Subordination:

(a) Subordination Agreements Enforceable: A subordination agreement is enforceable in a Bankruptcy case to the same extent that it would be enforceable under applicable non-bankruptcy law (ex: contract law).

(b) Subordination of Security Holder's Claim:

    1. Any of the following Claims arising from the purchase or sale of the Debtor's (or an Affiliate's) Security are subordinated to all Claims that are senior (or equal) to a Claim represented by the Security, for purposes of distribution:

       i. A Claim arising from rescission of a purchase or sale of the Debtor's (or one of its Affiliate's) Security; or

      ii. A Claim for damages arising from the purchase or sale of the Security; or

     iii. A Claim for reimbursement or contribution allowed under §502 on account of the Claim

    2. Common Stock Exception: If the Security is common stock, the above Claims have the same priority as the common stock would.

(c) Other Subordination of Claims: In addition to (a) and (b), the court may (after notice and a hearing):

    (1) Subordinate Allowed Claims: Subordinate an allowed Claim (or interest) for purposes of distribution to another allowed Claim (or interest), under principles of equitable subordination.14;

and (2) Transfer Liens: Order that any Lien securing such a subordinated Claim be Transferred to the estate.

---

14 Note: The legislature intended that the "principles of equitable subordination" follow case law and leave the development of the principle to the courts. Under existing law, a Claim is generally subordinated only if its holder is guilty of inequitable conduct, or the Claim itself is susceptible to subordination, such as a penalty or a Claim for damages arising from the purchase or sale of a Security of the Debtor. The fact that the Claim may be secured has no effect on the issue of subordination. However, it is rare that because a Claim is a secured Claim, that itself justifies equitable subordination.

5. Bifurcation - Determining Amount of Secured Claim (§506):

OVERVIEW ─────────────────────────────
- §506(a) breaks claims into two parts:
  - ☞ The Secured Claim
  - ☞ The Deficiency (unsecured) Claim
- The Deficiency Claim will not have the same priority as the Secured Claim (ex: If the secured collateral = $1,000 and the outstanding Debt = $1,200, $1,000 of the claim would be secured; the remaining $200 would be unsecured and would have a priority similar to other unsecured claims in its class).
- Proceeds of Collateral - since rent is considered to be "Proceeds from Collateral" (§552(b)), some courts allow rental income from the collateral to be used to secure the claim (while decreasing the deficiency claim, and allowing more interest to be secured) by adding its Value to the claim.
- Equity Cushion - if the Value of the collateral is greater than the claim amount, the excess collateral Value is known as an "equity cushion," which most courts will allow the secured Creditor to take advantage of (i.e. by using the equity cushion to secure accrual interest) (ex: The Creditor has a $1,000 claim against the Debtor, but has secured collateral worth $1,300. The Creditor's Equity Cushion = $300).
  - ☞ A Secured Party with an Equity Cushion is deemed to be an "Oversecured Creditor"
  - ☞ When an equity cushion exists, a court will be more likely to find that a Creditor has "Adequate Protection."
- Interest
  - ☞ Oversecured Creditors have a right to the post-Petition interest accrual in their collateral (to the extent of the equity cushion (in the excess of the collateral Value from the claim Value) (§506(b));
  - ☞ Undersecured Creditors are not guaranteed interest accrual on their clams – even as an unsecured claim. They are only entitled to it under §726(a)(5).

- Declining Value of Collateral: Some Courts hold that an Oversecured Creditor is not entitled to protection of its Equity

Cushion with the accrual of post-Petition interest if the Value of the collateral, itself, is declining.

- Increasing Value of Collateral: If the Value of the collateral is increasing (ex: rental income on property) (as per §506(d)):
  - Some courts allow Creditors to obtain interest or reduce their deficiency claim by the increased Value amount (ex: Creditor had a $1,000 claim against the Debtor secured by property Valued at $800. The deficiency claim is $200; If the collateral is a piece of equipment being leased for $10 a month, the income on the collateral may be used to reduce the deficiency amount; thus, in 6 months, the Value of the collateral would = $860, leaving a deficiency of $140);
  - Other courts say that a claim is bifurcated at the time collateral is evaluated, and, thus, the deficiency claim can never become secured, and interest can never become secured by increased Value in the collateral (ex: In the above example, the $10 monthly income would not go to reduce the $200 deficiency claim.).
  - Some Courts allow the deficiency and interest claim to be converted into secured claims only if the underlying Lien/claim is not:
    1. From an illegal source (ex: a PMSI in drugs);
       or 2. Disallowed under §502 (PROOF OF CLAIMS)
       • Some Courts do not consider bifurcation to occur until either
       1. The collateral is sold
       or 2. A Chapter 11 or 13 plan is completed

• Adequate Protection - Decreasing Value of collateral: (see also "ADEQUATE PROTECTION" below)

- In Bankruptcy, the claim amount usually rises (because of post-Petition interest accrual) while the collateral Value usually declines (because of use by Trustee or depreciation).
- Value which must be protected: Since the Value of the collateral may depreciate, the Creditor would be at a loss if it remained in the estate and was not immediately sold. Thus, an Oversecured Creditor is not guaranteed to remain totally secured since it can't collect interest on its claims. Thus, Adequate Protection is needed to protect the Secured Creditor's interest in the

collateral.
• Some courts protect only the equity cushion from the date of Bankruptcy
• Other courts protect the Secured Party only up to the Value of the claim itself as of the date of Bankruptcy
• Some Courts only protect the equity cushion up to the claim amount (including interest) at the time the claim amount and collateral Value become equal (i.e.- when the decreasing Value of the collateral and the increasing Value of the claim meet)
• Other Courts say that once the equity cushion disappears and meets the claim amount, the Debtor may no longer take Value from the collateral (even if the Value later raises).

• When the Creditor is Entitled to Adequate Protection
  • Collateral is used, sold, or leased by the Trustee/DIP
  • The Creditor's Liens are primed by a senior or equitable Lien authorized by the court to allow the Trustee to obtain credit (i.e. "DIP financing").

• Secured Collateral must be "released" to pay the Secured Claims (as per §725) before proceeding to distribute funds to Unsecured Creditors under §726.

RELEVANT SECTIONS: §506

§506: Determination of Secured Status:

(a) Bifurcation:
   1. An "Allowed Secured Claim" is a claim secured by a Lien on estate property or subject to a setoff, and is secured only to the extent of:
      a) The Value of the Creditor's interest in the property (i.e. collateral)
      b) The Value of the Creditor's setoff (under §553)

2. An "Unsecured Claim/Non-Allowed Secured Claim" is the part of the claim that exceeds the Value of the collateral or setoff.
3. The Value of the collateral and claim is determined at a hearing, taking into account the purpose of the valuation and the intended use/disposition of the collateral.

(b) Allowable Interest to Oversecured Creditors:
1. If the Value of the Creditor's interest is greater than the Creditor's original claim together with the Trustee's fees (under (c) below), he is an "Oversecured Creditor."
2. Oversecured Creditors are allowed to take, in addition to the amount of their original claim:
     a) Post-Petition Interest
     b) Reasonable fees, costs or charges provided for under the Security Agreement

(c) Trustee's Recoverable Fees: The Trustee may recover the reasonable and necessary costs and expenses incurred to preserve or dispose of the property, to the extent the Secured Party benefits.
(d) Unsecured Claims: Unsecured Claims are void (for purposes of surviving Bankruptcy), unless:
(1) The claim was only disallowed under §502(b)(5) (UNMATURED CLAIMS) or §502(e) (REIMBURSEMENT CLAIMS); OR
(2) The only reason the claim is not an Allowed Secured Claim is because the Creditor neglected to file a proof of claim (under §501).

D) **RIGHT TO SETOFF**

OVERVIEW ────────────────────────────

- If the Debtor and the Creditor both owe each other <u>pre-Petition</u> Debts, they may "setoff" the other one's pre-Petition claim when settling the Debt (ex: Debtor owes Creditor $10,000 for goods. Debtor owes Creditor $1,000 for a breach of a warranty (ex: goods were not packed properly); Debtor may setoff Creditor's $10,000 Bankruptcy claim; thus, Creditor only has a Bankruptcy claim for $9,000).
- Creditors are considered to be "Secured" in the amount of their Setoff, and are subject to Adequate Protection laws.
- <u>Creditors</u> – can reduce their claim dollar for dollar by the setoff amount (§506(a) - and the Creditor will retain a Security Interest in Debtor's right to setoff) and are not required to pay their setoff Debt to the Debtor if the Debtor's Debt is greater (§542(b)) (ex: one may think that the Creditor would have to pay the Debtor the full $1,000 in warranty damages (above); this would make the Creditor worse off if he is unsecured, since he'll probably get little if anything out of his $10,000 invoice to the Debtor. Thus, the Creditor would be out $11,000 ($1,000 damage claim + $10,000 shipment of goods which will unlikely be recovered if unsecured); With §506(a), the Creditor is only at a loss for $9,000, since its as if he paid the full $1,000 to the Debtor, maintained a Security Interest in that money, and used it as collateral to collect on his $10,000 claim (of which he could only get the $1,000 "secured" amount)).

• Setoffs are subject to the Automatic Stay, although banks have a right to put a freeze on the Debtor's Account (§362(a)(7)).

- <u>Requirements for Setoff:</u>
  - ☞ Must be a "<u>Mutual Debt</u>"
  - ☞ Must reflect Pre-Petition Debt
  - ☞ Creditor cannot have improved its position (applies to setoffs during the Preference-period)
  - ☞ <u>Cannot be either</u>:
    - ➢ A Disallowed Claim
    - ➢ Or An Assignment for purposes of obtaining a Setoff (to secure the claim) during the Preference Period
    - ➢ Or A Setoff Debt which was incurred during the Preference Period with <u>Intent</u> to obtain setoff right

- **Allowable Setoff Amount:** The following formulas help calculate the amount of setoff a Creditor is entitled to:

> Setoffable Amount = Total Debt $_{\text{owed to Creditor}}$ - "Takeback"

> "Takeback" = ("Insufficiency" $_{\text{at setoff date}}$)
> x ("Insufficiency" $_{\text{Later of 1st \underline{Date of Insufficiency} and 1st Date of the Preference Period}}$)

> Insufficiency = $ owed to Creditor - $ owed to Debtor

> Unsecured Amount = Total Debt $_{\text{owed to Creditor}}$ - Setoffable Amount

- If Undersecured Creditors receive payments on the "unsecured" amount, the payments will be "Voidable Preferences" (see "Voidable Preferences" below).

RELEVANT SECTIONS: §362(a)(7); §506(a); §553

§362(a)(7): Automatic Stay:
The Automatic Stay applies to and affects all entities involved in any setoff of a Debt to the Debtor for any Claim against the Debtor for any obligation to the Debtor which arose before the Petition was filed

§506(a): Bifurcation:
1. An "Allowed Secured Claim" is a claim secured by a Lien on estate property or subject to a setoff, and is secured only to the extent of:
   a) The Value of the Creditor's interest in the property (i.e. collateral)
   b) The Value of the Creditor's setoff (under §553)
2. An "Unsecured Claim/Non-Allowed Secured Claim" is the part of the claim that exceeds the Value of the collateral or setoff.

3. The Value of the collateral and claim is determined at a hearing, taking into account the purpose of the valuation and the intended use/disposition of the collateral.

§553: Setoff:
(a) Right to Setoff:
   i) The rights of a Creditor to offset are not affected by Bankruptcy Provisions (except the Automatic Stay (§362) and §363) if:
      1) The Debt is a Mutual Debt; AND
      2) The Debt arose before the commencement of the case
   ii) Exceptions: Setoffs may not be made to the extent that:
      (1) Disallowed Claim: The Creditor's claim is disallowed
      (2) Assignment: The Claim was Transferred to the Creditor by another entity, either:
        (A) After the Commencement of the Case; OR
        (B) During Insolvency:
           (i) Within the 90 day Preference Period; OR
           (ii) While the Debtor was Insolvent
      (3) Bad Intent: The Creditor incurred its obligation to the Debtor:
        (A) Within the 90 day Preference Period
        (B) While the Debtor was Insolvent
        (C) Intent: For the purpose of obtaining a right of setoff against the Debtor
(b) Limitation for Setoff: The Creditor may be no better than he would have been without having taken the Setoff:
   (1) If the Creditor made the Setoff during the Preference Period, the Trustee may recover from the setoff amount the difference between:
      1. The Insufficiency on the later of:
        (A) 90 Days before Petition Date; AND
        (B) The first day (during the Preference Period) in which there is an insufficiency; AND
      2. The Insufficiency on the date of the Setoff
   (2) "Insufficiency" is the amount Debtor owes the Creditor less that amount the Creditor owes the Debtor
(c) Presumption of Insolvency: The Debtor is presumed to be Insolvent during the 90-day Preference Period.

E) LIQUIDATION AND PRIORITY OF DISTRIBUTION OF ESTATE:

OVERVIEW ——————————————————————————

- In a Chapter 7 proceeding, the Bankruptcy estate is liquidated and distributed in the following order:
  1. Payment to Superior Perfected Secured Creditors to the extent of their secured claim (§724(b)(1); §725).
  2. If there are Tax Liens: (§724)
     a) Payment of §507(a)(1)-(7) "Priority Claims" (as listed below) up to the Value of the Tax Lien
     b) Payment to the holder of the Tax Lien equal to:

Total Tax Lien - $ paid to all §507(a)(1)-(7) claimants   (in aggregate)

     c) Payment to Secured Parties Junior to the Tax Lien
     d) Any part of the Tax Lien's balance not paid above
     e) Payment to the Estate

  3. If there are no Tax Liens: (§726)
     a) Payment of §507(a) Priority Claims
     b) Payments to Allowed Unsecured Creditors
     c) Payment to Unsecured Creditors who filed late
     d) Payment of "Gap" fines, penalties, and damages
     e) Payment of interest on unsecured claims
     f) Remainder to the Debtor

  4. "Priority Claims"(in addition to §507(a) claims):
     a) §726(b) Claims from Converting a Case (as per §365(g) after conversion)
     b) §507(b) Claims for damages arising from inadequate protection
     c) §503 Administration Expenses
     d) "Gap" Claims (as per §502(f))
     e) Wages – within 90 Days – and up to $4,000
     f) Pension type plans
     g) Fisherman/Farmers
     h) Consumer deposits (up to $1,800)
     i) Alimony

---

j) Taxes [not in §724 distribution]
1) Income Tax for returns due within the past 3 years
2) Property Tax payable within 1 year of the Petition
3) Trust fund Tax
4) Employment Taxes within 3 years before Petition
5) Tax Penalties
6) Erroneous refunds (§507(c))
k) Unsecured Insurance Claims

RELEVANT SECTIONS: §724; §725; §726; §507; §503

§724: Treatment of Certain Liens:

(a) Fines and Penalties: The Trustee may avoid a Lien that secures a claim for any fine or penalty arising before the Trustee was appointed (as specified in §726(a)(4)).

(b) Tax Liens - Allowable, unavoidable secured claims subject to a tax Lien, (or proceeds of such property), shall be distributed as follows:

(1) To any holder of an allowed secured claim (as per §725) which is:
   a) Not avoidable under the Bankruptcy Code; AND
   b) Senior to the tax Lien

(2) To holders of claims under §507(a)(1)-(7) claims (i.e. not tax claims) to the extent the tax claim is secured by the Lien

(3) To the holder of the Tax Lien, in the amount exceeding the distribution of (2) above

(4) To secured parties junior to the tax Lien

(5) The balance of the tax Lien holder's claim (not paid under (3) above)

(6) To the estate (under §727)

(c) Competing Claimants: If two claimants would be entitled to distribution under the same section in §724(b) above, then the distribution would be divided up as if the claim were not governed by this section.

(d) Statutory Liens shall be treated as tax Liens if their priority is to be determined under Internal Revenue Code §6323.

§725: Distribution of Certain Property:

Before property is to be distributed under §726 (and after the Petition has been filed), the Trustee must dispose of any estate property if:
- a) A Creditor has an interest in it (i.e. it is the collateral of a Secured Party);
- and b) The property has not been disposed of under another Bankruptcy Code section;
- and c) There was notice and a hearing.

§726: Distribution of Property of the Estate

(a) Priority of Distribution: Property of the Estate (left over after paying Secured Parties, Administrative Expenses, and Tax Liens) shall be distributed as follows (subject to §510's subrogation rights):

(1) Payments of §507 claims (distributed as per §507)

(2) Payment of any Allowed Unsecured Claim (not falling under other subsections of §726) if:
  (A) It is timely filed under §501(a)
  (B) It is timely Filed under §501(b)
  (C) It is filed late, and:
    (i) The Creditor holding the claim did not have notice or actual knowledge of the Bankruptcy in time to file timely; AND
    (ii) The Proof of Claim is filed in time to permit payment

(3) Allowable Unsecured Claims which were filed late (and not excused under §726(a)(2)(C)).

(4) Payment of any Secured or Unsecured Fine, Penalty, Forfeiture, or Punitive Damage if:
  a) They arose before the earlier of:
    1. The time the Trustee was appointed; OR
    2. The time the Order of Relief was granted; AND
  b) The damages or money was not compensation for actual monetary losses suffered by the claim holder

(5) Payment of Interest of all of the above claims (at Legal Rate form date of filing)

(6) To the Debtor

(b) Claimants Under The Same Distribution Class: If there is not enough money to cover the entire class, they shall receive a pro rata payment for their share of claims in their class.
* * * *

(c) Distribution of Community Property * * * *

§507: Priorities:

(a) Expenses and Claims: The following <u>expenses</u> and <u>claims</u> have priority of distribution in the following order after the Secured Creditors have been paid (as per §725/§726: DISPOSITION/DISTRIBUTION OF PROPERTY):

(1) Administrative Expenses:
   a. Allowed under §503(b), including the following (Note: If there are competing claims, they get divided pro-rata):
      1. Actual and necessary costs and expenses of <u>Preserving the Estate</u> (§503(b)(1)(A))
      2. Wages, salaries, or commission for <u>Post-Petition Services</u> (§503(b)(1)(A))
      3. <u>Taxes</u> incurred by the estate (§503(b)(1)(B))
      4. Reimbursement and Compensation to the <u>Trustee</u> (§503(b)(2) and §330(a))
      5. Allowable Attorneys' and Accountants' <u>Fees</u> (§503(b)(4))
   b. Fees and Charges assessed against the estate (under 28 U.S.C. 123).

(2) §502(f) Post-Petition Unsecured Claims:
   a. The case is an Involuntary Case
   b. The claim arises out of the ordinary course of the Debtor's business or financial affairs
   c. The claims occur <u>after</u> the Petition is filed, but <u>before</u> the earlier of:
      1) The appointment of a Trustee; OR
      2) The Determination of the Order for Relief

(3) Up To $4,000[15] of Compensation Claims - to each entity if:
   i) It is earned by the earlier of:
      1. <u>90 days</u> before the Petition was filed; OR
      2. The date the business ceased to operate; AND

---

[15] $4,300 as of April 1, 1998.

ii) The claim was for either:
   (A) <u>Wages, Salaries or Commissions</u> - including vacation, sick, and severance pay earned by an individual; OR
   (B) <u>Sales Commissions</u> - earned by a corporation with only 1 employee acting as an Independent Contractor, as long as:
      1. The Sales Person sold goods/services for the Debtor in the ordinary course of business;
   and 2. The Sales Person earned 75% of his income from the Debtor in the last year.

(4) Allowed Unsecured Claims For Contributions to Employee Benefit Plans:
   (A) Benefits must arise from services rendered within <u>6 months</u> before the Petition was filed.
   (B) Allowable Amount:

((No. of Employees) * ($4,000)[16]) - Total Distributions under (3) + Distributions to other Employee Benefit Plans

(5) $4,000[17] of Unsecured Claims of Fishermen and Farmers:

(6) <u>$1,800[18] of Deposits on Consumer Goods/Services</u> - Up to $1,800[19] for each individual who gave the Debtor a deposit for consumer goods/services that were never tendered.

(7) Alimony and Child Support

(8) Taxes:
   (A) Income Tax for returns due within past <u>3 years</u>
   (B) Property Tax payable within <u>1 year</u> of Petition
   (C) Trust fund Tax
   (D) Employment Taxes within <u>3 years</u> before Petition
   (E) Excise Taxes within <u>3 years</u>
   (F) Custom Duties
   (G) Tax Penalties

---

[16] $4,300 as of April 1, 1998.
[17] $4,300 as of April 1, 1998.
[18] $1,950 as of April 1, 1998.
[19] $1,950 as of April 1, 1998.

(9) Unsecured Claims by Insurance Companies - in which the Debtor promised to make regular installment payments

(b) Secured Party's Attorneys' Fees:
The Secured Party's claim for Attorneys' Fees has priority over all other claims in this section if:
1) The Secured Party is secured by a Lien on the Debtor's property; AND
2) The Trustee provides Adequate Protection for the Secured Party; AND
3) The Creditor has a claim under §507(a)(1) for reimbursement of Attorneys' fees arising from lifting the Automatic Stay (under §362) or preventing the use, sale, or lease of property (under §363)

(c) Erroneous Tax Refund or Credit: The IRS has the same priority over regaining the erroneously made refund/credit as it did in the original taxed amount.

(d) Subrogation Rights: An entity that is subrogated to the rights of the holder of a claim specified in (a)(3)-(9) is not subrogated to the right of that claim holder to priority under that subsection.

§503: Allowance Of Administrative Expenses:

(a) Filing for Administrative Expenses:[20]
1. Timely Claims: Entities holding Claims for Administrative Expenses may timely file a request for payment.
2. Untimely Claims: An Entity may only file a late Claim if:
   a) It shows cause; AND
   b) The court grants permission to do so.

(b) Kinds of Administrative Expenses Allowed:

i) The following are various Administrative Expenses (in addition to those under §502(f)) allowed after notice and a hearing:
   (1) Expenses:
      (A) Costs of Preserving the Estate: The actual and necessary costs of preserving the estate, including:

---

[20] Note: The Rules of Bankruptcy Procedure will specify the time, the form, and the method of the filing

1. Wages; AND
2. Salaries; AND
3. Commissions for services rendered <u>after</u> the commencement of the case (e.g. Attorney's fees); AND
4. Payment to an individual Debtor for services rendered to the estate (ex: When the individual was a sole proprietor and was employed by the estate to run the business after the commencement of the case. (<u>Local Loan v. Hunt</u>, 292 U.S. 234, 243 (1943)).

(B) Taxes - Either:
    (i) <u>Post-Petition taxes</u> - incurred by the estate, except those specified in §507(a)(8) (Note: This includes taxes on capital gains from sales of property by the trustee and taxes on income earned by the estate during the case);

or (ii) <u>Taxes due as a result of an excessive carryover allowance</u> - which the Estate benefited from, regardless of whether the taxes related to a year ending before or after the Petition was filed.[21]

(C) Fines & Penalties (or reduction in credit) - relating to a tax specified in §503(B) (including interest on tax liabilities and certain tax penalties incurred by the trustee.)

(2) Compensation and Reimbursement - awarded under §330(a) (to a trustee, examiner, Debtor's Attorney, and other professionals)

---

21 Background: The tax code allows the trustee of an estate which suffers a net operating loss to carry back the loss against an earlier profit year of the estate/Debtor and to get a tentative refund for the earlier year. This is subject, however, to a later full audit of the loss which led to the refund. The IRS is required to issue a tentative refund to the trustee (whether the refund was applied for by the Debtor or by the trustee), but if the refund amount later proves to have been wrong, the IRS can request that the tax due because of the error be payable by the estate as an Administrative Expense.

(3) The actual and necessary expenses – incurred by any of the following (other than compensation and reimbursement specified in (4)):
   (A) A creditor that <u>files an involuntary Petition</u> (§303);
or (B) A creditor who (with the court's approval) <u>recovers property</u> for the benefit of the estate that the Debtor Transferred or concealed;
or (C) A creditor who incurred <u>expenses in a criminal prosecution</u> related to the bankruptcy case or the Debtor's business or property;
or (D) Any of the following who incur expenses in making a <u>substantial contribution</u> to a Chapter 9 or 11 case:
      1. A creditor;
   or 2. An Indenture trustee;
   or 3. An equity Security holder;
   or 4. A committee representing creditors or equity Security holders (other than an "official committee" appointed under §1102);
or (E) A <u>Custodian</u> superseded under §543 (and in addition to actual and necessary expenses, compensation for the Custodian's services which benefit the estate);
or (F) A <u>member of a committee</u> appointed under §1102, if the expenses are incurred in the performance of the committee's duties.

(4) Compensation for Professionals – allowed if:
   1. <u>Compensation is reasonable, based on the:</u>
      a. Time of the services; AND
      b. Nature of the services; AND
      c. Extent of the services; AND
      d. Value of the services; AND
      e. Cost of comparable services in a non-bankruptcy case; AND
   2. Services are of an <u>Attorney</u> or an <u>accountant</u>; AND
   3. The Entity incurring the Professional expenses is one listed in paragraph (3) above (i.e. an Entity for which necessary and actual expenses are allowed); AND
   4. Compensation represents reimbursement for <u>actual, necessary expenses</u> incurred by the Attorney or accountant

(5) Indenture Trustees:
   1. Reasonable Compensation for the service of an Indenture trustee making a substantial contribution in a Chapter 9 or 11 case
   2. The reasonableness of the compensation shall be based on the :
      a. Time of the services; AND
      b. Nature of the services; AND
      c. Extent of the services; AND
      d. Value of the services; AND
      e. Cost of comparable services in a non-bankruptcy case

(6) Fees and Mileage are payable pursuant to Title 28, Ch. 119 (§2041 et seq.).

ii) `None of the above Claims will be allowed if they are Claims or expenses allowed under §502(f), which include:
   a) Claims that arise in the ordinary course of the Debtor's business
and b) Claims that arise between the commencement of an involuntary case and:
   1. The appointment of a Trustee
   or 2. The Order for Relief

III. POWERS OF THE TRUSTEE/DIP

OVERVIEW ————————————————————

Upon filing of the Petition, either a "Trustee" or a "Debtor in Possession" is appointed to take-over the bankrupt estate.

- A "Trustee" is a third party which takes control of the estate in bankruptcy.
- A "Debtor-in-Possession" is the actual Debtor itself, who is entrusted to handle the affairs of the bankrupt estate.
- In almost all cases, a Debtor-in-Possession can enjoy all of the powers given to a Trustee under the code (§1107).
- Summary of Powers Over the Estate:
  - ☞ Turnover Orders - the Trustee may force third parties to return property they received from the Debtor during the Preference Period if such property is deemed "Property of the Estate" (§542).
  - ☞ Right to Avoid Executory Contracts - The Trustee may terminate contracts between the Debtor and a third party (§365).
  - ☞ Right to Avoid Liens - The Trustee may use its "Strong-Arm Power" to avoid any "unperfected" Liens placed on Estate Property, thereby causing Secured Parties who are unperfected to be unsecured (§544; §545; §546).
  - ☞ Right to Sell, Lease, or Use Collateral - The Trustee may sell, use, or lease assets secured as collateral by a Secured Party, as long as it assures that the Secured Party's interest in the collateral gets "Adequate Protection" (§363).
  - ☞ Right to Avoid Preferences - The Trustee may require any "voidable" Transfers made during the Preference Period to be turned-over to the estate (§547).
  - ☞ Right to Avoid Fraudulent Conveyances - The Trustee may require Transfers made as a "Fraudulent Conveyance" within 1 year of the bankruptcy filing, to be turned-over to the estate (§548).

A) **TURNOVER ORDERS (§542)**

OVERVIEW

- The Trustee has the power to obtain a "Turnover Order" under §542. This order forces a third party to return the actual Estate Property it received from the Debtor, to the Trustee.
- §542(a) allows the Trustee to order property returned to the Estate if:
  1) The Trustee wants to Use, Sell, or Lease it (under §363).
  Or 2) It is property which may be exempt by the Debtor (under §522).
- In other cases in which the Trustee is entitled to avoid certain Transfers, it may require the "Value" of the asset Transfer red to be returned to the Estate, rather than the actual asset itself.
- Requirements to enforce a Turnover Order against certain property:
  1. Debtor must have an "Interest" in the property ("no matter how small")
  and 2. Either:
      a) Property of the Estate may be Used, Sold, or Leased (under §363)
      or b) Property would be Exempt (under §522)
- Debtor's Interest in Property:
  - ☞ The Debtor will be deemed to have an interest in the property if it has any interest in it, regardless of how small or unpowerful (compare this to §363 interest requirements, which requires the Debtor to have at least a minimal interest in the property);
  - ☞ The Debtor will even be considered to have an interest if there is a hypothetical possibility that it will get Value from the surplus of the sale of its collateral -- no matter how remote or Valueless.
    - ➢ Example: The IRS must send a notice of levy to a property owner; the right to the notice is enough to show the Debtor has an interest in the property.

- Property Subject to Turnover Orders:

  1) Proceeds: If collateral was sold before it was turned-over, the Trustee has a right to the proceeds.

2) Property Perfected by Possession: When a Trustee takes collateral from a Secured Party which was perfected by possession, the Trustee must give Adequate Protection to the Secured Party.

☞ The Secured Party's status as a "Secured Creditor" will not be reduced even though it no longer has possession of the collateral (ex: Negotiable Instruments, perfected by possession under Article 9, will lose their perfected status if the Secured Party loses possession for more than 21 days. If the Trustee wants to take the negotiable instrument it must provide the Secured Party Adequate Protection that the Secured Party will not be hurt by the loss in perfection of the instrument.).

3) Property Repossessed By Secured Party: may be recovered by the Trustee until the Secured Party sells it to a "bona-fide Purchaser" (as long as "Adequate Protection" is assured).

4) Collateral Subject to a Tax Lien: (§724(b))

☞ Collateral given to any Lien Holder senior to the IRS may have to return property pursuant to the Trustee's Turnover Order.

☞ Garnished Accounts – If the IRS levies an asset (ex: a bank Account), the Debtor still has an interest in the Account until the Debt is actually extinguished; therefore, it may be subject to the Turnover Order.

• Property Not Subject to Turnover:

1) Property Transfer red to a Bona-Fide Purchaser: If the property is Transfer red:
a) In Good Faith
b) Without Knowledge of the bankruptcy
c) To an Entity other than the Trustee
☞ Note, that, although not subject to the Turnover Order, the Transferee may be responsible for returning the Value of the Transfer to the Trustee (under §550).

2) Valueless Collateral: If the property is of "inconsequential Value or benefit" to the estate and the Trustee does not want to pursue obtaining it (§542(a)).

3) Special Custodian Rule - Property of the Estate held with a
    Custodian (ex: the Sheriff, a Trustee, guardian, etc.) may not be
    used or distributed; rather, the Custodian must turn over such
    property to the Trustee (§543(a),(b)) ;
- Exception:
    ☞ The Custodian does not have to turn-over such property to
       the Estate if (§543(d)(2)):
       1. The Custodian is an Assignee for the benefit of a
           Creditor,
    and 2. The Custodian was appointed as such an Assignee, or
           took charge of the property at least 120 Days before
           the Petition was filed
    and 3. No fraud or injustice would result
- The Custodian may, in the court's discretion, be excused from
  turning over property in its control if :
  1. The court deems it to be in the best interest of the Creditors
      (§543(d)(1)).
  And 2. The Debtor is not Insolvent
  and 3. The Equity holders of the Debtor will be better served by
           the Custodian retaining possession of the property.

RELEVANT SECTIONS: §542, §543

§542: Turnover of Property of the Estate:

(a) Return of Property to the Estate: The Trustee may order property
     to be returned to the estate if it falls under §363 (SALE/USE OF
     PROPERTY) or §522 (EXEMPT PROPERTY) unless the property is
     of inconsequential Value or benefit to the estate.
(b) **Debts to the Estate**: Entities that owe money to the estate must
     pay their debts when they are due (either matured, or they are
     debts payable in demand or order) less any setoffs (under §553:
     SETOFF)
(c) Property Not Subject to Turnover: Property will not be subject to
     Turnover if the Creditor:
     1. Had no actual notice or actual knowledge of the
         commencement of the case
     2. Transferred the property in Good Faith
     3. Transferred to an entity other than the Trustee

(d) Life Insurance Companies may receive property of the Debtor under particular circumstances, as when the property is used to pay premiums under a life insurance contract that was entered into before the Petition date.

(e) Books and Records:
1. The Court may order records and documents relating to the Debtor's property to be turned over or disclosed to the Trustee.
2. Privileges that may apply remain intact.
3. There must be <u>notice</u> and a <u>hearing</u>.

§543: Turnover of Property by A Custodian:

(a) Actions Prohibited by Custodian:
1. A Custodian (defined in §101(11)) who knows that a bankruptcy case was started may not <u>disburse</u> or <u>administer</u> any of the following property in the Custodian's estate:
   a. Property of the Debtor
   b. Proceeds, product, offspring, rents, or profits of the property
   c. Property of the Estate
2. <u>Exception</u>: The Custodian may administer property if necessary to preserve it.

(b) Turnover by Custodian - A Custodian must:
(1) <u>Turnover</u>: Deliver to the trustee any of the above-listed property held by the Custodian or Transferred to the Custodian that is in the Custodian's custody control on the date that the Custodian first knew of the starting of the case
and (2) <u>Accounting</u>: File an accounting of any of the above-listed property of the Debtor that the Custodian controlled at any time

(c) Disbursements: After notice and a hearing, the court shall:
(1) Protect all parties that the Custodian has become obligated to with respect to the Debtor's such property
(2) Award the Custodian reasonable compensation for services and expenses incurred
(3) <u>Custodian Liable for Wrongful Disbursements</u>:
   a. The court shall hold the Custodian liable for any improper or excessive disbursement
   b. <u>Exceptions</u>:

1. If the Custodian is an assignee for the benefit of the creditors that was appointed or took possession more than 120 days before the Petition date.
2. The disbursement was made in accordance with applicable law.
3. The disbursement was approved:
   a. By a court of competent jurisdiction
   and b. After notice and a hearing
   and c. Before the start of the bankruptcy case

(d) Exceptions to Turnover: After notice and a hearing, the bankruptcy court:
   (1) May excuse the Custodian from subsection (a), (b), or (c) in the best interests of creditors and equity Security holders (if the Debtor is not Insolvent).
   (2) Must excuse the Custodian from subsections (a) and (b)(1) if:
   a. The Custodian is an assignee for the benefit of the Debtor's creditors.
   and b. The Custodian was appointed or took possession more than 120 days before the Petition date.
   and c. Compliance is not necessary to prevent fraud or injustice.

B) TRUSTEE'S USE OF COLLATERAL: (§363)

OVERVIEW ───────────────────────────────────

- The Automatic Stay (§362) keeps the collateral in the estate; The Trustee may retain possession over any property it has an interest in (remember, "no matter how small or remote") (see §541(a)).
- Ordinary Use of Collateral – The Trustee may use collateral or its proceeds, interest free, before distributing it to the secured parties, as long as it is in the ordinary course of business (§363) .
- Not in the Ordinary Course: When the Trustee wants to use the collateral out of the ordinary course of the Debtor's business, Notice, Hearing, and Court Approval are required (if the Creditor objects to such proposed use)(§363(b)(1)).
- Use of CASH COLLATERAL:

  - Cash collateral (as defined in §363(a)) may not be used by the Trustee unless:
    - ➤ The Court allows
    - or ➤ The Creditor agrees

  - ☞ "Cash Collateral" includes
    - ➤ Cash
    - ➤ Negotiable Instruments
    - ➤ Documents of Title
    - ➤ Securities
    - ➤ Deposit Accounts
    - ➤ Proceeds, rents, and profits
    - ➤ Other cash equivalents

  - ☞ Oversecured Creditors will get interest from any Value leftover from the proposed use or sale of its Collateral -- Unsecured Creditor' will not be entitled to get this interest (§362(a)).

  - ☞ Adequate Protection Defense: Secured Parties may use the "Adequate Protection" defense to prevent the Sale, Use, or Lease of its collateral.
    - • Burden of Proof: The Creditor must show that the Value of the collateral will not be adequately protected while used or leased by the Trustee, and that the collateral will diminish in Value.

69

• <u>Giving Adequate Protection</u> - The Trustee may provide Adequate Protection in 3 ways (§361):
1. Cash Payments - to the Creditor, reflecting the depletion in Value
2. Extra Collateral - to the Creditor to Account for depletion of original collateral
3. Indubitable Equivalent - give the Creditor an "equivalent" type of Security.

• Minor Interest Defense: Property in which the Debtor only holds Equitable Title, and <u>not</u> Legal Title (i.e. no possession; ex: a trust) is not subject to §363. Such property includes:
• Beneficiary to a trust where the Debtor is the Trustee
• Beneficiary to a will whose Executor is the Debtor
• Mortgages, where the mortgagor is the Bankrupt Debtor.

RELEVANT SECTIONS: §361, 363

§361: Adequate Protection

A. Adequate Protection may be provided by:

(1) Cash Payments: Requiring the trustee to make <u>Cash Payments</u> to the extent that the actions by the Trustee (under §362, §363, and §364) result in a decrease in Value of the Creditor's interest in the property

or (2) Extra Liens: Providing the Creditor with an <u>Additional or Substituted Security Interest</u> to the extent that actions by the Trustee (under §362, §363, and §364) result in a decrease in Value of the Creditor's interest in the property

or (3) Other Relief: an "indubitable equivalent" of the Creditor's interest (other than giving the Creditor payment as a §503(b)(1) Administrative Expense).

B. Sections 362 (AUTOMATIC STAY), §363 (USE, SALE, AND LEASE
    OF PROPERTY), or §364 (OBTAINING CREDIT) may require
    "Adequate Protection" of a Person's interest in property.

§363: Use, Sale, or Lease of Property:

(a) "Cash Collateral" - In this section, "Cash Collateral" means:
    1. Cash
    2. Negotiable Instruments
    3. Documents of Title
    4. Securities
    5. Deposit Accounts
    6. Other cash equivalents subject to a Security Interest under
        §552(b) that the estate and an Entity other than the estate
        have an interest in, including:
        a) Proceeds
        b) Products
        c) Offspring
        d) Rents
        e) Profits for lodging properties (including fees, charges,
            Accounts or other payments for rooms/facilities at a
            hotel, motel or other lodging facility)

(b) Not in the Ordinary Course of Business:
    (1) Notice and Hearing Required: The trustee may use, sell, or
         lease Property of the Estate other than in the Ordinary
         Course of Business, only after notice and a hearing.
    (2) Cases Where Notification is Required by §7A of the
         Clayton Act * * * *

(c) In The Ordinary Course of Business:
    (1) The Trustee may Use, Sell or Lease estate property in the
         Ordinary Course of Business, without notice and a hearing
         if:
        a) The business of the Debtor is authorized to continue
            (under §§721, 1108, 1203, 1204, or 1304)
        b) The Court does not order otherwise
            (2) Cash Collateral - The Trustee may not Use, Sell or
                 Lease Cash Collateral (under §363(1)) unless:
                 (A) Everyone with an interest in the Cash
                      Collateral consents.

71

or (B) The court authorizes such Use, Sale or Lease after <u>notice</u> and a <u>hearing</u>.

(3) Hearings Under §363(c)(2)(B):

    a. These hearings may be preliminary hearings or consolidated with a §363(e) hearing.

    b. Either way, the hearing must be scheduled in accordance with the Debtor's needs.

    c. If the hearing is a preliminary hearing, the court may authorize the use, sale or lease only if there is a reasonable likelihood that the Trustee will prevail at the final hearing (§363(c)).

    d. The court shall act quickly on a request for authorization for the Trustee to use, sell or lease property (under §363(2)(b)).

(4) Trustee's Duty Not to Commingle Funds: The Trustee shall segregate (and account for) any Cash Collateral in its Possession, Custody, or Control (except as provided in §363(2)).

(d) Limitations on Use: The Trustee may only use, sell or lease property to the extent not inconsistent with other relief granted under §362(c), §362(d), §362(e) or §362(f).

(e) Adequate Protection: Notwithstanding any other provision, the court shall prohibit or condition the Use, Sale or Lease of estate property (and property that is subject to any unexpired lease of personal property) <u>to the extent that</u> it is necessary to provide Adequate Protection of any parties' interests in the property (and Adequate Protection cannot otherwise be provided).

(f) Sale of Property: The Trustee may sell property (under (b) and (c) above) <u>free and clear</u> of any interest in such property only if:

    (1) <u>Law Permits</u> - applicable non-bankruptcy law permits the sale free and clear of the interest

or (2) <u>Consent</u> - The Creditor consents

or (3) Beneficial Sale:

    a) The Creditor's interest is a Lien

and b) The property will be sold for a Value greater than the aggregate Value of all Liens on the property

or (4) Bona-fide Dispute - The Creditor's interest in the property is
in dispute

or (5) Entitled only to Monetary Interest - The Creditor could be
compelled to accept a money satisfaction of its interest in a
legal or equitable proceeding.

(g) Sale of Right in Dowery: The Trustee may sell property under
§363(b) or (c) free and clear of any dowery or courtesy right
(vested or contingent).

(h) Sale of Co-Owned Property:
The Trustee may sell both the estate's interest and the interest of
any co-owner of property, if:
(1) Splitting ("partition of") the interests in the property is
impracticable
and (2) The Sale of the estate's interest would yield significantly
less than the sale of the property free and clear of the co-
owner's interest.
and (3) The benefit to the Estate outweighs the detriment to the co-
owners
and (4) The property is not used to assist public utilities (heat, light,
power)
and (5) At the time of the Petition, the Debtor had an undivided
interest as either a:
a) Tenant in Common
b) Joint Tenant
c) Tenant by the Entirety

(i) Purchase of Property By Spouse/Co-owner:
The spouse or co-owner of the property of a Debtor has the first
right to purchase the following estate property if a sale is about
to take place:
1. Property being sold under §363(g) (COURTESY AND DOWER)
2. Property under sold under §363(h) (TENANT IN COMMON,
JOINT TENANT, TENANT BY THE ENTIRETY)
3. Property that was community property immediately before
the commencement of the case.

(j) Distribution of Proceeds to Co-Owners: Upon sale of co-owned
property under (g) or (h), the Trustee shall distribute the
proceeds of the sale to the co-owner (or spouse) less the costs

and expenses of the sale (but not the trustee's compensation since it is paid by the Bankruptcy Estate).

(k) Purchase By Lien-holder: The holder of a Lien on property to be sold under (b) (above) may bid at a sale for the property, and may offset the Value of the Lien-holder's Claim from the sale price of the property.

(l) "Ipso Facto" Clauses Not Effective: The Trustee will maintain its right to <u>use</u>, <u>sell</u> or <u>lease</u> property (under §363(b) or (c) or under a bankruptcy plan) even if the contract contains an "<u>Ipso Facto</u>" provision, which is a provision that requires the Debtor's interest in the property to be terminated, modified or forfeited by any of the following events:
1.   The Debtor's insolvency or financial condition
or   2.   The filing of a bankruptcy Petition
or   3.   On a Bankruptcy Trustee's appointment or taking possession
or   4.   On a non-bankruptcy Custodian's taking possession

(m) Reversal on Appeal - If the authorization to sell or lease property is later reversed or modified on appeal, the sale or lease is <u>not</u> affected if:
1.   The Purchaser acted in good faith, regardless of whether or not he knew of the appeal.
and 2.   The authorization to sell or lease was not stayed (pending the decision of the appeal).

(n) Voiding "Rigged" Sales:
1.   The Trustee may "avoid" a sale of the property if the bidders planned together to bid for property at a certain price.
2.   The Trustee may recover damages (Value of property – price paid), all costs, fees and expenses, and punitive damages in certain cases (ex: in cases of willfulness).

(o) Burdens of Proof: In hearings under this section for use, sale and lease of property:
(1) <u>Trustee's Burden</u>: To prove that a Creditor has Adequate Protection

74

(2) <u>Creditor's Burden</u>: To prove the validity and priority of its
interest

C) RIGHTS OVER EXECUTORY CONTRACTS OR LEASES: (§365)

OVERVIEW ────────────────────────────

- The Trustee has the power to assume or reject "Executory Contracts" and "Unexpired Leases":
  - An "Executory Contract" is a contract which requires substantial performance by one or both sides in order not to be deemed an "excuse" for the other party to perform (some courts require both sides to have outstanding obligations to be performed; others only require one side to).
  - An "Unexpired Lease" must be a "true lease" (i.e.- not a "Security Interest disguised as a lease" under the UCC (see §1-201(37))) under the State Uniform Commercial Code.

- The Trustee must either Assume, Assign, Reject, or Abandon, the Estate's contracts or leases. However, court approval is necessary for the Trustee to assume or reject them.
  - Business Judgment Rule Test – Most courts approve the Trustee's decision under a "business judgment rule test," and only overrule the Trustee's decision upon a showing of Bad-faith or Gross Abuse of Discretion .
  - Balancing of the Equities Test – A minority of courts use a balancing test. These courts would allow a contract or lease to be rejected if the harm to the third-party is not disproportionate to the benefit of the Bankrupt Debtor upon the rejection.

- The Trustee must assume or reject a contract or lease in its entirety; it cannot pick and choose portions of the contract or lease it wishes to keep.
- Time Limitations:

  - Chapter 7 proceeding: The Trustee must assume a contract within 60 days after the Order for Relief is made. If there is no assumption, the contract/lease will be deemed rejected.

    - Chapter 11, 12, & 13 proceedings:

- Executory Contracts & Residential Leases – may be rejected/assumed at any time before the Plan is confirmed, unless the third-party is granted an "expedited decision" (§365(d)(2)).
- Nonresidential Leases - must be assumed or rejected within 60 days after the Order for Relief is made, unless the court grants an extension.

- Requirements to Assume Contracts/Leases in Default:

1) A Trustee must meet the following requirements if he wishes to assume a contract of which it is already in default (§365(b)(1)):
   a) Cure – The Trustee must cure the default
   b) Compensate - The Trustee must compensate the other party for any monetary loss caused by the default.
   c) Adequate Assurance of Future Performance
2) Further Assurances - If Trustee cannot cure or compensate, it can provide adequate assurance to the third party that it will cure and/or compensate it for defaults.
3) Defaults Caused by Bankruptcy – A contract or lease will not be deemed to be in default (for purposes of §365(b)(1)) if the default is caused by an "Ipso-facto Clause" (i.e. a clause which creates a default if the Debtor goes bankrupt or becomes Insolvent).

- Agreements Which May Not Be Assumed:

1) Personal Service Contracts (§365(c)(1)): A contract may not be assumed if:
   - Applicable non-bankruptcy law allows the other party to be excused from performance
   and - The contract is assigned to another party, (ex: Debtor Picasso is under contract to paint a portrait for John. Under applicable State law, if Personal service contract such as this, is assigned by Picasso, John would be excused from performing under the contract).

2) Contracts to Loan Money or to Issue Securities

3) Nonresidential Leases Terminated Before Bankruptcy - if the termination occurred under non-bankruptcy law.

§365: Executory Contracts and Unexpired Leases:

(a) Trustee's Strong-Arm Power: The Trustee may <u>assume</u> or <u>reject</u> any Executory contract or Unexpired lease of the Debtor, subject to:
   1. The Court's Approval
   2. Reasonable notice and a hearing
   3. §365(b), (c), and (d)
   4. §765-§766 (CUSTOMER PROPERTY)

(b) Executory contracts Defaulted by Debtor:

   (1) If the Debtor previously defaulted on an Executory contract/Unexpired lease, the Trustee may only assume it if he:
      (A) <u>Cures the Default</u>, or provides <u>Adequate Assurance</u> that he will cure soon
   and (B) <u>Compensates</u> the other party for any actual monetary loss arising from the default or provides <u>Adequate Assurance</u> that the Trustee will compensate.
   and (C) Provides <u>Adequate Assurance</u> of future performance under the contract/lease
   (2) <u>Exceptions</u>: §365(b)(1) does not apply if the default is a breach of an ipso facto provision relating to:
      (A) The <u>Insolvency or Financial Condition</u> of the Debtor (at any time before the closing of the Bankruptcy case)
   or (B) The Commencement of a Bankruptcy case
   or (C) The <u>Appointment of a Trustee</u> under Bankruptcy (or the taking of possession by a non-bankruptcy Custodian.)
   or (D) The <u>Satisfaction of any Penalty Rate/Provision</u> relating to a default from the Debtor for non-performance of a <u>non-monetary obligation</u> under the executory contract
   (3) Definition of "Adequate Assurance" (as used in §365(b)(1) and (f)(2)(b)) for future performance of a real property lease in a <u>shopping center</u> ***

   (4) <u>Supplies and Services Incidental to Unassumed Lease</u>: If there is an unexpired lease in default (but not one described in (b)(2) (OBLIGATIONS UNDER IPSO FACTO PROVISIONS)), the lessor <u>does not</u> have to give services or supplies

78

incidental to the lease unless the Trustee pays (by the terms
of the lease) for services or supplies given before the lease is
assumed.

(c) Restrictions - When Trustee May Not Assume or Assign - The
trustee may not Assume or Assign an executory
contract/unexpired lease (whether or not the contract
prohibits/restricts assignment of rights), if:
    (1) Applicable Law Excuses Performance:
       (A) Applicable law excuses the other party from performing
the contract with an Entity other than the Debtor .
    and (B) The party does not consent to an Assumption or
Assignment.
or   (2) Contracts to Make Loans: The contract is a commitment to
loan money to the Debtor or to issue a Security of the
Debtor.
or   (3) Commercial Leases - The lease is a non-residential lease
which has been terminated under applicable non-bankruptcy
law before the Order for Relief was filed.
or   (4) Airport Terminal Leases * * *

(d) Time Limit:
    (1) Residential Real/Personal Property in Chapter 7: If the
Trustee in a Chapter 7 case does not assume a contract/lease
within 60 days after the Petition (may be extended by Court
within the 60 days), the contract/lease is presumed rejected.
    (2) Residential Real/Personal Property in Chapters 9,11,12, or
13:
       a. The Trustee may assume the contract at any time before
Confirmation of the Plan.
       b. Upon motion, a court may require the Trustee to make a
determination by a specific time.
    (3) Trustee's Obligations under Unexpired lease of Non-
Residential Real Property:
       a. After the Order for Relief, the Trustee must perform all
obligations under an unexpired lease of non-residential
real property until the lease is Assumed or Rejected.
       b. Duties Excluded: Duties under §365(b)(2)
         (OBLIGATIONS UNDER IPSO FACTO PROVISIONS).
    (4) Non-Residential Real Property Leases (any Chapter): If the
Trustee does not Assume or Reject the lease within 60 days

of the Order for Relief, the lease is deemed Rejected (the
property must be surrendered to the Lessor)

(5) Leases of Aircraft Terminals or Gates * * *
(6) Leases of Aircraft Terminals or Gates * * *
(7) Leases of Aircraft Terminals or Gates * * *
(8) Leases of Aircraft Terminals or Gates * * *
(9) Aircraft * * *
(10) Trustee's Obligations under Unexpired lease of Personal
     Property - Chapter 11:
     a. The Trustee must perform all obligations arising after
         60 days of the Order for Relief until the lease is
         Assumed or Rejected
     b. The Court may order otherwise (regarding the timing or
         the obligations themselves), if:
         1. There is notice and a hearing.
     and 2. The equities of the case favor a modification.
     c. Duties Excluded: Duties under §365(b)(2)
         (OBLIGATIONS UNDER IPSO FACTO PROVISIONS).
     d. The Lessor does not waive his rights under the lease or
         under the Code by accepting performance of the
         Debtor's obligations by the Trustee.

(e) Modifications Not Allowed:

     (1) The Debtor may not modify or terminate an executory
          contract/unexpired lease (including contracts for personal
          property, but not property that was relieved from the
          Automatic Stay of §362) based soley on an Ipso Facto
          provision relating to:
          (A) The Insolvency or Financial Condition of the Debtor (at
              any time before the closing of the Bankruptcy case)
     or   (B) The Commencement of a Bankruptcy case
     or   (C) The Appointment of a Trustee under Bankruptcy (or the
              taking of possession by a non-bankruptcy Custodian).

     (2) Exception: §365(e)(1) does not apply (i.e. ipso facto clauses
          will be effective) to the following types of Contracts/Leases:
          (A) Non-assignable Contract/Lease – if:
              (i) Applicable law excuses a party from accepting/
                   rendering performance to a Trustee or Assignee

and (ii) The party does not consent to an Assumption or
Assignment

or (B) <u>Contracts to Make Loans</u> – if the contract is a
commitment to loan money to the Debtor or to issue a
Security of the Debtor.

(f) When Trustee May Assign:
(1) The Trustee may <u>assign</u> an executory contract or unexpired
lease (regardless of a restriction clause or prohibiting law).[22]
(2) Requirements for Assignment:
(A) The Trustee <u>assumes</u> the contract/lease
(B) The Assignee gives Adequate Assurance of Future
Performance (whether or not there is a default)
(3) The Contract/Lease terms cannot be terminated or modified
because of the assumption or assignment by the Trustee
(regardless of a termination or modification clause or
applicable law).

(g) Time of Breach: The rejection of an executory
contract/unexpired lease of the Debtor will be considered a
<u>breach</u> as of the following dates:

(1) Unassumed Contract/Lease – The breach is deemed to have
occurred <u>immediately before Petition date</u> if the
contract/lease has not been assumed either:
a) under §365
or b) under a Chapter 9, 11, 12 or 13 Plan

(2) Assumed Contract/Lease -
(A) <u>NON-CONVERTED CASE</u>: The breach is deemed to
have occurred <u>at the time of rejection</u> if the lease case
not been converted to a Chapter 7 proceeding (under
§1112, 1208 or 1307).
and (B) CONVERTED CASES:
(i) Immediately before the time of Conversion if:
a) It was assumed before the Conversion
and b) It was rejected after the Conversion

or (ii) At The Time Of Rejection if:

---

[22] With the exception of leases of airport terminals and gates.

a)   It was assumed after the Conversion
and b)   It was rejected after the Conversion

(h) Debtor as Lessor of Real Property Lease:
   (1) Real Property Leases:
      (A) Lessee's Rights in Rejected Lease:
         (i)   If the Trustee's Rejection of the Unexpired Real
               Property Lease would allow the Lessee to treat the
               lease as terminated (under the lease itself,
               applicable law or an agreement), the Lessee may
               treat the lease as terminated.
         (ii) If the lease term has begun, the Lessee may retain
               its leasehold rights[23] for the remainder of the lease
               term to the extent they are enforceable under
               applicable non-bankruptcy law
      (B) Lessee's Right to Setoff: If the Lessee elects to retain
           control of the property, it may setoff any damages from
           Debtor's non-performance before it pays its rent (but
           only rent reserved for the remainder of the term after
           the date of rejection).
      (C) Rejection of a Lease of Real Property in a Shopping
           Center * * *

   (2) Rejection of Timeshares * * * *

   (i)   Executory Contract to Sell Real Estate:
      (1) Purchaser's Possessory Rights: If the trustee rejects
           an executory contract to sell real estate, and the
           Purchaser remains in possession of the property,
           the Purchaser may either:
           a)   Treat the contract as terminated
      or b)   Remain in Possession of the Property
      (2) Purchasers Retaining Possession: If the Purchaser
           retains possession of the property then the parties
           will have the following duties:
         (A) The Purchaser's Duty to Pay:
            1.   He shall continue to make all payments to
                 the Estate

---

[23] Includes rights relating to the amount of rent and the timing of payments; rights of
use, possession, quiet enjoyment, subletting, assignment, hypothecation.

2. He may offset any damages occurring
after the date of rejection from
nonperformance by the Trustee
- (B) The Trustee's Duty to Deliver Title:
  1. The Trustee must deliver title to the
  Purchaser, as per the contract
  2. The Trustee is <u>not</u> required to perform all
  other obligations of the contract

(j) Purchaser's Lien:
  1. Applicability - Purchasers not electing §365(i)(2): This
  section applies to:
     a) A Purchaser whose executory contract is rejected and
     who treats it as terminated under §365(i).
     b) A Purchaser whose executory contract is rejected and
     he is not in <u>possession</u> of the property.
  2. Rights: The above Purchasers will maintain a <u>Lien</u> on the
  property for the portion of the purchase price already paid.

(k) Automatic Novation: An assignment of an executory contract or
unexpired lease by the Trustee will relieve the Trustee and the
Estate from any liability for a breach occurring after the
assignment.

(l) Lessor's Right to Security: If the Debtor is a <u>lessee,</u> the landlord
may require the same deposit or Security from the Assignee as
the one he would have obtained from a similar tenant at the
beginning of the lease term.

(m) Rental Agreements: Leases of real property shall include any
rental agreement to use real property (for purposes of,
§541(b)(2) (PROPERTY OF THE ESTATE), §362(b)(10)
(EXCEPTIONS TO AUTOMATIC STAY), and this section).

(n) Intellectual Property

  (1) If the Debtor is a Licensor of an Intellectual Property right
  under an executory contract, and the Trustee rejects the
  contract, the Licensee may either:

E-Z RULES FOR BANKRUPTCY

(A) <u>Treat the contract as terminated</u> – If the Trustee's
rejection is the equivalent of a breach that would allow
the Licensee to treat the contract as terminated by:
1. Its own terms
or 2. Applicable non-bankruptcy law
or 3. An agreement made by the Licensee with another
party

(B) Retain its Rights:
1. The Licensee may retain its rights under the
contract (and any supplementary agreement) to the
Intellectual Property as they existed before the case
commenced.
2. <u>Rights Included</u>:
a. Right to enforce exclusivity provisions in the
contract.
b. The rights retained <u>do not</u> include the right to
specific performance.
3. <u>Time for Retention of Rights</u>:
(i) Until the end of the contract period
or (ii) Until any period that the contract is extended
as of right by applicable non-bankruptcy law
(2) <u>Licensee's Rights</u>: If the Licensee chooses to retain its rights
(under (1)(B)):
(A) The Trustee must allow the Licensee to exercise its
rights.
and (B) The Licensee must make any royalty payments due
under the contract for the entire time the Licensee
retains its rights.
and (C) The Licensee is deemed to waive:
(i) Any setoff right it might have with respect to the
contract (under the Bankruptcy Code or under
applicable non-bankruptcy law).
or (ii) Any Claim allowable under §503(b) arising from
performance of the contract.

(3) <u>Trustee's Responsibilities</u>: If the Licensee chooses to retain
its rights (under (1)(B)), and the Licensee makes a <u>written</u>
request, then the Trustee must:
(A) Provide the Intellectual Property (and any embodiment)
held by the Trustee.

and (B) Not interfere with the Licensee's rights, including the
right to obtain the property from a third party.
(4) So long as the Trustee does not reject the contract, and the
Licensee makes a <u>written</u> request, the Trustee must:
(A) To the extent provided in the contract:
(i) Perform the contract.
and (ii) Provide the Intellectual Property (and any
embodiment) held by the Trustee.
and (B) Not interfere with the Licensee's rights, including the
right to obtain the property from a third party.

(o) Commitments to Federal Depositories Assumed

1. In a Chapter 11 case, the Trustee is deemed to have assumed
any commitment by the Debtor to an agency regulating
federal depository institutions to maintain the capital of an
insured depository institution.
2. The Trustee shall immediately cure any deficiency under
any such commitment.
3. Any Claim for a later breach of the Debtor's obligations is
entitled to priority under §507 (PRIORITIES).
4. This subsection <u>does not</u> extend any commitment that would
otherwise be terminated by an act of the regulatory agency.

D) STRONG -ARM POWER TO AVOID LIENS (§544; §545;§546)

OVERVIEW

- The Trustee may avoid certain Liens on Estate Property, thereby causing an unperfected secured party to become unsecured.
- Section 544(a) gives the Trustee its "Strong Arm" power, giving the Trustee the "hypothetical" status of a <u>Judicial Lien Creditor</u> and a <u>Bona-fide Purchaser of Real Property</u>.
  - ☞ Thus, any Lienholder who would be subject to a Judicial Lien Creditor or a bona-fide Purchaser of Real Property would lose out to the Trustee (ex: Secured Party has a perfected Security Interest in Debtor's printing press under Article 9 of the UCC. According to Article 9, a Judicial Lien Creditor arising <u>after</u> Secured Party perfected its interest in the machine would <u>not</u> have priority over the Secured Party. However, if the Secured Party had attached, but not perfected before the Judicial Lien Creditor arose, Article 9 would give the Judicial Lien Creditor priority over the Secured Party (see UCC §9-301(1)(b)). Thus, in the latter case, a Bankruptcy Trustee, stepping into the shoes of a Judicial Lien Creditor, would take priority over the unperfected Secured Party and would be able to avoid its unperfected Lien under §544(a)(1)).

RELEVANT SECTIONS: §544, §545, §546

---

§544: Avoiding Powers:

"The Strong-Arm Statute"

(a) Trustee's Avoidance Powers:
    i)   At the commencement of the case, the Trustee shall have the
        1.   Rights and powers of any Creditor
        2.   Right to avoid any Transfer of Debtor's property
        3.   Right to avoid any obligation incurred by the Debtor
    ii) These powers are received regardless of the Trustee or any Creditor knowledge

iii) Scope of Avoidance Powers: Avoidance powers apply to
obligations/ Transfers that are voidable by:
(1) A Creditor that:
  a)   Extends credit to Debtor by Petition date
and b)   Obtains a Judicial Lien with respect to such credit
  1.   At Petition date
  and 2.   On all property on which a Creditor on a
            simple contract could have obtained such a
            Judicial Lien, regardless of whether a Creditor
            actually exists (i.e. a "Hypothetical Lien
            Creditor")
or (2) A Creditor that:
  a)   Extends credit to the Debtor by the Petition date
and b)   Obtains an execution against the Debtor that is
          returned unsatisfied, regardless of its actual
          existence (i.e. "Hypothetical Lien Creditor")
or (3) A Bona-Fide Purchaser of Real Property (other than
          fixtures) that buys from a Debtor:
  a)   Against whom applicable law permits such
        Transfer to be perfected
  b)   That obtains the status of Bona-Fide Purchaser
  c)   Who has a perfected such Transfer by the Petition
        date, regardless of whether or not such a Purchaser
        actually exists (i.e. "Hypothetical Lien Creditor")

(b) Property and Interests the Trustee May Avoid:
The Trustee may avoid any Transfer of interest of the Debtor in
property/any obligation or Debt incurred by the Debtor that is:
a.   Voidable (under applicable law) by an unsecured Creditor
      who has an allowable claim under §502 (ALLOWANCE OF
      CLAIMS OF INTERESTS)
or b.   Not allowable only under §502(e) (CLAIMS FOR
      CONTRIBUTION OR REIMBURSEMENT)

§545: Statutory Liens:

The Trustee may avoid the fixing of a Statutory Lien on the Debtor's
property if:

(1) The Statutory Lien became effective against the debtor:
(A) When the Bankruptcy Petition was filed

87

    (B) When an Insolvency (other than under this Title) proceeding against the debtor was commenced

    (C) When a Custodian is Appointed or Authorized to take (or actually takes) possession of Debtor's property

    (D) When the Debtor becomes Insolvent

    (E) At the execution of the property which was levied by another Lien-holder

or   (2) Unperfected Liens: The Lien is not Perfected or Enforceable against a Bona Fide Purchaser at the time the Bankruptcy Petition is filed.

or   (3) Rents: It is for rent

or   (4) It is a Lien of Distress for Rent

§546: Exceptions To Avoiding Powers:

(a) Time Limitation: An action (under §544, §545, §547, §548, or §553) must be commenced after the earlier of:

    (1) 2 Years after Trustee's appointment

    (2) The time the case is closed or dismissed

(b) Trustee's avoidance powers are subject to:

    1) Any generally applicable law permitting perfection to relate-back in time (thereby allowing a later Security Interest to be effective against an earlier interest in the same property).

    2) An interest in property shall be perfected by notice if:

        a) Such law dictates that perfection can only be accomplished by either:

            1. Seizure of property

        or 2. Commencement of an action

        b) There has been no seizure or commencement by Petition date.

    3) Notice must be made within the time fixed by the law requiring seizure or commencement (for perfection).

(c) Reclamation Rights:

The rights and powers of a Trustee (under §544(a), §545, §547, and §549) are subject to any rights (statutory or common law) of a Seller of Goods to reclaim goods sold to Debtor.

    (1) Requirements:

a. Goods are sold in the Ordinary Course of the Seller's
Business
b. Debtor received goods while Insolvent
c. Seller makes a <u>written</u> demand within <u>10 days</u> after the
Debtor received the goods

(2) Seller's Right to Reclamation may be denied if the Court:
(A) Grants Seller's claim under §503(b)(ADMINISTRATIVE
EXPENSES ALLOWED)
or   (B) Secures Seller's claim by a Lien

(d) Crops * * *
(e,f) Trustee Cannot Avoid Margin Payments * * *
(g) Trustee Cannot Avoid "Swap Agreements" * * *

E) <u>RIGHT TO AVOID VOIDABLE PREFERENCES</u>:

THIS SECTION PRIMARILY APPLIES TO UNDERSECURED
OR UNSECURED CREDITORS since Transfers to Oversecured
Creditors will usually not be Voidable Preferences.

1) The Voidable Preference:

OVERVIEW ————————————————————————

- A "Preference" is a Transfer made during the pre-Petition
Preference Period. As mentioned above, the "Preference Period" is
<u>90 days</u> before the Debtor files the bankruptcy Petition (this is
extended to <u>1 Year</u> if the Transfer is made to an "Insider").
- Like the Automatic Stay , the Voidable Preference mechanism is
used to maintain fairness between the Creditors. Without the
Voidable Preference power, a Debtor could get rid of most of its
assets to certain Creditors whom it "prefers," to give them to,
leaving a worthless estate for the remaining Creditors when it files
for Bankruptcy. This would leave all of the other Creditors at a
disadvantage.
- If a Transfer is a Voidable Preference, the Trustee can "reverse" the
Transfer and order the "preferred Creditor" to return the
preferentially Transfer red property (or the Value of such property)
to the Estate.

- Not all Transfers made during the Preference Period are Voidable Preferences (For example, Transfers made to an Oversecured Creditor during the Preference Period is not a Voidable Preference, since the Oversecured Creditor would have received just as much from the Bankruptcy estate after the Petition was filed (see §547(b)).
- When a Transfer is a "Voidable Preference": The following requirements must all be met in order for a Transfer to be deemed a Voidable Preference (§547(b)):

1. A Transfer of <u>Debtor Property</u> (i.e.-Debtor had an interest in it) (§547(b))

and 2. The Transfer was to or for the benefit of the Creditor (§547(b)(1).

and 3. The Transfer was made on Antecedent Debt (i.e., the Debt was incurred by the Debtor before the Transfer was made) (§547(b)(2)).

and 4. The Transfer was made during Preference Period (i.e.- <u>90 days</u> before the Petition is filed, or <u>1 year</u> if the Transfer is to an "Insider" (§101(31)); (§547(b)(4))

and 5. The Transfer was made while the Debtor was Insolvent (§547(b)(3) (note: if during the <u>90 day</u> Preference Period, there is a <u>rebuttable</u> presumption that the Debtor is Insolvent (§547(f));

and 6. By keeping the Preference, the Creditor will be receiving more than it would under §726 (§547(b)(5)) :

  ☞ <u>Secured Party</u>: This will never occur if the Creditor is Oversecured

  ☞ <u>Priority Creditor</u>: This will not occur if the Creditor is a Priority Creditor (ex: IRS Lien).

  ☞ <u>Unsecured Creditor:</u> Under-secured Creditors can't keep Transfers made during the Preference Period unless the Transfer was made specifically to reduce the Creditor's Security Interest in the Debtor's collateral property (ex: if a Security Interest =$500,000 and loan = $1M (i.e.-$500,000 unsecured), a check for $300,000 would be a Preference because the Secured Party would still have a $500,000 secured loan + now only a $200,000 unsecured loan (instead of a $500,000 unsecured loan); if the Secured Party specifically reduced his Security Interest to $200,000 the $300,000 check wouldn't be a Preference because he'll still have a $500,000 unsecured loan)).

90

- **General Approach to a Preference Problem:**
  - ☞ Look at the Time Transfer Occurred (§547(e))
  - ☞ Check to See if §547(b)'s Requirements are met (§547(b))
  - ☞ Check §547(c)'s Savings Clauses for Defenses (§547(c))
  - ☞ If collateral is inventory or Accounts: see if there is any "Takeback" (under §547(c)(5))

---

2) TIMING RULES:

OVERVIEW ————————————————————————

- In the case of Preferences, timing is everything!

  - ☞ Timing issues, addressed in §547(e), are extremely important to examine. Simply put, the actual date of Transfer may not be the "Date of Transfer " in the eyes of the Bankruptcy Code. Section 547(e) dictates when a Transfer or perfection occurs for purposes of determining whether a Preference has been made.

  - ☞ Perfection:
    - ➤ Real Estate: Perfected when recorded in Real Property Records or when a subsequent "Bona-fide Purchaser" cannot take superior title to the property.
    - ➤ Personalty: Perfected when a "Judicial Lien Creditor cannot get a better Security Interest" (as per §9-301(1)(b) of the UCC (i.e.- this usually means when the Creditor has a Perfected Security Interest by filing or by possession)).

  - ☞ Time of Transfer :
    - ➤ Actual Time of Transfer : if perfected within <u>10 days</u> of the Transfer .
    - ➤ Upon Perfection: if perfected after <u>10 days</u> from the Transfer (but before Bankruptcy).
    - ➤ Immediately before Bankruptcy: if never perfected
    - ➤ Note: Even if a Secured Party perfected after Bankruptcy, if perfection occurs within the <u>10 day</u> grace period (under

---

§547(e)(2)(A)), the Secured Party will be considered to be perfected before the Petition was filed (i.e. it is not subject to the Automatic Stay under §362(b)(3)) (ex: Day 1: Creditor advances money for Debtor to purchase a machine, which Debtor immediately purchased. On Day 4, Debtor files for Bankruptcy; on Day 8 Creditor perfects. Creditor is deemed to have been perfected on Day 1. Note also that the Automatic Stay did not prevent the Creditor from perfecting after the Petition was filed).

- **SPECIAL TIMING RULES:**
  - Mortgagees:
    - ☞ Mortgages are considered <u>recorded</u> on the day the papers are given to the County Clerk (and not when the clerk actually records them)
    - ☞ Payment by Check:
      - ➤ A Check is considered Transfer red when it is actually <u>cashed</u>.
      - ➤ Teller's Checks: Transfer occurs when the check is written by the bank
    - ☞ Future Advances: Considered to be made when they are given or committed to.
  - After-Acquired Property:
    - ☞ Considered Transfer red (and perfected under UCC §9-203) when it becomes Debtor's property, and is thus perfected when Debtor obtains possession.
    - ☞ Usually considered to have been given on Antecedent Debt, and thus a Voidable Preference
  - Execution Liens on Personalty: See State law.
  - Execution Liens on Realty: See State law.

3) THE SAVINGS CLAUSES:

OVERVIEW ————————————————————————

- The following rules describe when something is considered a Voidable Preference and when a Voidable Preference can be "saved" from the Trustee's power to avoid them.
  - ☞ Section 547(b) discusses when a Transfer is a Voidable Preference.
  - ☞ The "Savings Clauses" under §547(c) list situations when voidable Transfers can become "unavoidable Transfers " (thereby allowing the Transferee to keep the property Transfer red).

- The following list can prevent Transfer avoidance <u>to the extent that</u> they fulfill the exceptions

- <u>Contemporaneous Exchange:</u> (§547(c)(1))
  - ☞ Must be intended to be Contemporaneous and actually is substantially contemporaneous (ex: check cashed within 30 days considered contemporaneous)
- <u>Contemporaneous Exchange and §547(e) Grace Period:</u>
  - ☞ Some Courts say that if something is substantially contemporaneous, but it exceeds the <u>10 day</u> grace period for perfection under §547(e), the transaction isn't a Voidable Preference.
  - ☞ Others say that even if it exceeds the <u>10 day</u> period, it will be considered "contemporaneous" if the Transfers are made within a close proximity of each other (i.e. 12 or 13 days), and it was intended to be contemporaneous.
- <u>Ordinary Course:</u> (§547(c)(2))
  - ☞ Payment made in the Ordinary Course to repay a Debt incurred in the Ordinary Course is not a Voidable Preference (ex: paying a bill for office supplies).
  - ☞ We look at the <u>method</u> of payment (ex: wire Transfer) and <u>purpose</u> of payment (ex: regular interest installment payment)
- <u>Considerations for Ordinary Course</u>: Courts look at the following when determining whether a Transfer was made in the Ordinary Course:

☞ <u>Payment made in the ordinary course of the Debtor's business</u> - i.e.- the payment method and purpose is usual and customary for Debtor
☞ <u>Payment made according to Ordinary Business Terms</u>
☞ <u>The Debt was incurred in the Ordinary Course of Business</u>
☞ <u>Prior course of dealings between the Parties</u> shows that the payment in question is not unusual
☞ <u>Time of the Transfer</u> - late payments are usually <u>not</u> deemed to be made in the ordinary course (although some courts may find it in the ordinary course if prior dealings between the parties show consistently late payments as the accepted norm).
☞ <u>The Size of the Payment</u>
   ➤ Continuous Payments of Interest - are considered "payments in the ordinary course."
   ➤ Dishonored/Bounced Checks:
      ⇒ Redeposited dishonored checks are usually <u>not</u> considered to be paid in the Ordinary Course.
      ⇒ If the Debtor sends a certified check after its check bounces, such a payment is not in the Ordinary Course (i.e. it is not ordinary for check to bounce nor for the Debtor to pay by Cashier's check)

• <u>PMSIs ("Purchase Money Security Interests")</u>: (§547(c)(3))
  ☞ Property attached pursuant to a Purchase Money Security Interest ("PMSI") is <u>not</u> a preferential Transfer .
  ☞ Money must be advanced <u>After</u> or <u>While</u> the Security Agreement is made (i.e.- NOT before).
  ☞ Money advanced must be used to purchase the collateral secured
  ☞ Perfection must occur within the applicable grace period (usually between 10 - 20 days, depending on the state's UCC) .
• <u>Special Attachment for Banks</u>: Since Banks have an automatic right to Setoff (§553), §506 gives them an Automatic Security Interest in the Debtor's Accounts in the amount of the PMSI loan they give the Debtor.

• <u>New Value</u>: (§547(c)(4)):
  ☞ A Transfer will be avoided if it is made in exchange for New Value.
  ☞ New Value is defined in §547(a)(4) and includes:
    ➤ A release of a <u>valid</u> Security Interest.
    ➤ Money

⇒   Goods or services
⇒   Commitment or extension of credit

• **Proceeds in Sold Collateral**: Some courts consider New Value to be given if collateral is exchanged for proceeds which are harder to perfect, since the Security Interest would not be as valuable to a Creditor as it was before it was sold (ex: proceeds have a risk of becoming commingled funds and can lose their Value under UCC §9-306(4)(d) (only secured up to amount deposited within <u>10 days</u> of Bankruptcy (see "Heavy Money Rule")).

• <u>Floating Liens In Inventory and Accounts</u>: (§547(c)(5))
  ☞ Unlike other collateral, Liens in inventory and Accounts receivable are often "floating Liens." Since inventory is constantly sold and replenished (and, similarly, Accounts receivable are constantly paid for and re-created) a "floating Lien" is created. When inventory is sold (or Accounts are paid) the Lien on the inventory "floats" from the sold inventory to the new inventory purchased by the Debtor.
  ☞ Thus, in reality, the Creditor is obtaining a new perfected Security Interest in the Debtor's inventory each time the Debtor receives new goods.
  ☞ One must determine the amount of the Creditor's interest in the inventory/Accounts that is considered to be secured at the beginning of the Preference Period, since payments for that amount will not be a Voidable Preference.

• SPECIAL PREFERENCE CASES:

1. <u>Proceeds:</u> The delivery of Proceeds to a Secured Creditor is Never a Voidable Preference.

2. <u>Cash Collateral</u>: (as defined in §363(a))
    • The Surrender of Cash Proceeds of collateral is NEVER a Voidable Preference (as long as it is not commingled).
    • <u>Commingled Funds:</u> Heavy Money Rule:
       ☞ Cash proceeds are not reduced unless the Account dips below the proceeds level.
       ☞ Once the level drops, you can <u>Never</u> recover the dropped amount, for any new money placed in the Account is not

considered to replace the cash collateral.
- Checks written from a Commingled Account - will be considered a Voidable Preference unless the Security Interest is simultaneously reduced.
- Perfection: Note: that under UCC §9-306(4)(d), the Creditor will only be secured up to the amount of cash collateral in the Account within 10 Days of Bankruptcy .

3. Stock Dividends:
- Stock dividends received (Transfer red as per below) during the Preference Period are usually Voidable
- Dividends as Proceeds:
  ☞ Most courts consider Stock Dividends to be Proceeds of stock (and, thus not voidable) (except for the 11th Circuit).
  ☞ Stock Dividends will be considered Transfer red when Debtor receives them (not when they are declared).

4. Withholding Taxes:
- Payments to the IRS during the Preference Period are NOT Voidable Preferences (since withholding taxes are not Debtor Property to begin with. It is considered to be held by the Debtor as Trustee for the IRS (Exempt from the estate under §541))
- Commingled Tax Money: If the funds are commingled, the IRS will obtain a Lien on the entire estate.

5. Exempt Property: If Exempt Property is Transfer red/becomes subject to a Lien during the Preference Period, a Voidable Preference will arise when the Debtor Transfers the exempt property (since the exemption would have been waived under §522(g)).

6. Letters of Credit:
- It is important to realize that money paid under a Letter of Credit is not part of the Debtor's estate (according to most opinions). The Bank has an independent obligation to pay the Letter of Credit. Thus,
  ☞ Payment under a Letter of Credit is not a Voidable Preference
  ☞ Payment under a Letter of Credit is not subject to the Automatic Stay .
- If the Bank pays under the L/C, it will not be liable under §550(a) (for paying a voidable Transfer) since the Bank's

obligation to pay has no relationship with the Debtor's
obligation to perform under its contract with the beneficiary of
the L/C.

7.   After –Acquired Property:
     • Perfection usually occurs when the Debtor gets rights in the
       collateral.
     • If the AAP is acquired During the Preference Periods it will be
       considered a Voidable Preference unless the Creditor is
       Oversecured
8.   Future Advances:
     • Each Future Advance is considered to be a new Security Interest
       (although priority will be the same as in the original)
     • Even if the initial Future Advance is considered a Voidable
       Preference , subsequent Future Advances will not be considered
       Voidable Preferences since they will be considered New Value
       (as per §547(a)(2) and §547(c)(4)) :
       ☞ Any Future Advance given which is covered by the
         collateral, will be considered secured because it is a
         contemporaneous exchange.
       ☞ Any Future Advance that exceeds the collateral Value will
         not be a Voidable Preference because it is New Value.
9.   Security Interests in Executory Contracts:
     • A Security Interest in income from an Executory Contract is
       considered to be an Account Receivable, and any payments
       during the Preference Period to the Creditor arising out of the
       Contract will be considered Proceeds and are Not voidable.
     • The Executory Contract must oblige the Debtor to perform
       (can't be optional to perform).
10. Wage Garnishments:
     • Payments to the Sheriff by a garnishee are not considered
       Voidable Preferences since income is considered to be an
       Account Receivable.
     • Since, like Executory Contracts, money is assumed to be coming
       in, payments are not Voidable Preferences.
11. Refinancing: Money given to refinance a loan isn't considered to be
     Debtor property (like a constructive trust), and, thus, is not a
     Voidable Preference.

```
╔═══════════════════════════════════════════════════════╗
║ RELEVANT SECTIONS: §547                                ║
╚═══════════════════════════════════════════════════════╝
```

§547: Preferences:

(a) Definitions

   (1) Inventory - Personal Property which is:
   - a. Leased or furnished
   - b. Held for sale or lease
   - c. To be furnished under a contract for service
   - d. Raw Materials
   - e. Work-in-process
   - f. Materials used or consumed in business
   - g. Farm products held for lease (such as crops or livestock)

   (2) New Value:
   - a) This includes:
        - 1) Money
   - or 2) Money's worth in goods, services or new credit
   - or 3) Release by a Transferee of property (which was previously Transferred to it) in a valid transaction by the Debtor (or Trustee under applicable law) including proceeds of such property.

   - b) An obligation substituted for an existing obligation is not considered new Value.

   (3) Receivable - a right to payment (whether or not such right has been earned by performance)

   (4) A Debt for a tax is incurred on the day when the tax is last payable without penalty (including any extensions).

(b) Voidable Preferences - A Trustee may avoid any Transfer of interest of the Debtor, in property which is:
   - (1) To or for the benefit of a Creditor
- and (2) For/on account of an Antecedent Debt (i.e. a past debt, owed by the Debtor before the Transfer was made, and not a contemporaneous exchange as in §547(c)(1))
- and (3) Made while the Debtor was Insolvent
- and (4) Made either:

(A) Within <u>90 days</u> of the Petition date
(B) Within <u>1 Year</u> of the Petition date for <u>Insiders</u> (as per §101)

and (5) A Transfer that enables the Creditor to receive more than he would if:
(A) The case were under Chapter 7 (Liquidation (i.e. not over-secured as per §725))
(B) The Transfer had not been made
(C) Creditor received payment of Debt under the Bankruptcy Code

(c) Exceptions (Savings Clauses):
(1) <u>Contemporaneous Exchanges</u>: Transactions will be considered "contemporaneous" to the extent they were both:
(A) Intended to be a Contemporaneous Exchange for <u>new Value</u> (ex: A check that is cashed within <u>30 days</u> is considered contemporaneous).
(B) In fact substantially a Contemporaneous Exchange (see §547(e)).

(2) <u>Ordinary Course of Business</u> - Transfers qualify if:
(A) It was a payment of a Debt that was incurred in the <u>Ordinary Course of Business.</u>
and (B) It was made in the <u>Ordinary Course of Business</u> or financial affairs of the Debtor and the Transferee (ex: regular bond payments, regular installments on a loan).
and (C) Made according to Ordinary Business Terms.

(3) <u>PMSI's</u> - Qualify only if:
(A) The Security Interest secures <u>new Value</u> that was:
(i) Given at or after signing a Security Agreement (Security Agreement must contain description of new collateral)
and (ii) Given by the Secured Party
and (iii) Given as a PMSI (i.e. to enable Debtor to acquire property)
and (iv) Was actually used by Debtor to acquire property (i.e. a "true PMSI").
(B) It was perfected within <u>10 days</u> after the Debtor receives possession of the property.

(4) <u>New Value</u>: A Transfer given to the Creditor who gave <u>new Value</u> after the Debtor made the Transfer , if:

(A) The new Value was not secured by an unavoidable Security Interest (i.e. not perfected and, thus, subject to a Judicial Lien or the Trustee's Avoiding Powers under §546)

(B) The Debtor did not make the Creditor better off than he would have been if the Creditor never gave the Debtor new Value (ex: over-secures, to extend to past debts)

(5) Floating Liens: New Perfected Security Interests in Inventory or Receivables, including their proceeds: As long as the Security Interest does not prejudice unsecured creditors by "over-securing" to cover debts made during the later of:
   (A) Either:
      (i) 90 Days before the Petition date (for a Transfer applying to §547(b)(4)(A)).
      (ii) 1 Year before the Petition date, if the Transfer was made by an "Insider" (as per §547(b)(4)(B)).
   (B) The date that new Value was first given under the Security Agreement (i.e. the Security Agreement which created the Security Interest).

(6) Unavoidable Statutory Liens (ex: Tax Liens, pursuant to §545) * * * *

(7) Payments to Ex-Spouses: * * * *

(8) Property of a Personal Debtor if:
   a)   The Debtor's debts are primarily Consumer Debts
and b)   The total Value of all affected Transferred property is less than $600

(d) Avoiding Transfers to a Surety
   1) The Trustee may avoid a Transfer of an interest in the Debtor's property which is to or for the benefit of a Surety if:
      a)   It is to secure reimbursement of the Surety
      b)   The Surety furnished a bond or other obligation to dissolve a Judicial Lien (which the Trustee could have avoided under 547(b)).
   2) The liability of the Surety under such a bond/obligation shall be discharged to the extent of either:

100

a) The Value of such property recovered by the Trustee
or b) The amount paid to the Trustee

(e) Time of Transfer (for purposes of this section)
(1) Perfection:
(A) Real Property (other than fixtures): Perfection occurs
when a Bona-Fide Purchaser who buys from the Debtor
(against whom applicable law permits such a Transfer
to be perfected) cannot acquire an interest that is
superior to that of the Secured Party (i.e. Recorded).
(B) Personal Property (including fixtures): Perfection
occurs when a Creditor cannot acquire a superior
Judicial Lien to that of the Secured Party (i.e. Perfected,
so it has superiority to Judicial Liens under UCC §9-
301(1)(b)).
(2) When Transfer is Made:
(A) When the Transfer is actually made, if it is perfected
within 10 days of Transfer
or (B) Upon perfection, if perfected after 10 days from the
Transfer
or (C) Immediately before Petition is filed if it is not perfected
by the later of:
(i) The commencement of the case (Petition date)
or (ii) 10 days after the Transfer is actually made
(3) Debtor must acquire rights in property for Transfer to be
made.

(f) Preference Period: The Debtor is presumed to have been
Insolvent within the 90 days immediately preceding the Petition
date (for purposes of this section).

(g) Burden of Proof - For purposes of this section:
1. The Trustee has the burden of proving avoidability of a
Transfer under §547(b).
2. The Creditor (or Party in Interest against whom the Trustee
is seeking recovery or avoidance) has the burden of proving
non-avoidability under §547(c).

5) WHO TRUSTEE MAY RECOVER VOIDABLE
PREFERENCES FROM: (§550)

OVERVIEW ─────────────────────────────

• The Trustee may recover Preferentially Transfer red property or its
equivalent Value from the following (§550(a)):
     • The initial Transferee (ex: If Creditor assigned his
     right to payment to Holder and Debtor preferentially
     pays Holder, Holder will be liable for the Preference).
     • The Actual Transferee/Creditor
     • Any future Transferee (after the initial Transferee)
     • The Entity to whom the Transfer was designed to
     benefit (ex: Creditor owed Bill $100 and Debtor owed
     Creditor $100. Instead of paying Bill, Creditor told
     Debtor to pay the money it owed Creditor to Bill. If such
     payment is deemed a Voidable Preference, the
     Bankruptcy estate may recover from Bill or Creditor --
     since Creditor was the Person to whom the Transfer
     was intended to benefit).

• Good Faith Purchaser Exception: The Trustee can't get property back if
it was sold to a "Good Faith Purchaser" (§550(b)). The Transferee must
     • Have no knowledge that the Transfer was voidable
     • Have taken the Transfer in Good Faith
     • Have taken Value in exchange (i.e.- "satisfaction or
     securing of a present or antecedent Debt (§501(b)(1))

• Guarantors - if payment is made to a Transferee before the Preference
Period began, the Trustee may still be able to recover the Transfer if the
guaranty on the loan was made by an Insider, since the Insider benefited
from the payment to the Transferee.

RELEVANT SECTIONS: §550

§550: Liability of Transferee of Avoided Transfers:

(a)   Persons Whom Trustee May Recover From:
     i)   To the extent that a Transfer is avoided (under §544, §545,
       §548, §549, or §724(a)), the Trustee may recover (for the
       benefit of the estate):

1) The Transferred property

or   2) The Value of the property (if the court consents)

ii)   The Trustee may recover such property or Value from:

(1) Either:

a)   The Initial Transferee

or   b)   The Entity for whose benefit the Transfer was made

or   (2) Any Immediate or Intermediate Transferee of the initial Transferee

(b) Persons Whom Trustee May Not Recover From:

(1) A Transferee (from the initial Transferee) who is a Good Faith Purchaser, taking the property:

a)   For Value (see definition above)

and b)   In Good Faith

and c)   Without knowledge that the Transfer was voidable

(2) Any immediate or intermediate Good Faith Transferee of the Good Faith Purchaser

(c) Insiders: The Transferee may only recover property (under §550(a)) from an "Insider" if:

(1) The Transfer was avoided under §547(b).

and (2) The Transfer was made for the benefit of a Creditor who was an Insider at the time of the Transfer .

and (3) The Transfer was made within 1 year of the filing, but before the 90 day Preference Period.

(d) Trustee Limited to Loss: The Trustee is only entitled to a single satisfaction under §550(a).

(e) Transferee's Rights in Recovered Property:

(1) Transferee's Lien on Recovered Property:
A Good Faith Transferee (from whom the Trustee may recover property under §550(a)) will obtain a Lien on the recovered property in an amount equal to the lesser of:

(A) The cost the Transferee incurred in improving the property less any profit realized from it

(B) Any increase in Value of the property resulting in the improvement

(2) "Improvement" under this section includes:

(A) Physical additions or changes to the Transferred property

    (B) Repairs
    (C) Payment of any Tax on the property
    (D) Payment of any Debt secured by a Lien on the property
         (that is superior or equal to the rights of the trustee)
    (E) Preservation of the property

(f) Time Limit: An action or proceeding to recover property under
    §550 may not be commenced <u>after</u> the <u>earlier of</u>:
    (1) <u>1 year</u> after the Transfer is avoided
or (2) The time the case is dismissed

§551: Automatic Preservation of Avoided Transfer :

1.   The following avoided Transfers or Liens are automatically
    preserved for the benefit of the estate:
    a.   Any Transfer avoided under §522, §544, §545, §547, §548,
         §549, or §724(a)
or b.   Any Lien void under section 506(d)
2.   These Liens are preserved only with respect to Property of the
    Estate (this prevents the trustee from asserting an avoided tax
    Lien against after acquired property of the Debtor).
3.   If a preserved Lien does not benefit the estate, the trustee may
    abandon it under §554.
4.   The section prevents junior Lienholders from improving their
    position at the expense of the estate when a senior Lien is
    avoided.

F) RIGHT TO AVOID FRAUDULENT CONVEYANCES:

OVERVIEW ――――――――――――――――――――

- A Fraudulent Conveyance may be avoided by the Trustee (under §548) or by the Creditors (under the applicable State law (such as the UFCA and UFTA))

- "Fraudulent Conveyance"
  ☞ A Fraudulent Conveyances will be found when Transfers are made:
    ➢ With Actual Intent to defraud Creditors (§7)
    or ➢ Without Fair Consideration (as per §3) where the Conveyor is Insolvent "(as per §2) (see also §4,§5,§6 of the UFCA)
    ➢ Time: When determining whether a Fraudulent Conveyance exists, we look at the transaction at the time of the Conveyance and not later.

- The Fraudulent Conveyance Rule: (UFCA)
  ☞ If a Fraudulent Conveyance is established, a Creditor may:
    ➢ Have the conveyance set aside (to the extent necessary to get its claim enforced) (§9 and BRC §548 -says "may avoid Transfer " ONLY within 1 Year of BANKRUPTCY))
    or ➢ Disregard the conveyance and proceed to attach and sell the property as if it were never Transfer red (the Person possessing the conveyance is like a Bailor) (Only §9 of the UFCA)

- The Good Faith Purchaser Exceptions:
  ☞ This rule will not apply if the property is sold to a Good Faith Purchaser (from the Person initially receiving the Fraudulent Conveyance)
- Requirements for Good Faith Purchaser:
  1. Must purchase in Good Faith
  2. Either: The Purchaser shall
     a) Under UFCA: Have No Knowledge(§9(1))
     b) Under BRC: Have taken the property for New Value (§548(c))
  3. Must Purchase for Fair Consideration (if there is no Fair

Consideration, the Transferee may keep the property as a
"Security for Repayment" of the Value it actually did pay
(see §9(2)).

- Estoppel By Deed: Normally, anyone purchasing from a Good Faith
  Purchaser will also take free and clear of a Fraudulent Conveyance
  Avoidance.
  - However, under the doctrine of "Estoppel by Deed," if the
    "wrongdoer" or a non-innocent party purchases the
    property from a Good Faith Purchaser, the wrongful
    Purchaser will be subject to Fraudulent Conveyance
    Avoidance.

- Creditor's Entitlement:
  - Even though property was sold to a GFP (from the Person
    initially receiving the Fraudulent Conveyance), the Creditors are
    entitled to the proceeds from the Conveyance Sale.
  - Rational: under the UFCA , the Creditor can levy/attach
    property even though it was conveyed to the Transferee; thus, if
    the Transferee sold the property, it would be entitled to the
    proceeds, since the Transferee is considered to be a
    "Bailor/Agent," holding the property and/or whatever proceeds
    are derived from it, in Trust.
  - Creditors must return to the Transferee the money it paid (even
    if it is far less than fair consideration) to get the property back
    from the Transferee.
- Who May Avoid Transfer :
  - UFCA: Any Creditor may assert Fraudulent Conveyance rights
    (not just a Secured Party or Lien-holders)
  - BRC:
    - The Trustee
  - or • A Perfected Secured Creditor (since only they can avoid the
    Trustee's Avoidance Powers)

- Protection for Transferee: In order to avoid Fraudulent Conveyance
  law, the Transferee should obtain a warranty of title and a written
  statement that the parties are not trying to make a Fraudulent
  Conveyance.

• APPLICATIONS:

1) Foreclosure Sales: Foreclosure sales will not be considered
   Fraudulent Conveyances (even if sold for less Value than Fair
   Market Value) if they are properly administered under State law.

2) Exempt Property: Exempt property purchased by the Debtor before
   Bankruptcy will probably be considered a Fraudulent Conveyance
   because there may be an "intent to defraud Creditors." Thus, the
   Transfer would be voidable, and the exempt property purchase will
   not be subject to discharge of §522 protection since §727(a)(2)
   disallows discharge where the Debtor tried to defraud Creditors.

3) Subrogation Rights as Fair Consideration: Rights of Subrogation are
   normally considered fair consideration, but we do look to the
   solvency of the company at the date of subrogation to determine the
   Value of the right.

4) Corporate Dividends: Dividends by an Insolvent company are
   Fraudulent Conveyances under §4 of the UFCA if:
   a) The Debtor Corporation is Insolvent
   and b) No Fair Consideration is exchanged (a company has no
   obligation to give dividends and gets nothing in return for it)
   • §9(2) will not help the shareholder (Transferee) since it
   paid nothing to get back.

5) Upstream Guarantees: Are considered to be Fraudulent Conveyances
   even if the Corporation making the guarantee does not actually pay the
   guarantee while Insolvent.
   • By simply assuming the obligation it has made a Fraudulent
   Conveyance.
   • Definition: Upstream Guarantees occur when:
   a) A Corporation guarantees the Debts of its Major
   Shareholders
   or b) A Subsidiary Corporation guarantees the Debts of its Parent
   Corporation.

   • Exception: Fair Consideration Given:
   ☞ If the loan obtained by the Shareholder was used to be re-

invested in the Debtor Corporation then a Fraudulent
Conveyance will not arise since <u>Fair Consideration</u> would
be given (Note: Banks often prefer Shareholders to take out
loans for their Corporations, and have the Corporations
guarantee them, since Corporations have limited liability
for loan and Shareholders don't)
- ☞ Some may argue that Fair Consideration is received by
  Debtor Corporation since it has a "Right of Subrogation."
- ☞ Many courts look to the Value of the Right of Subrogation
  to see if it is a Fraudulent Conveyance.

6) <u>Downstream Guarantees:</u> Usually not considered a Fraudulent
Conveyance.
- • Definition: A <u>Shareholder</u> or <u>Parent Company</u> guarantees a loan
  for an "affiliated" company or subsidiary.
- ☞ In this case, the Debtor Corporation gets a "Right of
  Subrogation" as Fair Consideration, and also benefits by
  having its interests improved.

7) <u>Cross-stream Guarantees:</u> Usually considered Fraudulent
Conveyances:
- • Definition: Sister or Subsidiary to Subsidiary corporate
  guarantees
- • A Right of Subrogation will = the "Fair Consideration" Value,
  if the Value of the Subrogation right is adequate (look at the
  company's solvency at time of Guarantee)
8) <u>Leveraged Buy-outs ("LBO's"):</u>
- • Normally, LBO's will survive an Fraudulent Conveyance
  challenge
- • When LBO's are <u>under-capitalized</u>, and designed to cheat
  Creditors, courts may find a Fraudulent Conveyance under §7
  (intent to defraud)

RELEVANT SECTIONS: §548; UFCA

§548: Fraudulent Transfers:

(a) Avoiding Transfers - A Trustee may avoid Transfers made
within 1 year of the Petition date if:
   (1) The Debtor made the Transfer with actual intent to hinder,
    delay or defraud any other Creditors (including those
    created after the Transfer).
and (2) Either:
    (A) Received less than a reasonable equivalent in exchange
      (for the Transfer /obligation)
    (B) The Debtor was:
      (i) Insolvent either:
        1) As a result of the Transfer /obligation
      or 2) When the Transfer was made
    or (ii) Undercapitalized
    or (iii) The Creditor knew/should have known that the
         Debtor could not "afford" the Transfer

(b) Trustee of a Partnership: A Trustee can generally avoid
Transfers by an Insolvent partnership to a general partner if the
Debtor was Insolvent when the Transfer was made (or became
Insolvent as a result of the Transfer).

(c) Exception: Unless a Trustee can avoid the Transfer (under §544,
§545, §546, or §547), a Creditor may retain its interest if it takes
the Transfer or obligation:
  1) For New Value
  2) In Good Faith
  3) For a "fair" price

(d) Terms of Transfer :
   (1) Time of Transfer (for purposes of this section):
    a) A Transfer is made when it is so perfected that even a
      Bona-Fide Purchaser who buys from the Debtor
      (against whom applicable law permits such a Transfer
      to be perfected) cannot acquire an interest superior to
      that of the Transferee.
    b) If such a Transfer is not so perfected (as indicated
      above) before the Petition date, then the Transfer will
      be deemed made immediately before the date of the
      filing of the Petition.

   (2) Value:
    (A) "Value" – General Definition:

1. "Value" means:
    a. Property
or b. Satisfaction of a present or antecedent debt
or c. Securing of a present or antecedent debt

2. "Value" does not include an unfulfilled promise to support the Debtor or the Debtor's family.

(B) A stock broker or commodity broker take "Value" if they:
1. Receive a <u>margin payment</u> (defined in §101, §741 or §761)
or 2. Receive a <u>settlement payment</u> (defined in §101 or §741)

(C) A "Repo" participant takes "Value" if he:
1. Receives a <u>margin payment</u> (defined in §101, §741 or §761)
2. Receives a <u>settlement payment</u> (defined in §101 or §741)

(D) A swap participant takes for Value if he receives a Transfer in connection with a Swap Agreement.

Selected Provisions from the
Uniform Fraudulent Conveyances Act

§2: Insolvency:

(1) Person: A Person is Insolvent when the Present Market Value of the Person's assets is less that that amount required to pay debts as they become due.

* * * *

§3: Fair Consideration:

Fair consideration is deemed to have been given if:

(a) Conveyance of Property/Release of Debt is made in exchange for:
1. A fair equivalent
and 2. In good faith

(b) Security Interest: A Security Interest is given:
1. To secure a present advance or antecedent debt
and 2. The amount of the claim is not disproportionately small to the Value of the property

§4: Conveyance by an Insolvent:

A Fraudulent Conveyance is deemed to exist (for Creditor of the Conveyor) if:

a) The Person conveying the property is Insolvent
and b) Fair Consideration (under §3) is not given (regardless of actual intent)

§5: Conveyance by a Person in Business:

A Fraudulent Conveyance is deemed to exist (for creditors of the Conveyor and of the transaction) if:
a) The Person making the conveyance is engaged in a business.

and b)   The Conveyance is made without <u>Fair Consideration</u> (under §3) (regardless of actual intent).

and c)   The "Conveyor" has an unreasonably small capital left after the conveyance.

§6: Conveyance by a Person About to Incur Debts:

A Fraudulent Conveyance is deemed to exist (for present and future creditors) if:

a)   The Person conveying the property <u>intends</u> or <u>believes</u> that he is about to incur debts beyond his ability to pay them as they become mature (i.e. he knows he will soon be Insolvent).

and b)   <u>Fair Consideration</u> (under §3) is not given (regardless of actual intent).

§7: Conveyance Made With Intent to Defraud:

A Fraudulent Conveyance is deemed to exist if it is made with actual intent to <u>hinder, delay,</u> or <u>defraud</u> Creditors (present or future creditors).

§9: Rights of Creditors Under Fraudulent Conveyance Law:

(1)   The Fraudulent Conveyance Rule
   i)   Rights of Creditors
      (a)   <u>Set Aside Conveyance</u> or <u>Annul Obligation</u> to the extent necessary to collect on his claim
   or   (b)   <u>Disregard the Conveyance</u> and Attach or Levy Execution upon the conveyed Property
   ii)   <u>Exception:</u> Creditor may not assert such powers if the property has been sold:
      a)   To a Good Faith Purchaser:
         1)   A Purchaser
         2)   For Fair Consideration
         3)   Without knowledge of the Fraudulent Conveyance upon purchase
   or   b)   Someone who obtained title from a Good Faith Purchaser

(2) Rights of Non-GFP Innocent Purchaser - A non-Good Faith
Purchaser may keep the property as <u>Security for Repayment</u> if:
    a)   He is a Purchaser
and b)   The Purchaser gave less than fair consideration for the
         property
and c)   The Purchaser did not have <u>actual fraudulent intent</u>

* * * *

IV. Other Rights

A) CHAPTER 13 PROCEEDINGS:

OVERVIEW ───────────────────────────────

- **Payment of Creditors:** *(§1322; §1325)*
  - ☞ In a Chapter 13 proceeding, the Debtor will be able to keep all pre-Petition property, yet must give the Estate all <u>Post-Petition Wages</u>.
  - ☞ The amount of wages the Debtor must give up must put the Creditors in as good a position as they would have been in under a Chapter 7 proceeding (§1325(a)(4))
  - ☞ A Chapter 13 <u>Plan</u> will be created, dictating the details of how the Debtor will pay its pre-Petition Debts in the future.

- **Secured Claims:**
  - ☞ Secured Creditors must approve the Chapter 13 plan.
  - ☞ Debtor can't modify his Security Agreement on perfected property (ex: Home Mortgage), but may cure defaults (§1325(b)(2))

- **Sufficiency of Plan:**
  - ☞ <u>Good Faith</u> – is required; some courts hold that not paying unsecured Creditors is not good faith, even if they would've received nothing under chapter 7.
  - ☞ The Plan cannot last for more than <u>3 years</u> (§1322(d)) unless extended for "Cause"
  - ☞ <u>"Cause" to Extend:</u> A court may extend a plan if:
    1. The extension will allow the Debtor to pay 100% on the dollar of all claims.
    - or 2. The extension will allow the Debtor to pay 70% of the Debt Creditors would have received under a Chapter 7 liquidation.
    - or 3. The plan has been confirmed and the Debtor has had an emergency, requiring it to leave its job for a while
  - ☞ <u>Charity</u> - allowed to be given by a Debtor, but must be in moderation.

RELEVANT SECTIONS: §1321, §1322, §1323, §1324, §1325, §1326

§1321: Filing of Plan:

The Debtor shall file a plan.

§1322: Contents of Plan:

(a) Mandatory Provisions - The plan must contain the following:

   (1) Payment of Debtor's Future Income: The plan must give to the Trustee's supervision and control, whatever portion of the Debtor's future income that is needed to implement the plan.
   (2) Payment of Priority Claims:
       a. The plan must provide for full payment of all §507 priority Claims.
       b. Payment is to be made in deferred cash payments.
       c. Exception: The holder of a particular Claim may agree to a different treatment of his Claim.
   (3) Identical Treatment of Claims: The plan must provide identical treatment for all Claims in a class.

(b) Optional Provisions - Subject to (a) and (c), the plan may contain the following provisions:

   (1) Designation of Classes:
       a. The plan may designate classes of unsecured Claims (as provided in §1122)
       b. The plan may not discriminate unfairly against any class
       c. The plan may treat Claims for a consumer Debt differently than other unsecured Claims if there is a co-Debtor who is liable on the Debt
   (2) Rights of Claim Holders:
       a. The plan may modify the rights of both secured and unsecured Claim holders
       b. Exception: The rights of a secured Claim holder may not be modified if the Security Interest is in the Debtor's principal residence.
       c. The plan may also leave the rights of holders of any class of Claims unaffected.

(3) <u>Defaults</u>: The plan may provide for <u>curing</u> or <u>waiving</u> defaults.

(4) <u>Joint Payment of Claims</u>: The plan may provide that payments on any unsecured Claim are to be made together with payments on other (secured or unsecured) Claims.

(5) <u>Maintaining Payments</u>: The plan may provide (even if it modified the rights of Claim holders in (2), above):

    a.   That any default be cured within a reasonable time.

and b.   That payments be maintained while the case is pending on any Claim (secured or unsecured), where the last payment is scheduled to be due <u>after</u> the final payment under the plan is due.

(6) <u>Payment of Post-Petition Claims</u>: The plan may provide for the payment of any Claim (or a part of a claim) allowed under §1305.

(7) <u>Executory Contracts/Unexpired Leases</u>: The plan may provide that (subject to §365: EXECUTORY CONTRACTS AND UNEXPIRED LEASES) any executory contract or unexpired lease of the Debtor not previously rejected under §365 be <u>assumed, rejected,</u> or <u>assigned</u>.

(8) <u>Payment of Claims</u>: The plan may provide that any Claim (or a part) against the Debtor be paid from the estate's property or from the Debtor's property

(9) <u>Vesting of Property</u>: The plan may provide that Property of the Estate vest in the Debtor (or any other Entity) either when:

    a.   The plan is confirmed

or b.   At a later time

(10) <u>Other Provisions</u>: The plan may include any other appropriate provision not inconsistent with the Bankruptcy Code.

(c) Special Rules for Debtor's Principal Residence: Notwithstanding (b)(2) and applicable non-bankruptcy law:

(1) Curing Default Causing Lien on Property: A default with respect to, or that gave rise to, a Lien on the Debtor's principal residence may be cured under §1322(b)(3) or §1322(5) until the residence is sold at a legal foreclosure sale.

(2) Modifying Payment Schedule under Mortgage: In a case where the last mortgage payment (on the original payment schedule for the Claim) is due before the final payment

under the plan, the plan may provide for the payment of the Claim as modified under §1325(a)(5).

(d) Limit on Pay Period
1. The pay period under the plan is limited to 3 years.
2. Exception: The court may approve a 5-year period for cause.

(e) Availability of Funds to Cure Defaults
1. If it is proposed in a plan to cure a default, the amount necessary to cure the default is determined in accordance with:
   a. The underlying agreement
   and b. Applicable non-bankruptcy law
2. This subsection applies regardless of the provisions of subsection (b)(2) and §506(b) and 1325(a)(5) (ALLOWED SECURED CLAIMS).

§1323: Modification of Plan Before Confirmation:

(a) Modification - When Allowed:
1. The Debtor may modify the plan without approval at any time before confirmation.
2. The Debtor may not modify the plan if the modified plan does not meet the requirements of §1322 (CONTENTS OF PLAN).

(b) Effect of Modification: After the Debtor files a modification under §1323 (MODIFICATION BEFORE CONFIRMATION), the modified plan becomes the plan.

(c) Effect of Acceptance/Rejection: If a secured Claim holder accepts or rejects a plan, the acceptance or rejection remains binding unless:
1. The modified plan changes the rights of the holder
and 2. The holder withdraws or alters his earlier acceptance or rejection.

§1324: Confirmation Hearing:

a. A Party in Interest may object to confirmation of the plan (distinguished from merely rejecting a plan).

117

b. The bankruptcy judge is required to provide <u>notice</u> and an opportunity for <u>hearing</u> objections to confirmation.

§1325: Confirmation of Plan:

(a) Mandatory Confirmation: The Court must confirm a plan (except as provided in (b)) if:

(1) <u>Satisfaction of Plan Requirements</u>: The plan satisfies the provisions of Chapter 13 and other applicable provisions of the Bankruptcy Code.

(2) <u>Fees Paid</u>: Any required fees (under 28 U.S.C. Chapter 123 or the plan) have been paid.

(3) <u>Good Faith Proposal</u>: The plan has been proposed:
   a.   In good faith
and b.   Not by any illegal means

(4) <u>Distributions at Least as Large as Under Liquidation</u>: The property to be distributed under the plan for each allowed unsecured Claim is equal to or greater than what would be paid on the Claim if the estate were liquidated under chapter 7 on the plan's effective date.

(5) <u>Secured Claims</u> - For Allowed Secured Claims In the Plan:
   (A) <u>Acceptance by Secured Creditors</u>: The Claim holder has accepted the plan.
or (B) <u>Creditor's Liens</u>:
      (i) The plan provides that the holder of such Claim retain the Lien securing such Claim
   and (ii) The property to be distributed under the plan for the Claim is equal to or greater than the allowed amount of the Claim on the plan's effective date.
or (C) <u>Debtor Surrenders Collateral to Secured Creditor</u>: The Debtor surrenders the collateral to the Claim holder.

(6) <u>Debtor's Compliance Feasible</u>: The Debtor will be able to:
   a.   Make all payments under the plan
and b.   Comply with the plan

(b) When Court May Not Approve Plan

(1) Objections to Plan:
   a.   The court may not approve the plan if any of the following object to its confirmation:
      1.   The Trustee

118

or   2.   The holder of an allowed unsecured Claim
b.   Exception: If either of the following is true as of the plan's effective date:
(A) Value of Property: The property to be distributed under the plan for the Claim is equal to or greater than the Claim amount
or   (B) Debtor's Income Is Applied to Payments:
1.   The plan provides that all of the Debtor's projected disposable income for the plan's first 3-years will be applied to make payments under the plan.
or   2.   The 3-year period begins on the date that the first payment is due under the plan.

(2)   "Disposable Income" - In §1325(b) "Disposable Income" means income which is:
1.   Received by the Debtor
and 2.   Not reasonably necessary to be spent for any of the following:
(A) The Debtor's (or a dependent's) maintenance or support
and (B) If the Debtor is engaged in business - Expenses needed to continue, preserve, and operate the business.
(c)   Payment of Income to Trustee: The court is authorized to order any Entity (defined in §101(15)) to pay any income of the Debtor to the Trustee (Note: Any Governmental Unit is an Entity subject to such an order).

§1326: Payments:

(a)   Debtor's Payments Under The Plan:

(1)   Time: The Debtor must start making the payments proposed by the plan within 30 days after the plan is filed (unless the court may order otherwise).
(2)   Payments Made Before Confirmation:
a.   The Trustee must hold all payments made (under §1326(a)) until the plan is either confirmed or denied.
b.   If a plan is confirmed, the Trustee must distribute any payment as soon as practicable.
c.   If a plan is denied:

        i.   The Trustee must return any payment to the Debtor

       ii.   The Trustee may deduct any unpaid Claim allowed
under §503(b) (ADMINISTRATIVE EXPENSES).

(b) Recurring Payments: Before or at the time of each payment to creditors under the plan, the following must be paid:

    (1) Administrative Expenses: Any unpaid Claim for Administrative Expenses (under §507(a)(1))

and (2) Trustee's Fee: The Standing Trustee's fixed fee (under 28 U.S.C. §586(e)(1)(B)) if a Standing Trustee (appointed under 28 U.S.C. §586(b)) is serving in the case.

(c) Payments to Creditors

    1.   The Trustee must pay the creditors under the plan.

    2.   Exceptions – If otherwise provided in:

       a.   The plan

   or b.   The order confirming the plan

B) REDEMPTION RIGHTS: (§9-505)

OVERVIEW ─────────────────────────────────────

- Who May Redeem
  - ☞ Debtor: The Debtor has a right to redeem property before the Creditor disposes of it
  - ☞ Junior Creditor: A junior Secured Party has a right to redeem the property from the senior Secured Parties.

- Redemption Price
  - ☞ Normally, the redemption price =

All Debt expenses
+ Accrued Interest
+ Expenses Secured Party incurred to take property

- Redemption by Individuals: (§722)
  - ☞ Availability
    1. UNDER A CHAPTER 7 CASE
    2. It is intended for Personal, Household use
    3. The Debtor is an "individual"
    4. The property is Exempt or Abandoned by the Trustee
    5. The Debt is otherwise dischargeable (Courts anticipate if a Debt can be discharged)
  - ☞ Special Consumer Redemption Price:
    - ➤ Value of the Claim Secured by the collateral (thus, if the collateral = $80, and the claim = $100, Redemption Price = $80, because it is the secured amount; the remaining $20 becomes unsecured Debt. Whereas, the regular redemption would include the total $100 + interest + expenses).
    - ➤ Redemption must be made in one lump sum, not in installments.

RELEVANT SECTIONS: UCC §9-505; §722

§722: Redemption:

a) Redeemable Property: An individual Debtor may redeem tangible personal property if:

1)   It is intended for personal, family, or household use
and 2)   It was secured by a Lien securing a dischargeable consumer
          debt
and 3)   It has either been:
          a.   Exempt (under §522)
or   b.   Abandonment (under §554)

b)   Method of Redemption: Property may be redeemed when the
      Debtor pays the holder of the Lien the amount that the holder is
      secured by the Lien.

§9-505: Disposition Of Collateral:

(1) Compulsory Disposition Of Collateral
      a)   A S/P who has taken possession of the collateral must
            dispose of it under §9-504 within 90 Days after he takes
            possession if:
            1)   The Debtor has paid 60% of either:
                  a.   The cash price of a Consumer Goods PMSI
or   b.   The loan of any other S/I in Consumer Goods
            and 2)   The Debtor has not signed a statement after default,
                  renouncing or modifying his rights under this Part
      b)   If the S/P does not dispose of the collateral (pursuant to §9-
            504) within 90 Days, the Debtor may recover on the S/P's
            liability either
            1)   In conversion
or   2)   Under §9-507(1)

(2) Acceptance of Collateral as Discharge of Obligation
      a)   In all other cases (not specified in §9-505(1)) the S/P may
            propose to retain the collateral as Discharge of debtor's
            obligation (i.e. Strict Foreclosure)
      b)   Notice:
            1)   If the Debtor has not signed a statement renouncing or
                  modifying his rights under this subsection, the S/P
                  shall, after default send written notice of his proposal
                  (to keep the collateral in satisfaction of the debt).
            2)   Additional Notice:
                  a.   Consumer Goods: No other notice is required
                  b.   Other Cases: S/P must send a copy of the notice to
                        all other Secured Parties who:

     1. Have sent the S/P a <u>written</u> notice of their claim to interest in the collateral

and 2. S/P has received the notice <u>before</u> either:

       i)   The Debtor renounced or modified its rights

    or ii) S/P sends Debtor notice to accept collateral as discharge.

3) If anyone entitled to receive notice (including Debtor) objects to the S/P's proposal within <u>21 Days</u> after notice was sent, S/P must dispose of the collateral (under §9-504).

4) The S/P may keep the collateral in satisfaction of the Debtor's obligation if he does not receive any written objection (within <u>21 days</u>).

C) Conflicts Between Lien Creditors And Secured Parties

OVERVIEW ————————————————————————

- If property is already in possession of a Secured Party, a Sheriff may not take the property pursuant to an execution
- In order to get such property from an Secured Party, the Judgement Creditor must obtain a Turnover Order; upon execution of the order, the Judgement Creditor could sell the land subject to the Security Interest to the Buyer (thus, Secured Party is still secured by collateral and if the buyer defaults, the Secured Party may foreclose under UCC §9-504).
- Secured Status: In order to perfect a Security Interest in property, the secured party must complete the following:
  1. Attachment must occur (UCC§9-203(1): Writing, Value, Debtor's Equity)
  2. Perfection must occur (UCC §9-301(1))
- Lien Creditor Status under the UCC - Judgement Creditor likely becomes a Lien Creditor upon serving the Execution to the Sheriff
- Conflicts between Secured Party and Letter of Credit ("L/C"):
  - ☞ Secured Party takes priority over any subsequent L/C's (UCC §9-301(1)(b) - thus, if a Judgement Creditor and a Secured Party "perfected" simultaneously, the Secured Party would win because the Judgement Creditor must arise Before the Security Interest is perfected in order to have priority)
- First to Levy or Perfect
  - ☞ When the Security Interest "arises" in between a Judgement Creditor's execution and levy, the first to levy or perfect wins
  - Note that State law might allow the Secured Party to win only if the Security Agreement was   made after the execution (since if the Security Agreement was made before there would be no Purchase, just an improved Lien)
  - Future Advances – have the same priority as the original advance (UCC §9-312(7);§9-301(4)) if the future advance money is given:
    1) Before the Judgement Creditor arises
  - or 2) Within 45 Days after the Judgement Creditor arises
  - or 3) Without Knowledge of the Judgement Creditor
  - or 4) Pursuant to a Prior Commitment
    - After-Acquired Property - If Both the Execution and Security

> Interest were made before the After-Acquired Property came
> into the Debtor's possession, the Secured Party wins since UCC
> §9-301(b) requires the execution to arise before the Security
> Interest (not simultaneously as it does here since attachment
> occurs as to both when Debtor gets possession of collateral)
> • **Rights of Inferior Parties:** Inferior/non-selling parties have a
>   right to the surplus proceeds (as per UCC §9-306).

RELEVANT SECTIONS: UCC §9-504; §9-203(1); §9-30; §9-312(7);
§9-306

§9-504: Secured Party's Right To Dispose After Default:

(1) Disposition of Collateral:
    i)   Upon default, a S/P may sell, lease, or otherwise dispose of
         collateral, either:
         a.   In its present condition
    or   b.   Following any commercially reasonable Preparation or
            Processing

    ii) Any sale of goods is subject to the Article on Sales
         (Article 2)
    iii) Proceeds of the disposition shall be applied in the order of
         the following:
         (a) Selling Expenses - the reasonable expenses of retaking,
             holding, preparing for sale/lease, and selling/leasing
             (including reasonable attorney/legal expenses involved
             (to the extend provided for by S/A (and not prohibited
             by law)))
         (b) Satisfaction of Debt - under his Security Agreement
         (c) Satisfaction of other Debts - secured by any
             Subordinate S/I holders if:
             1) Written notice of demand is received before
                distribution of the proceeds is completed
       and 2) Reasonable proof of S/I is presented (upon S/P's
               request)

(2) Deficiency and Surplus:

a) If the S/I secures an <u>Indebtedness</u>, then, <u>unless
   otherwise agreed</u>:
   1) The Debtor is entitled to surplus of the sale from the
      S/P
and 2) The S/P (seller) is entitled to deficiency from the
      Debtor
b) If the underlying transaction was a <u>Sale of Accounts</u>
   or<u>Chattel Paper</u> then, <u>ONLY if the Security Agreement
   provides</u>:
   1) Debtor is entitled to surplus of the sale from the S/P
and 2) S/P (seller) is entitled to deficiency from the Debtor

(3) <u>Notice of Disposition</u>:
   a) Disposition may be made by public or private proceedings.
   b) Disposition may be made as a one whole sale, or in separate
      transactions (under separate contracts).
   c) Disposition sale must be made under any commercially
      reasonable terms (including the method, manner, time, and
      place of the sale)
   d) S/P is not required to sell all collateral to one party.
   e) Secured Party must notify Debtor of time and place of sale
      <u>unless</u>:
      1) After default, the Debtor agrees not to be notified
   or 2) Collateral is perishable
   or 3) Collateral is very sensitive to market (Value changes
         quickly)
   or 4) Collateral is of a type customarily sold on a recognized
         market
   f) <u>Notification</u>:
      1) For Consumer Goods, no other notification must be
         sent
      2) For all other goods, notification must be sent to all
         other Secured Parties who sent Selling S/P a written
         notice of claim of an interest in the collateral.
   g) The S/P may purchase the collateral:
      1) At any Public Sale
   or 2) At a Private Sale, if
         a. The collateral is of the type sold in a recognized
            market
      or b. The collateral is of a type which is subject to a
            widely distributed standard price quotation.

126

(4) Even if the Secured Party files to make a proper sale, a
Purchaser takes Free of the S/P's (and any other subordinate's)
right/interest in the collateral if:
 (a) Collateral sold public sale:
   1) Collateral is sold at a Public Sale.
 and 2) Purchaser has no knowledge of any defects in sale
   process.
 and 3) Purchaser does not buy in collusion with another
   Secured Party, the Person conducting the sale, or other
   bidders.
and (b) The Purchaser acts in Good Faith (in all other sales (i.e.
 private sale)).

(5) Non-Qualifying Sales or Dispositions:
 a) A Person has rights and duties of a S/P if:
   1) She is liable to a S/P under either a:
     a. Guaranty
   or b. Indorsement
   or c. Repurchase Agreement
   or d. The like
 and 2) She either:
     a. Receives a Transfer of collateral from the S/P
   or b. Is subrogated to her rights
 b) Such a Transfer of collateral is not considered to be a "Sale
   or Disposition of Collateral" under Article 9.

§9-203(1): Requirements for Attachment:

i) A Security Interest Attaches ONLY If:

 (a) The collateral is Secured with either:
   1. Possession: In the Possession of the Secured Party
     (pursuant to agreement)
   or 2. Security Agreement: Debtor has signed a Security
     Agreement which:
     a. Is in WRITING
     and b. Describes the Collateral (as per §9-110)
       (Note: When collateral is crops or timber, a
       description of the land is required)
   or 3. Control of Investment Property - If:
     a. The collateral is INVESTMENT PROPERTY

and b.   The Secured Party has Control over the Investment
Property (as per §9-115(1)(e))
and c.   The Secured Party is Controlling it pursuant to an
agreement

and (b) Value has been given

and (c) Debtor's Rights: The Debtor has Rights in the collateral

ii) Requirements are subject to
a)   §4-208 for Security Interests of a Collecting Bank
b)   §9-115 and §9-116 for Security Interests in Investment
Property
c)   §9-113 for Security Interests arising under the Article of
Sales (Article 2)

§9-301: Priority Over Unperfected Security Interests:

(1) Classes of People who take Priority over an Unperfected
Security Interest:
(a) A Perfected S/P entitled to priority under §9-312
or   (b) A Person who becomes a Lien Creditor before the Security
Interest is Perfected (but see (2))
or   (c) A Buyer: Requirements to qualify as a "Buyer":
1)   The Buyer must be either:
a)   A Buyer not in the Ordinary Course of Business
or   b)   A Bulk Transferee
or   c)   A Buyer of Farm Products - in the Ordinary Course
of Business
and 2)   The Buyer cannot be a Secured Party.
and 3)   The Buyer must:
a)   Have No Knowledge of the S/I
and b)   Give Value
and c)   Receive delivery (of collateral) before the S/I is
perfected
and 4)   The Collateral must either be:
a)   Goods
or   b)   Instruments
or   c)   Documents
or   d)   Chattel Paper
or   (d) Transferee of Accounts, General Intangibles or Investment
Property who:

128

1) Gives Value before they are perfected
and 2) Is without knowledge of S/I
and 3) Is not a Secured Party

(2) PMSI Exception: A Secured Party takes priority over any Lien Creditor or "Bulk Transferee" (whose rights arise between the time of attachment and filing) if the Secured Party files a PMSI:
   a) Before Debtor receives the collateral (i.e. before attachment)
or b) Within <u>10 Days</u> after Debtor receives Possession of the collateral

(3) A <u>Lien Creditor</u> is
   a) A <u>Creditor who obtains a Lien</u> on property involved by attachment, levy, or the like
or b) An <u>Assignee for the Benefit of Creditors</u> from the time of assignment
or c) A <u>Trustee in Bankruptcy</u> from the date of the filing of the Petition
or d) A <u>Receiver in Equity</u> from the time of appointment

(4) A Person who becomes a <u>Lien Creditor after a S/I is perfected,</u> takes subject to that S/I only to the extent that it:
   a) Secures Future Advances made to Debtor:
      1. Before the Third Party becomes a Lien Creditor
   or 2. Within <u>45 Days</u> after the Third Party becomes a Lien Creditor
or b) Is made Without Knowledge of the Lien
or c) Is made pursuant to a Prior Commitment entered into without knowledge of the Lien

§9-312(7) Priorities in Future Advances:

a) A S/P will maintain the <u>SAME PRIORITY</u> (under (5) above or §9-115(5)) in <u>Future Advances</u> (as per §9-301(4)) as he did in his original advance (loan) if the Future Advances are made:
   1) After the original S/I is perfected (by filing or possession (or under §9-115 or §9-116 on Investment property))
or 2) Before/while the S/I is perfected

b) In all other cases, a perfected S/I has priority from the date the advance was made (i.e. if you perfect collateral worth $10M and initial Lien is for $2M (covering a $2M cash advancement), a

subsequent advance for $6M will have the same priority as the
first loan's Lien).

§9-306: Rights In "Proceeds":

(1) "Proceeds"
   a) Proceeds may be obtained from:
      1. Whatever is received upon:
         a. Sale
      or b. Exchange
      or c. Collection
      or d. Other disposition (of collateral or proceeds)
   or 2. Insurance payable from the loss/damage of the
         collateral, unless the insurance check is made payable
         to a non-party of the Security Agreement (Note: can
         be endorsed by Third Party to become valid)
   or 3. Any payments or distributions made with respect to
         investment property collateral.

   b) Proceeds may be in the form of:
      1. Cash Proceeds - Money, checks, deposit accounts, etc.
   or 2. Non-Cash Proceeds - all other proceeds

(2) Continuation of the S/I: Unless otherwise provided by the UCC,
    a S/I in collateral continues in:
    a) Collateral - even if it is sold/disposed of, unless the
       disposition was authorized by the Secured Party
and b) Proceeds - ONLY if the proceeds are IDENTIFIABLE

(3) The Security Interest in Proceeds
    i) A S/I in Proceeds is considered Continuously Perfected if
       the original collateral was "re-perfected" within 10 Days (of
       "conversion" to proceeds) (i.e. the date of perfection in the
       Proceeds relates back to date the original collateral was
       perfected).
    ii) The Proceeds becomes unperfected 10 Days after the Debtor
        receives the proceeds - Unless they are "re-perfected"
        (within the 10-day period).
    iii) A S/I in proceeds can only be perfected by the rules spelled
         out in the UCC, for original collateral of the same type
         (except as provided in this section).

iv) Perfection can be continuously maintained in Proceeds if:
 (a) AUTOMATIC RE-PERFECTION occurs; Automatic
   re-perfection occurs if either:
   1. Non-Cash Proceeds: (ex: a car for a car)
    a. The filed Financing Statement covers the
      original collateral
    and b. The proceeds are collateral in which a S/I may
      be perfected by filing (i.e. not cash) in the
      office where the Financing Statement was filed
      (even if you don't re-file) (Default Rule:
      silence means you have a S/I in proceeds)

   or 2. Non-Cash Proceeds bought with Cash Proceeds: If
      the non-cash proceeds on are acquired with cash-
      proceeds, perfection continues if the Financing
      Statement indicates the types of property
      constituting the proceeds (ex: a car for cash, to buy
      a new car).

 or (b) Proceeds are CASH PROCEEDS (ex: Accounts), AND:
   1. Cash-proceeds are identifiable
  and 2. A filed Financing Statement covers the original
    collateral
 or (c) The original collateral was Investment Property and the
   proceeds are Identifiable Cash proceeds
 or (d) The S/I in the proceeds is perfected before the 10 Day
   period expires.

(4) S/I In Proceeds of an Insolvent Debtor - A S/P (with a perfected
  S/I in proceeds) can only maintain a S/I in:

 (a) Non-Cash Proceeds, which are
   1. Identifiable
  and 2. In a separate deposit account, containing only proceeds

and (b) Money Cash-Proceeds, which are
   1. Identifiable
  and 2. In the form of money
  and 3. Not commingled with other money
  and 4. Not deposited into a deposit account prior to insolvency

and (c) Instrument Cash-Proceeds (i.e. checks, notes), which are

1. Identifiable

and 2. Not deposited in a deposit account prior to insolvency
proceedings

and (d) Cash-Proceeds in Accounts - In all cash and deposit
accounts of the Debtor (in which proceeds have been
commingled) perfection may be maintained, yet it will be:
  (i) Subject to any right to set-off

and (ii) Limited to:

> An "Amount" (<= any cash-proceeds received by
> Debtor within 10 days of
> insolvency)   less - (I)
> Payments to S/P on "account of cash
> proceeds" (within 10 Day period)
> less - (II) Cash Proceeds received by
> Debtor during 10 Day period

(5) Priorities with Returned/Repossessed Goods
  i) Requirements for Priority:
    a) The Sale of goods must result in an Account or Chattel
       Paper which is Transferred by the seller to the S/P.
  and b) The goods must be returned or repossessed by the
       Debtor or the S/P.

  ii) Rules of Priorities for Returned/Repossessed Goods
    (a) RE-PERFECTION: The Original Security Interest
       re-attaches to the goods, continuing perfection if:
       1. The goods were collateral at the time of the sale
    and 2. The Debt attached to collateral not paid at the sale
    and 3. It was perfected when the goods were sold
    and 4. Either:
       a. If Perfection by Filing: S/P files a new F/S
          only if the original Filing is not still effective
       or b. If Non-Filed Perfection: S/P takes possession
          of goods or file a new F/S

    (b) CHATTEL PAPER:
       1. An unpaid Transferee of the Chattel Paper
          maintains a S/I in the goods against the
          Transferor.
       2. If Transferee of Chattel Paper is entitled to priority
          (pursuant to §9-308), then he takes priority over
          RE-PERFECTED Secured Parties (see (a)above).

132

(c) ACCOUNTS:
1.   An unpaid Transferee of an account has a S/I in goods against the Transfer or.
2.   This S/I is subordinate to a re-perfected S/I (see (a) above)

(d) A S/I of an unpaid Transferee (pursuant to (b) and (c)) must be perfected to protect themselves against
1.   Creditors of the Transfer or
and 2.   Purchasers of the returned/repossessed goods

D) CHAPTER 11 PROCEEDINGS:

OVERVIEW ——————————————————————

• Chapter 11: Chapter 11 is similar to Chapter 13 in that a plan of reorganization is created and the Debtor aims to reorganize itself for continued existence.

•   Eligibility: Any <u>Person</u>, <u>Partnership</u>, or <u>Corporation</u> with a domicile in the U.S. may file under Chapter 11, except for:
  • Railroads
  • Banks and Insurance Companies
  • Individuals or Family Farmers who were Debtors in a Bankruptcy Proceeding dismissed within <u>180 days</u>.

•   The Chapter 11 Plan is the focal point of the Chapter 11 proceeding since it dictates how creditors will be paid and treated.

•   The Creditors of the Chapter 11 Debtor:
  • All Creditors are divided into different classes (§1122).
  • Each class will contain creditors of "substantially similar" claims and interests (§1122(a))

•   <u>Requirements for the Plan</u>: Each plan must contain the following (§1123(a)):

  1. <u>Designation of Classes</u> - the plan must designate classes of Claims and interests (except for §507 Priority Claims (§1121(a)(2))
  2. <u>Unimpaired Claims</u> - The plan must specify Claims or interests that are unimpaired by the plan (ex: Secured Claims).
  3. <u>Impaired Claims</u>: the plan must specify the treatment of any class of Claims or interests that is impaired under the plan.
  4. <u>Equal Treatment Within a Class</u> - the plan must provide the same treatment for each Claim or interest in a particular class (unless holders of a claim agree to be treated less preferentially).
  5. <u>Execution of the Plan</u>: the plan must provide adequate means for it's the reasonable reorganization of the Debtor.
  6. <u>Voting Power for Classes of Securities</u>:
     • The plan must prohibit the issuance of non-voting equity securities, by requiring a provision to this effect in the

Debtor's charter
- The plan must provide for an appropriate distribution of voting power among the various classes of equity securities (ex: if one class has a preference over another with respect to dividends, the plan would have to provide for the election of directors representing the preferred class in the event of default in the payment of such dividends).
7. Selection of Officers, Directors, Trustees over the Estate.

- Acceptance of the Plan:
  - At any particular time, there may be competing reorganization plans proposed for the Debtor. These plans may be made by different groups of Creditors or the Debtor.
- Solicitation for Acceptance – The Code is very specific on who may solicit creditors to approve of a particular reorganization plan (§1125).
  - The soliciting party must provide "Adequate Information" in all related communications.
  - A "Safe Harbor" checklist of required disclosures is provided in §1125(e) to help soliciting parties comply with this rule.
    - Who may Vote for Plan: Only creditors who are holders of claims or interest in the Estate may vote to accept or reject a plan.
    - Required Amount of Acceptances for a Class of Interests (§1126(d)): A plan is "accepted" by a class of interests if:
      1. The plan has been accepted by creditors holding at least 2/3 the amount of the allowed interests of the class that are voted.
      and 2. The plan has been accepted by creditors holding at least ½ the number of the allowed interests of the class that are voted.
    - A class (and each Claim holder in the class) that is not impaired under a plan is conclusively presumed to have accepted the plan (§1126(f)).

- Confirmation of the Plan: The court must confirm a plan if:
  1. Compliance with Code: The plan complies with the applicable provisions of the Bankruptcy Code
  and 2. Solicitation Compliance – by the proponents and solicitors of the plan.
  And 3. Good Faith - The plan has been proposed in good faith and not by any unlawful means.

And 4. <u>Payments Made are Reasonable</u> under the Plan
And 5. <u>Sufficient Disclosure is Made</u> - as to the identity of Officers, Directors and Insiders
And 6. <u>Approval of Governmental Agency</u> affected by the Plan or regulating the Debtor.
And 7. <u>Consent by Classes of Claims</u> -
- <u>Unsecured Claims:</u>
  (i) <u>Unanimous consent</u> of all affected Claim holders.
  or (ii) Each Claim holder will get (or retain) property equal to or greater than what the creditor would get if the Debtor were liquidated under Chapter 7 on the plan's effective date.
- <u>Secured Claims (Claim holder makes an election under §1111(b)(2)):</u> That each Claim holder will get (or retain) property equal to or greater than the creditor's share of the estate's interest in the collateral on the plan's effective date.
And 8. <u>Priority Claims (under §507) Must be Paid in Full</u>
and 9. <u>Impaired Classes</u>: At least one class of Claims that is impaired (not including Insiders) under the plan has accepted the plan (if there are any impaired classes).
and 10. <u>Liquidation Is Not Likely</u>:
and 12. <u>Bankruptcy Fees</u> will be paid

RELEVANT SECTIONS: §1121, §1122, §1123, §1125; §1126

§1121: Who May File A Plan:

(a) The Debtor
1. The Debtor may file a reorganization plan.
2. Time for Filing:
   a. Voluntary Case: At any time or with the Petition that commenced the case
   b. Involuntary Case: At any time after the Petition is filed

(b) 120-Day Rule - Debtor's Exclusive Right to File:
1. Only the Debtor may file a plan during the first <u>120 days</u> after the Order for Relief is made.
2. <u>Exceptions</u>: See §1121(c).

(c) When Any Party in Interest Files Plan:

    i)   Any Party in Interest may file a plan before the <u>120-day</u> waiting period (in §1121(b)) if:
        (1) A Trustee has been appointed
or (2) The Debtor does not file a plan within <u>120 days</u> after the Order for Relief
or (3) The Debtor fails to file an plan that was accepted within <u>180 days</u> of the Order for Relief by each class of Claims or interests that is impaired under the plan.

    ii) "Party in Interest" includes:[24]
        a. The Debtor
        b. The Trustee
        c. A creditors committee
        d. An equity Security holders committee
        e. A creditor
        f. An equity Security holder
        g. Any Indenture trustee

(d) Extension of Deadlines: The court may increase or reduce the 120-day and 180-day periods if:
    i. A "Party in Interest" makes a request within the periods
and ii. There is <u>notice</u> and a <u>hearing</u>[25]

(e) Small Business Exception: If the Debtor elects to be considered a Small Business:
    (1) The Debtor may file a plan until <u>100 days</u> after the Order for Relief is filed.
    (2) All plans must be filed within the first <u>160 days</u> after the Order for Relief is filed.
    (3) Extensions and Reductions:
        i. The court may:
            (A) <u>Reduce</u> the <u>100-day</u> period ((e)(1)) or the 160-day period ((e)(2)) for cause
      and (B) <u>Increase</u> the <u>100-day</u> period ((e)(1)), only if the Debtor shows that the extension is needed because of circumstances which he did not cause.

---

[24] This list is not exhaustive (ex: In the case of a public company, a Trustee is appointed within 10 days of the Petition; then, for most purposes any Party in Interest may file a plan).

25 Note: Under §1121(a) the Debtor has an exclusive privilege for 6 months to file a plan. Therefore, the legislative notes to §1121 State that an extension should be based on a showing of probable success; an extension should not be used as a tactical device to put pressure on parties in interest to yield to a plan they might not agree with.

    ii.   Requirements:
        A.   A "Party in Interest" makes a request within the period.
    and B.   There is notice and a hearing.

§1122: Classification of Claims or Interests:

(a) Interests and Claims in Same Class: A Claim or an interest may be placed in the same class if it is "substantially similar" to the other Claims or interests in that class.

(b) Exception: The plan may designate a separate class of Claims for unsecured Claims which are not "substantially similar" if:
1.   Each Claim in the class is <u>less than</u> (or reduced to) a certain "approved amount."
2.   The "approved amount" is found by the court to be <u>reasonable and necessary</u> for administrative convenience.

§1123: Contents of Plan:

(a) Requirements for the Contents of a Plan – The following is required in a Reorganization Plan (regardless of any other applicable non-bankruptcy law):

    (1) Designation of Classes:
        i.   The plan must designate classes of Claims and interests (subject to §1122).
        ii. <u>Priority Claims Exception</u>: Priority Claims (specified in §507(a)(1), §507(a)(2), or §507(a)(8)) are not required to be classified (since they may not have arisen when the plan is filed).
    (2) <u>Unimpaired Claims</u>: The plan must specify Claims or interests that are unimpaired by the plan (ex: Secured Claims).
    (3) Impaired Claims:
        i.   The plan must specify the treatment of any class of Claims or interests that is impaired under the plan.

ii.   This paragraph applies to Claims, not creditors.[26]

(4) Equal Treatment Within a Class:

    i.   The plan must provide the same treatment for each Claim or interest in a particular class.

    ii.   Exception: The holder of a particular Claim or interest can agree to a different treatment of that Claim, so long as it is not better.

(5) Execution of the Plan:

    i.   The plan must provide adequate means for its execution.

    ii.   These means may include the following:

        (A) Retain Property: The Debtor retains all (or any part of) the estate's property.

        (B) Transfer Property: The estate's property is Transferred (all or any part) to 1 or more entities, whether organized before or after the plan is confirmed.

        (C) Merger or Consolidation: The Debtor merges or consolidates with 1 or more Persons.

        (D) Sale of Property: The Property of the Estate (all or any part) is sold. The sale is either subject to or free of:

            1.   Any Lien

      or   2.   The distribution of the estate's property (all or any part) among "interested parties"

        (E) Satisfaction or modification of any Lien.

        (F) Cancellation or modification of any Indenture or similar instrument (This might include a deposit with an agent for distribution (not an Indenture trustee)).

        (G) Any default is cured or waived.

        (H) Changing Terms of Outstanding Securities - For example:

            1.   An extension of a maturity date

      or   2.   A change in an interest rate

      or   3.   A change in some other term

        (I)   The Debtor's charter is amended.

---

[26] Therefore, if a creditor is under-secured, and so has both a secured Claim and an unsecured Claim, this paragraph will be applied to each of his Claims.

(J) The securities of the Debtor (or any other Entity referred to in (B) or (C)) are issued for:
1. Cash
2. Property
3. Existing securities
4. In exchange for Claims or interests
5. For any other appropriate purpose

(6) Voting Power for Classes of Securities:
i.   The plan must prohibit the issuing of non-voting equity securities, by requiring a provision to this effect in the Debtor's charter (if the Debtor if a Corporation; otherwise, in the charter of any Corporation referred to in (5)(B) or (5)(C)).
ii. The plan must provide for an appropriate distribution of voting power among the various classes of equity securities (ex: if one class has a preference over another with respect to dividends, the plan would have to provide for the election of directors representing the preferred class in the event of default in the payment of such dividends).

(7) <u>Selection of Officers, Directors, Trustees</u>: The plan's provisions for the selection of officers, directors and trustees (and their successors) <u>must be</u> consistent with:
i.   The interests of creditors and equity Security holders
and ii. Public policy

(b) Matters That a Plan May Propose (subject to (a)):
(1) The plan may impair or leave unimpaired any class of Claims (secured or unsecured) or interests.
And (2) <u>Executory Contracts</u>: The plan may provide that any executory contract or unexpired lease of the Debtor that was not previously rejected under §365, be:
a. assumed
or b. rejected
or c. assigned.
and (3) <u>Pursuing Claims and Interests</u> - The plan may provide for:
(A) the <u>settlement</u> or <u>adjustment</u> of any of the Debtor's or the estate's Claims or interests
or (B) the <u>retention</u> and <u>enforcement</u> of any Claim or interest by:
1. The Debtor

   2. The Trustee
   3. A representative of the estate appointed for that
       purpose
and (4) Sale of Property (This would be a "liquidating plan") - The
         plan may provide for:
         a. The sale of (all or substantially all) of the estate's
             property
    and b. The distribution of the sale proceeds among Claim
             holders
and (5) Modification of Rights of Claim Holders:
         a. The plan may modify the rights of holders of secured
             Claims.
         b. This does not include a Claim secured only by a
             Security Interest in the Debtor's principal residence.
         c. The plan may also leave the rights of holders of any
             class of Claims unaffected
and (6) Other Provisions: The plan may include any other
         appropriate provision not inconsistent with the Bankruptcy
         Code.

(c) Cases Concerning Individuals: To protect individual Debtors, a
     plan may not provide for the use, sale, or lease of property
     exempted under §522, unless:
     1. The plan is proposed by the Debtor
 or 2. The Debtor consents

(d) Curing Defaults: If a plan proposes to cure a default, the amount
     necessary to cure the default is to be determined by:
     1. The underlying agreement
and 2. Applicable non-bankruptcy law (regardless of subsection (a)
         and §506(b), 1129(a)(7), and 1129(b))

§1124: Impairment of Claims or Interests:[27]

a) Definition of "Impaired" Claim - A class of Claims or interests
    is "impaired" under a plan unless:
    (1) The plan does not change the rights (legal, equitable, and
         contractual) that each Claim in a class entitles its holder.

---

[27] Note: This section does not include payment "in property" other than cash. Except
for a rare case, Claims payable in property (by their terms), but a plan may provide
that and any affected Persons may accept or reject the proposed plan. They may not be
forced to accept a plan declaring the holders' Claims or interests to be "unimpaired."

or (2) <u>Defaults</u>:
    (A) The plan cures any default (other than those described
        in §365(b)(2), i.e. a default under an ipso facto or
        bankruptcy clause) that occurred before or after the
        commencement of the case.
and (B) The plan reinstates the original maturity date of a Claim
        or interest.
and (C) The plan pays the Claim holder for any damages
        resulting from his reasonable reliance on a contractual
        provision or law that would entitle him to accelerate
        payment after the default.
and (D) The plan does not otherwise change the rights (legal,
        equitable, and contractual) of the Claim holder.

b) <u>Exception</u>: Consent to less-favorable treatment under
    §1123(a)(4) is <u>not</u> an "impairment."

§1125: Post-Petition Disclosure and Solicitation:

(a) Definitions for this Section:

   (1) "Adequate Information"

       a. <u>Definition</u>: Information that would enable (by its type
          and detail) a hypothetical reasonable investor (typical
          of Claim holders of the relevant class) to make an
          informed judgment about the plan.

       b. Both the kind and form of information are left to the
          court's discretion, guided by what is reasonably
          practicable, taking into account:
          1. The nature and history of the Debtor
      and 2. The condition of the Debtor's books and records

       c. "Adequate Information" <u>does not</u> have to include
          similar information about other possible or proposed
          plans

   (2) "Investor typical of holders of Claims or interests of the
      relevant class" is an investor that has:
      (A) A Claim or interest of the relevant class

and (B) A relationship with the Debtor that is similar to all other Claim holders of the class.

and (C) The ability to obtain information (other than the disclosure required by this section) from sources that the other Claim holders of the class generally have.

(b) Solicitations for Plan: An acceptance or rejection of a plan may <u>only</u> be solicited from a Claim holder if:

    1. The solicitation is made after the commencement of the case

and 2. The following is sent to the solicited Claim holder either during or before the solicitation:

    a. The plan or a summary of the plan

and b. A written disclosure statement containing "Adequate Information," as approved by the court:

      i. The court determines "Adequate Information" in a <u>hearing</u> with <u>notice</u>.

      ii. The court may approve a disclosure statement without a valuation of the Debtor or an appraisal of the Debtor's assets (Note that in some cases, a valuation or appraisal will be necessary to develop Adequate Information).

(c) Similarity of Disclosure Statements:

    1. The same disclosure statement shall be transmitted to each Claim holder of the same class.

    2. Different classes may be sent different disclosure statements (i.e. differing in amount, detail, or kind of information).

(d) Determining the Adequacy of a Disclosure Statement:

    1. The court does not have to follow any otherwise applicable Federal or State law in determining if there is "Adequate Information" in the submitted disclosure statement.

    2. An agency or official who administers or enforces such a law <u>may</u> be heard on the issue of whether a disclosure statement has "Adequate Information."

    3. The agency or official <u>may not</u> appeal an order approving a disclosure statement.

(e) "Safe Harbor" Provision for Good Faith Solicitation

    1. <u>General Rule</u>: A Person that solicits or participates in the <u>offer, issuance, sale</u> or <u>purchase</u> of securities in good faith is not responsible for violating any law governing such

solicitation or offers, issuances, sales, or purchases of
securities (anti-fraud laws), if:

    a.   Good Faith Requirement: The Person that solicits
        acceptance or rejection of a plan, or participates in the
        securities dealings must do so in good faith

and b.   In compliance with the provisions of the Bankruptcy
        Code

and c.   Securities in Offer, Issuance, Sale or Purchase belonged
        to:

        i.   The Debtor

    or ii. An Affiliate participating in a joint plan with the
           Debtor

    or iii. A successor to the Debtor newly organized under
           the plan

2.   Note: §1125(e) does not affect civil or criminal liability for
      defects and inadequacies that are beyond the limits of good
      faith.

(f) Small Businesses:

    i.   A "Small Business" is a Debtor who has elected under
       §1121(e) to be considered a Small Business

    ii. Special Rules for Small Businesses (notwithstanding
       subsection (b)):

      (1) The court may conditionally approve a disclosure
          statement (subject to final approval after notice and a
          hearing).

      (2) A conditionally approved disclosure statement may be
          used to solicit acceptances and rejections of a plan, as
          long as:

          a.   The Debtor provides Adequate Information to each
              solicited Claim holder.

          b.   The conditionally approved disclosure statement is
              mailed at least 10 days before the hearing on
              confirmation of the plan.

      (3) A hearing on the disclosure statement may be combined
          with a hearing on confirmation of a plan.

§1126: Acceptance of Plan:

(a) Who May Accept:

1. The holder of a Claim (allowed under §502) may <u>accept</u> or <u>reject</u> a plan.
2. The Secretary of the Treasury may <u>accept</u> or <u>reject</u> the plan on behalf of the United States if the U.S. is a creditor or equity Security holder.

(b) Pre-Petition Solicitation: For the purposes of §1126(c) and (d), a Claim holder that has accepted or rejected the plan before the commencement of the case is deemed to have accepted or rejected the plan (as the case may be) if:
　　(1) <u>Applicable Non-Bankruptcy Law</u>: The solicitation was in compliance with any applicable non-bankruptcy law that governs whether disclosure in connection with the solicitation is adequate.
or　(2) <u>If there is no Law or Rule:</u> The solicitation occurred after disclosure of "Adequate Information" (defined in §1125(a)) to the holder.

(c) Acceptances by An Entire Class of Claimants: A plan is "accepted" by a class of Claims if:

1. The plan has been accepted by creditors holding at least 2/3 <u>the amount</u> of the allowed Claims of the class that are voted.

and 2. The plan has been accepted by creditors holding at least ½ <u>the number</u> of the allowed Claims of the class that are voted.

and 3. The creditors are not entities discounted under §1126(e)(Acceptance or Rejection in Bad Faith).

(d) Required Amount of Acceptances for a Class of Interests: A plan is "accepted" by a class of interests if:
1. The plan has been accepted by creditors holding at least 2/3 <u>the amount</u> of the allowed interests of the class that are voted.
and 2. The plan has been accepted by creditors holding at least ½ <u>the number</u> of the allowed interests of the class that are voted.
and 3. The creditors are not entities designated under §1126(e).

(e) Exclusions from Calculations for Acceptance or Rejection in Bad Faith:

      1.   The following Claims are excluded from the calculations in (c) and (d):

          a.   Claims not voted in good faith

and b.   Claims procured or solicited not in good faith

and c.   Claims procured or solicited not in accordance with the Bankruptcy Code

      2.   Requirements for Such an Exclusion:

          a.   A Party in Interest makes a request

and b.   <u>Notice</u> and a <u>hearing</u>

(f) Presumed Acceptance of Plan – Unimpaired Classes:

      1.   A class (and each Claim holder in the class) that is not impaired under a plan is conclusively presumed to have accepted the plan (regardless of any other provision in §1126).

      2.   Acceptances from the Claim holders of the class therefore do not have to be solicited.

(g) No Presumed Acceptance of Plan – Classes With No Priority: A class of Claim holders that is not entitled under the plan to receive (or retain) any property under the plan on account of their Claims is deemed <u>not</u> to have accepted a plan (regardless of any other provision in §1126).

Table of Contents

CHAPTER 1: GENERAL PROVISIONS

§101: SELECTED DEFINITIONS THAT APPLY IN THE BANKRUPTCY CODE: 158
(1) "Accountant"..158
(2) "Affiliate" 158
(4) "Attorney"..159
(5) "Claim" 159
(6) "Commodity Broker"...159
(7) "Community Claim" 160
(8) "Consumer Debt"..160
(9) "Corporation"..160
(10) "Creditor"..160
(11) "Custodian"...160
(12) "Debt" 161
(12A) "Debt For Child Support" 161
(13) "Debtor"..161
(14) "Disinterested Person" 161
(15) "Entity" 162
(16) "Equity Security" 162
(17) "Equity Security Holder" 162
(21B) "Federal Depository Institutions Regulatory Agency" 162
(22) "Financial Institution"..163
(23) "Foreign Proceeding"...163
(24) "Foreign Representative" 163
(25) "Forward Contract"...163
(26) "Forward Contract Merchant"...164
(27) "Governmental Unit" 164

CHAPTER 3: CASE ADMINISTRATION

SUBCHAPTER I – COMMENCEMENT OF A CASE

§301: COMMENCEMENT OF A VOLUNTARY CASE   170
1. Filing of Petition. 170
2. Order for Relief...170
§303: INVOLUNTARY CASES   170
(a) Against Whom an Involuntary Case can be commenced.................170
(b) Who May Commence an Involuntary Case.....................................170
(c) Joining Additional Creditors 171
(d) Filing an Answer..172
(e) Indemnity Bond...172
(f) Debtor's Use and Possession of Property 172

Table of   E-Z RULES FOR BANKRUPTCY
Contents

(g) Interim Trustee 172
(h) Order for Relief 173
(i) Damages 173
(j) Dismissal of Involuntary Petition 174
(k) Foreign Banks 174
§307: UNITED STATES TRUSTEE   174

SUBCHAPTER III – ADMINISTRATION

§347: UNCLAIMED PROPERTY   175
(a) Property Paid Into Court 175
(b) Property Returned to the Debtor 175
§348: EFFECT OF CONVERSION   175
(a) Date of Order for Relief in Conversion 175
(b) Exception for Standard Order of Relief Date 176
(c) Conversion Order as Order for Relief 176
(d) Pre-Conversion Claims 176
(e) Effect in Trustee 176
(f) Conversions from Chapter 13 176

SUBCHAPTER IV – ADMINISTRATIVE POWERS

§361: ADEQUATE PROTECTION   178
§362: AUTOMATIC STAY   178
(a) The Automatic Stay 178
(b) Exceptions To The Automatic Stay 179
(c) Duration of Automatic Stay 181
(d) Relief From The Automatic Stay 182
(e) Lifting the Stay 182
(f) Irreparable Damage 183
(g) Burden of Proof 183
(h) Recovery of Actual Damages 183
§363: USE, SALE, OR LEASE OF PROPERTY   184
(a) "Cash Collateral" 184
(b) Not in the Ordinary Course of Business 184
(c) In The Ordinary Course of Business 184
(d) Limitations on Use 185
(e) Adequate Protection 185
(f) Sale of Property 185
(g) Sale of Right in Dowery 186
(h) Sale of Co-Owned Property 186
(i) Purchase of Property By Spouse/Co-owner 186
(j) Distribution of Proceeds to Co-Owners 186
(k) Purchase By Lien-holder 186
(l) "Ipso Facto" Clauses Not Effective 187
(m) Reversal on Appeal 187
(n) Voiding "Rigged" Sales 187
(o) Burdens of Proof 187

§364: Obtaining Credit   188
(a) In the Ordinary Course of Business..188
(b) Out of the Ordinary Course of Business.....................................188
(c) Secured or Super-Priority Credit 188
(d) First Priority Lien on Previously Encumbered Property................188
(e) Effect of Appeal 189
(f) Effect on T.I.A. 189
§365: Executory Contracts and Unexpired Leases   189
(a) Trustee's Strong-Arm Power...189
(b) Executory contracts Defaulted by Debtor 189
(c) Restrictions - When Trustee May Not Assume or Assign 190
(d) Time Limit 190
(e) Modifications Not Allowed...191
(f) When Trustee May Assign...192
(g) Time of Breach...192
(h) Debtor as Lessor of Real Property Lease 193
(i) Executory Contract to Sell Real Estate 193
(j) Purchaser's Lien..194
(k) Automatic Novation 194
(l) Lessor's Right to Security..194
(m) Rental Agreements...194
(n) Intellectual Property 195
(o) Commitments to Federal Depositories Assumed...........................196

CHAPTER 5: CREDITORS, DEBTOR, AND THE ESTATE

SUBCHAPTER I – CREDITORS AND CLAIMS

§501: Filing Proofs of Claims and Interests   197
(a) Who May File..197
(b) Alternate Filers..197
(c) Debtor's Filing. 197
(d) Special "Relation Back" Claims...197
§502: Allowance of Claims or Interests   198
(a) Presumption that Claim is Allowed...198
(b) Procedure Upon Objection 198
(c) Estimations..199
(d) Other Disallowed Claims 200
(e) Claims for Contribution or Reimbursement 200
(f) Claims Arising Out of the Ordinary Course...................................200
(g) Claims Resulting From Rejected Contracts and Leases 201
(h) Claims Resulting From Recovered Property 201
(i) Claims Arising From Post-Petition Tax Assessment......................201
(j) Reconsideration of Allowed/Disallowed Claims............................201
§503: Allowance Of Administrative Expenses   202

Table of   E-Z RULES FOR BANKRUPTCY
Contents

(a) Filing for Administrative Expenses 202
(b) Kinds of Administrative Expenses Allowed...............................202
§504: SHARING OF COMPENSATION   205
(a) Sharing Prohibited...205
(b) Exceptions..205
§506: DETERMINATION OF SECURED STATUS   206
(a) Bifurcation..206
(b) Allowable Interest to Oversecured Creditors 206
(c) Trustee's Recoverable Fees...206
(d) Unsecured Claims 206
§507: PRIORITIES: 207
(a) Expenses and Claims..207
(b) Secured Party's Attorneys' Fees 208
(c) Erroneous Tax Refund or Credit 209
(d) Subrogation Rights...209
§509: CLAIMS OF CO-DEBTORS   209
(a) Right of Subrogation 209
(b) Exceptions to Subrogation 209
(c) Subordination Allowed Claims of Co-Debtor 210
§510: SUBORDINATION   210
(a) Subordination Agreements Enforceable. 210
(b) Subordination of Security Holder's Claim 210
(c) Other Subordination of Claims..210

SUBCHAPTER II – DEBTOR'S DUTIES AND BENEFITS

§522: EXEMPTIONS   212
(a) Definitions..212
   (1) "Dependent"..212
   (2) "Value" 212
(b) Available Exemptions 212
(c) Effect of Exemption 212
(d) §522(b)(1) Exemptions 213
(e) Waivers Unenforceable 214
(f) Avoiding Liens on Exempt Property...215
(g) Exempting Recovered Property..216
(h) Avoiding Exempted Property...216
(i) Exempting Property Recovered From Setoffs.................................216
(j) Exempting Other Property. 216
(k) Administrative Expenses..217
   (l) Debtor's Filing...217
   (m) Joint Exemptions...217
§523: EXCEPTIONS TO DISCHARGE   218
(a) Debts that are Excepted from Discharge 218
   (1) TAXES..218
   (2) DEBTS FOR PROPERTY RECEIVED UNDER FALSE
PRETENSES OR BY CONSUMERS 218
   (3) UNSCHEDULED DEBTS...219

(b) Debts Discharged in Prior Bankruptcy 224
(c) Notice and Hearing 224
(d) Protection to Honest Consumer Debtors 225
(e) Fiduciary Status 226
§524: EFFECT OF DISCHARGE   226(A)
EFFECTS OF DISCHARGE   226
(b) Exception to §524(a)(3) 227
(c) Reaffirmation Agreements 227
(d) Discharge Hearing 228
(e) Liability of Other Entities 229
(f) Voluntary Repayment 229
(g) Other Injunctions 229
(h) Application to Existing Injunctions under Chapter 11 236

SUBCHAPTER III – THE ESTATE

§541: PROPERTY OF THE ESTATE   237
(b) Exclusions from Estate 237
(c) Superceding Contract Clauses 238
(d) Debtor's Legal Title in Trust Property 238
§542: TURNOVER OF PROPERTY OF THE ESTATE   239
(a) Return of Property to the Estate 239
(b) Debts to the Estate 239
(c) Property Not Subject to Turnover 239
(d) Life Insurance Companies 239
(e) Books and Records 239
§543: TURNOVER OF PROPERTY BY A CUSTODIAN   239
(a) Actions Prohibited by Custodian 239
(b) Turnover by Custodian 239
(c) Disbursements 240
(d) Exceptions to Turnover 240
§544: AVOIDING POWERS   241
(a) Trustee's Avoidance Powers 241
(b) Property and Interests the Trustee May Avoid 241
§545: STATUTORY LIENS   242
§546: EXCEPTIONS TO AVOIDING POWERS   242
(a) Time Limitation 242
(b) Trustee's avoidance powers subject to 242
(c) Reclamation Rights 243
(d) Crops 243
(e,f) Trustee Cannot Avoid Margin Payments 243
(g) Trustee Cannot Avoid "Swap Agreements" 243
§547: PREFERENCES   243
(a) Definitions 243
(b) Voidable Preferences 244
(c) Exceptions (Savings Clauses) 244
(d) Avoiding Transfers to a Surety 246
(e) Time of Transfer 246

(f) Preference Period...247
(g) Burden of Proof...247
§548: FRAUDULENT TRANSFERS   247
(a) Avoiding Transfers...247
(b) Trustee of a Partnership 247
(c) Exception..247
(d) Terms of Transfer..248
§549: POST-PETITION TRANSACTIONS   248
(a) General Rule...249
(b) Involuntary Cases..249
(c) Good Faith Purchaser Exception 249
§550: LIABILITY OF TRANSFEREE OF AVOIDED TRANSFERS   250
(a) Persons Whom Trustee May Recover From.................................250
(b) Persons Whom Trustee May Not Recover From..........................250
(c) Insiders..250
(d) Trustee Limited to Loss...250
(e) Transferee's Rights in Recovered Property 250
(f) Time Limit..251
§551: AUTOMATIC PRESERVATION OF AVOIDED TRANSFER   251
§552: POST-PETITION EFFECT OF SECURITY INTEREST   252
(a) After-Acquired Property...252
(b) Exception - Post-Petition Proceeds 252
§553: SETOFF   252
(a) Right to Setoff..252
(b) Limitation for Setoff..253
(c) Presumption of Insolvency 253
§554: ABANDONMENT OF PROPERTY   253
(a) Grounds for Abandonment...253
(b) Court Ordered Abandonment 254
(c) Administered Property..254
(d) Property Not Abandoned..254

CHAPTER 7: LIQUIDATION

§ 706: CONVERSION   255
(a) Conversion by Debtor 255
(b) Conversion to Chapter 11 by Court..255
(c) Conversion to Chapter 12 or 13 by Court...................................255
(d) Eligibility Requirement...255

SUBCHAPTER II – COLLECTION, LIQUIDATION, AND DISTRIBUTION
OF THE ESTATE

§721: AUTHORIZATION TO OPERATE BUSINESS   256
§722: REDEMPTION   256
a) Redeemable Property...256
b) Method of Redemption..256
§724: TREATMENT OF CERTAIN LIENS   256

(a) Fines and Penalties 256
(b) Tax Liens 256
(c) Competing Claimants. 257
(d) Statutory Liens. 257
§725: DISTRIBUTION OF CERTAIN PROPERTY   257
§726: DISTRIBUTION OF PROPERTY OF THE ESTATE   257
(b) Claimants Under The Same Distribution Class 258
(c) Distribution of Community Property......................................258
§727: DISCHARGE   258

CHAPTER 11: REORGANIZATION

SUBCHAPTER II – THE PLAN

§1121: WHO MAY FILE A PLAN   263
(a) The Debtor 263
(b) 120-Day Rule - Debtor's Exclusive Right to File 263
(c) When Any Party in Interest Files Plan 263
(d) Extension of Deadlines..263
(e) Small Business Exception 264
§1122: CLASSIFICATION OF CLAIMS OR INTERESTS   264
(a) Interests and Claims in Same Class.......................................264
(b) Exception 264
§1123: CONTENTS OF PLAN   265
(a) Requirements for the Contents of a Plan 265
(b) Matters That a Plan May Propose 267
(c) Cases Concerning Individuals 267
(d) Curing Defaults...268
§1124: IMPAIRMENT OF CLAIMS OR INTERESTS   268
§1125: POST-PETITION DISCLOSURE AND SOLICITATION   268
(a) Definitions for this Section..268
(1) "Adequate Information"...269
(2) "Investor typical of holders of Claims or interests of the relevant
class" 269
(b) Solicitations for Plan...269
(c) Similarity of Disclosure Statements 270
(d) Determining the Adequacy of a Disclosure Statement..................270
(e) "Safe Harbor" Provision for Good Faith Solicitation 270
(f) Small Businesses..270
§1126: ACCEPTANCE OF PLAN   271
(a) Who May Accept..271
(b) Pre-Petition Solicitation 271
(c) Acceptances by An Entire Class of Claimants 271
(d) Required Amount of Acceptances for a Class of Interests 272
(e) Exclusions from Calculations for Acceptance or Rejection in Bad
Faith   272
(f) Presumed Acceptance of Plan – Unimpaired Classes 272

(g) No Presumed Acceptance of Plan – Classes With No Priority........272
§1127: MODIFICATION OF PLAN   273
    (a) Modification Prior to Confirmation...273
    (b) Modification After Confirmation 273
    (c) Compliance with §1125...273
    (d) Presumed Acceptance of Modification. 273
§1128: CONFIRMATION HEARING   274
§1129: CONFIRMATION OF PLAN   274
    (a) Requirements...274
    (b) The "Cram-Down": Alternatives for Confirmation of a Plan..........277
    (c) Multiple Plan Meeting Requirements – Confirmation of Best Plan   279
    (d) Denial of Confirmation 279

SUBCHAPTER III – POSTCONFIRMATION MATTERS

§1141: EFFECT OF CONFIRMATION   280
    (a) Persons Bound By Plan 280
    (b) Vesting of Property 280
    (c) Property Free and Clear of Claims and Interests 280
    (d) Discharge for Reorganized Debtor...281
    (1) Discharge of Debts..281
    (2) Exceptions to Discharge: Taxes 281
    (3) Exceptions for Debtor's Non-Cooperation...................................282
    (4) Waiver of Discharge..282
§1142: IMPLEMENTATION OF PLAN   282
    (a) Carrying Out Plan..282
    (b) Acts Necessary to Consummate Plan 282
§1143: DISTRIBUTION   282
§1144: REVOCATION OF AN ORDER OF CONFIRMATION   283
    a. When a Court May Revoke...283
    b. Requirements 283
    1. Request 283
    2. Time..283
    3. Notice 283
    c. Contents of Order of Revocation 283
§1145: EXEMPTION FROM SECURITIES LAWS   283
    (a) Exemption From Securities Laws..283
    (b) When a Creditor or Equity Security Holder May Resell Securities
    Received by the Plan 285
    (c) Offer or Sale Deemed Public Offering 286
    (d) Applicability of The Trust Indenture Act......................................287
§1146: SPECIAL TAX PROVISIONS   287
    (a) Termination of Taxable Period...287
    (b) Filing of Tax Returns 287
    (c) Exemptions From Tax 287
    (d) Advance Rulings from the IRS 287

CHAPTER 13: ADJUSTMENT OF DEBTS OF AN INDIVIDUAL WITH
REGULAR INCOME

SUBCHAPTER I – OFFICERS, ADMINISTRATION, AND THE ESTATE

§1301: Stay of Action Against Co-Debtor   288
    (a) Automatic Stay..288
    (b) Exception to Stay for Negotiable Instruments 289
    (c) Relief From the Automatic Stay....................................289
    (d) Lifting of Stay for Impaired Creditor............................290
§1302: Trustee   290
    (a) Appointment of Trustee..290
    (b) Duties of the Trustee...290
    (c) Duties When Debtor is in Business................................291
§1303: Rights and Powers of Debtor   292
§1304: Debtor "Engaged in Business"   292
    (a) Definition - "Engaged in Business"................................292
    (b) Permissible Operation by Debtor of Certain Business Activities....292
    (c) Requirement to File Reports on Operations 292
§1305: Filing and Allowance of Post-Petition Claims   293
    (a) Who May File...293
    (b) Allowance of Claims..293
    (c) Disallowed Claims. 293
§1306: Property of the Estate   293
    (a) Definition of "Property" 293
    (b) Possession of Property 294
§1307. Conversion or Dismissal   294
    (a) Conversion 294
    (b) Required Dismissal 294
    (c) Conversions to a Chapter 7 Case; Dismissal of Case For Cause 294
    (d) Conversion to Chapter 11 or 12 Case.............................295
    (e) Conversion when Debtor is a Farmer. 296
    (f) Conversions to other Chapters 296

SUBCHAPTER II – THE PLAN

§1321: Filing of Plan   296
§1322: Contents of Plan   296
    (a) Mandatory Provisions...296
    (b) Optional Provisions..296
    (c) Special Rules for Debtor's Principal Residence 297
    (d) Limit on Pay Period 298
    (e) Availability of Funds to Cure Defaults...........................298
§1323: Modification of Plan Before Confirmation   298
    (a) Modification - When Allowed.......................................298
    (b) Effect of Modification...298
    (c) Effect of Acceptance/Rejection 298
§1324: Confirmation Hearing   299

Table of   E-Z RULES FOR BANKRUPTCY
Contents

§1325: CONFIRMATION OF PLAN   299
(a) Mandatory Confirmation...299
(b) When Court May Not Approve Plan.............................300
(c) Payment of Income to Trustee.....................................300
§1326: PAYMENTS   300
(a) Debtor's Payments Under The Plan 300
(b) Recurring Payments 301
(c) Payments to Creditors 301
§1327: EFFECT OF CONFIRMATION   301
(a) Binding Effect of Confirmation....................................301
(b) Vesting of Property 301
(c) "Free and Clear"..302
§1328: DISCHARGE   302
(a) Discharge of Debts..302
(b) Discharge Where Payments Not Complete 302
(c) Discharge From Unsecured Debts.................................303
(d) Post-Petition Claims Not Discharged...........................303
(e) Revocation of Discharge 303
§1329: MODIFICATION OF PLAN AFTER CONFIRMATION   303
(a) General Rule Allowing Modification 303
(b) Additional Requirements and Results of Modification 304
(c) Limitation...304
§1330: REVOCATION OF AN ORDER OF CONFIRMATION   304
(a) Revocation Based on Fraud..304
(b) Disposition of Case 304

UNIFORM FRAUDULENT CONVEYANCES ACT

§2: Insolvency...306
(1) Person..306
§3: Fair Consideration 306
(a) Conveyance of Property/Release of Debt.....................306
(b) Security Interest 306
§4: Conveyance by an Insolvent...306
§5: Conveyance by a Person in Business.............................306
§6: Conveyance by a Person About to Incur Debts...............307
§7: Conveyance Made With Intent to Defraud 307
§9: Rights of Creditors Under Fraudulent Conveyance Law 307
(1) The Fraudulent Conveyance Rule 307
(2) Rights of Non-GFP Innocent Purchaser 307

SELECTED PROVISIONS FROM ARTICLE 9 OF THE UNIFORM
COMMERCIAL CODE

§9-203: ATTACHMENT AND ENFORCEABILITY OF SECURITY INTEREST   308
(1) Requirements for Attachment 308
(2) Time of Attachment 308
(3) Rights to Proceeds..309

Table of
Contents

§9-204: AFTER-ACQUIRED PROPERTY; FUTURE ADVANCES — 309
§9-301: PRIORITY OVER UNPERFECTED SECURITY INTERESTS — 309
§9-306: RIGHTS IN "PROCEEDS" — 311
§9-312: PRIORITIES AMONG CONFLICTING SECURITY INTERESTS IN THE SAME COLLATERAL — 314
§9-504: SECURED PARTY'S RIGHT TO DISPOSE AFTER DEFAULT — 316
§9-505: DISPOSITION OF COLLATERAL — 319

CHAPTER 1: GENERAL PROVISIONS

§101: Selected Definitions That Apply in the Bankruptcy Code:

(1) "Accountant" - includes an accountant, an accounting association, Corporation, or partnership authorized under applicable law to practice public accounting.

(2) An "Affiliate" is
    (A) Entity with Voting Control:
        1. An Entity that directly or indirectly has 20% or more of the outstanding voting securities of the Debtor, either by:
            i. ownership
    or ii. control
    or iii. holding them with the power to vote
        2. This does not include an Entity that holds these securities either:
            (i) As Fiduciary: in a fiduciary or agency capacity without sole discretionary power to vote
    or (ii) As Pledgee: solely to secure a Debt (so long as the Entity has not actually exercised its voting power)
  or (B) Corporation with Voting Control:
        1. A Corporation of which:
            i. the Debtor (directly or indirectly) (or an Entity described in (A)) has 20% or more of whose outstanding voting securities, either by ownership, control, or holding them with the power to vote
    or ii. An Entity (of the type described in (A) above) has 20% or more of whose outstanding voting securities, either by ownership, control, or holding them with the power to vote

        2. This does not include an Entity that holds these securities either:
            (i) As Fiduciary: in a fiduciary or agency capacity without sole discretionary power to vote
    or (ii) As Pledgee: solely to secure a Debt (so long as the Entity has not actually exercised its voting power)

  or (C) Property Controlled by Debtor:

1. A Person who operates his business under a lease or operating agreement by the Debtor

or 2. A Person substantially all of whose property is operated under an operating agreement with the Debtor,

or (D) Entity that Control's Debtor's Property: An Entity that operates either of the following under a lease or operating agreement:
1. The Debtor's the business
or 2. Substantially all of the Debtor's property

(4) "Attorney" includes: an Attorney, professional law association, Corporation, or partnership, authorized under applicable law to practice law.

(5) A "Claim" includes all of the following:
(A) Payment Claims: any right to payment whether or not such right is:
1. Reduced to judgment
2. Liquidated
3. Unliquidated
4. Fixed
5. Contingent
6. Matured
5. Unmatured
6. Disputed
7. Undisputed
8. Legal
9. Equitable
10. Secured
11. Unsecured

or (B) Equitable Claims for Breach: any right to an equitable remedy for breach of performance if that breach gives rise to a right to payment (as determined by (A) above).

(6) "Commodity Broker" – includes the following entities:
A. Futures commission merchant
B. Foreign futures commission merchant
C. Clearing organization
D. Leverage transaction merchant
E. Commodity options dealer (as defined in Sec. 761), with respect to which there is a customer (as defined in Sec. 761).

(7) "Community Claim" -a Claim:
   A. That arose before the commencement of the case
   B. Concerning the Debtor for which property of the kind
       specified in Sec. 541(a)(2) is liable (whether or not there is
       any such property at the time of the commencement of the
       case)

(8) "Consumer Debt" - Debt incurred by an individual primarily for
    a personal, family, or household purpose.

(9) "Corporation"
   (A) The definition includes:
       (i)   An association having a power or privilege that a
             private Corporation has (but not an individual or a
             partnership)
   or (ii) A partnership association organized under a law that
             makes only the capital subscribed responsible for the
             Debts of the association
   or (iii) A joint-stock company
   or (iv) An unincorporated company or association,
   or (v)   A business trust

   (B) The definition does not include a limited partnership.

(10) "Creditor" -
    (A) Any Entity that has a Claim:
        1. Against the Debtor
        2. That arose either at the time of or before the Order for
            Relief concerning the Debtor
   or (B) Any Entity that has a Claim against the estate of a kind
           specified in §§ 348(d), 502(f), 502(g), 502(h) or 502(i),
   or (C) Entity that has a community Claim.

(11) "Custodian" -
    (A) A receiver or trustee of any of the Debtor's property
        (appointed in a case or proceeding not under the Bankruptcy
        Code)
   or (B) An assignee under a general assignment for the benefit of
           the Debtor's creditors
   or (C) A Trustee, receiver, or agent under applicable law (or under
           a contract) that is appointed or authorized to take charge of
           property of the Debtor for the purpose of:

1. Enforcing a Lien against the property
or   2. General administration of the property for the benefit of the Debtor's creditors

(12) A "Debt" is a liability on a Claim

(12A) "Debt For Child Support" - the kind of Debt specified in Sec. 523(a)(5) for maintenance or support of a child of the Debtor

(13) "Debtor" - a Person or municipality about which a bankruptcy case has been commenced

(14) "Disinterested Person" - a Person that
(A) Is not:
    1. A Creditor
or   2. An Equity Security Holder
or   3. An Insider
(B) Is not (and was not) an investment banker for any outstanding Security of the Debtor
(C) Has not been either of the following within 3 years before the date the Petition was filed:
    1. An investment banker for a Security of the Debtor in connection with the offer, sale, or issuance of a Security of the Debtor
or   2. An Attorney for such an investment banker in connection with the offer, sale, or issuance of a Security of the Debtor
(D) Is not and did not hold any of the following positions with the Debtor within 2 years before the date the Petition was filed:
    1. Director of the Debtor
    2. Officer of the Debtor
    3. Employee of the Debtor
    4. Employee of an investment banker (as specified in (14) (B) or (C))

(E) Does not have a materially adverse interest to the estate, any class of creditors, or equity Security holders, by either having:
    1. Any relationship, connection, or interest (direct or indirect) with any interest (direct or indirect) in either:
        i. The Debtor

  or ii. An investment banker (as specified in (14) (B) or (C))
  2. Any other reason that may establish a material adverse interest.

(15) "Entity" includes a
 1. Person
 2. Estate
 3. Trust
 4. Governmental Unit
 5. United States Trustee

(16) "Equity Security" - includes:
 (A) Shares in a Corporation (whether or not Transfer able or called "stock") or similar Security
or (B) Interests of a limited partner in a limited partnership
or (C) Warrants or rights, other than a right to:
 1. <u>Convert</u> a share, Security, or interest (of the type described in (16) (A) or (B))
or 2. <u>Purchase</u> a share, Security, or interest (of the type described in (16) (A) or (B))
or 3. <u>Sell</u> a share, Security, or interest (of the type described in (16) (A) or (B))
or 4. <u>Subscribe to</u> a share, Security, or interest (of the type described in (16) (A) or (B)).

(17) "Equity Security Holder" – means a holder of an equity Security of the Debtor.

(21B)"Federal Depository Institutions Regulatory Agency" -
 (A) <u>The Federal banking agency</u> (as defined in section 3(q) of that Federal Deposit Insurance Act) - for an insured depository institution (as defined in section 3(c)(2) of the Act) for which no conservator or receiver has been appointed
 (B) <u>The National Credit Union Administration</u> - for an insured credit union (including an insured credit union for which the NCUA has been appointed conservator or liquidating agent)
 (C) <u>The Resolution Trust Corporation</u> - for any insured depository institution for which the RTC has been appointed conservator or receiver

(D) The Federal Deposit Insurance Corporation - for any insured depository institution for which the FDIC has been appointed conservator or receiver

(22) "Financial Institution" - a Person that
  A. Is one of the following:
    1. A commercial or savings bank
    2. Industrial savings bank
    3. Savings and loan association
    4. Trust company
and B. Such an Entity is acting as agent or Custodian for a customer in connection with a securities contract (as defined in Sec. 741)

(23) "Foreign Proceeding" -
  A. A proceeding in a foreign country in which any of the following were located at the commencement of that proceeding:
    1. the Debtor's domicile
    2. the Debtor's residence
    3. the Debtor's principal place of business
    4. the Debtor's principal assets
and B. The proceeding is for any of the following:
    1. to liquidate the estate
    2. to adjust Debts by:
      i. composition
      ii. extension
      iii. discharge
    3. those effecting a reorganization
  C. It is irrelevant whether the proceeding is judicial or administrative or whether or not it is under bankruptcy law.

(24) "Foreign Representative" – a duly selected trustee, administrator, or other representative of an estate in a foreign proceeding

(25) "Forward Contract" - a contract (other than a commodity contract) for the purchase, sale, or Transfer of any of the following:
  A. a commodity (as defined in Sec. 761(8))
  B. Any similar goods, articles, services, rights, or interests which is (or becomes) the subject of dealing in the forward contract trade.

C. Any product or byproduct of such an interest, with a maturity date more than 2 days after the date the contract is entered into, including a:
1. Repurchase transaction
2. Reverse repurchase transaction
3. Consignment
4. Lease
5. Swap
6. Hedge transaction
7. Deposit
8. Loan
9. Option
10. Allocated transaction
11. Unallocated transaction
12. Any combination of the above or option on it

(26) "Forward Contract Merchant" - a Person whose business consists (in whole or in part) of entering into Forward Contracts as or with merchants in similar commodities (as defined in §761(8)), goods, articles, services, rights, or interests which is (or becomes) the subject of dealing in the forward contract trade.

(27) "Governmental Unit" - includes
A. The United States
B. Any State of the U.S.
C. Any Commonwealth of the U.S.
D. Any District of the U.S.
E. Any Territory of the U.S.
F. Any municipality of the U.S.
G. A foreign State of the U.S.
H. Any department, agency, or instrumentality of the United States (but not a United States trustee while serving as a trustee in a bankruptcy case)
I. State of a foreign or domestic government
J. Commonwealth of a foreign or domestic government
K. District of a foreign or domestic government
L. Territory of a foreign or domestic government
M. Any municipality of a foreign or domestic government or other foreign or domestic government

(28) "Indenture" A document will be deemed an Indenture if it is:
A. Either a Mortgage, Deed of Trust, or Indenture

and B. There is outstanding <u>Security</u> (other than a voting-trust certificate) under such document

and C. The Security either:
1. Constitutes a Claim <u>against the Debtor</u>
or 2. Is <u>secured by a Lien</u> against any of the Debtor's property
or 3. Is an <u>Equity Security</u> of the Debtor

(29) "Indenture Trustee" – means any trustee under an Indenture

(30) "Individual with Regular Income" is an Individual
1. Whose income is "Sufficiently stable and regular" to enable such individual to make payments under a Chapter 13 plan
2. Who is <u>not</u> a Stock Broker or Commodity Broker

(31) "Insider" includes the following entities:
  (A) If the Debtor is an <u>Individual</u>:
    (i) A <u>Relative</u> of
      1) The Debtor
    or 2) A General Partner of the Debtor
    (ii) A <u>Partnership</u> – in which the Debtor is a General Partner
    (iii) A <u>General Partner</u> of the Debtor
    (iv) A <u>Corporation</u> of which the Debtor is either:
      a) A Director
      b) An Officer
      c) A "Person in Control" of the Corporation

  (B) If the Debtor is a <u>Corporation</u>: any
    (i) <u>Director</u>
    (ii) <u>Officer</u>
    (iii) "<u>Person in Control</u>" of the Debtor Corporation
    (iv) <u>Partnership</u> in which the Debtor Corporation is a General Partner
    (v) <u>General Partner</u> of the Debtor
    (vi) <u>Relative</u> of any of the above

  (C) If the Debtor is a <u>Partnership</u>: any
    (i) <u>General Partner</u> in the Debtor
    (ii) <u>Relative</u> of
      a) A General Partner of the Debtor
      b) A Director, officer, or "Person in control" of the Debtor

(iii) <u>Partnership</u> in which the Debtor is a General Partner
(iv) <u>General Partner</u> of the Debtor
(v) "<u>Person in Control</u>" of the Debtor

(D) If the Debtor is a <u>Municipality</u>: any elected official of the Debtor, or a Relative of an elected official.

(E) Any <u>Affiliate</u> or <u>Insider</u> of an Affiliate, as if such Affiliate where the Debtor itself,

(F) Any <u>Managing Agent</u> of the Debtor

(32) "Insolvent" means –
(A) <u>All Entities other than a Partnership or Municipality</u>:
    1.   A Person will be deemed to be "Insolvent" when the sum of the Entity's Debts is greater than all of its property
    2.   Valuation on Property: For purposes of determining the Entity's property Value
        (i) Exclude "Fraudulent Conveyances" - Any property Transferred, concealed, or removed with the intent to defraud the Entity's creditors should be excluded from the Value of the Entity's property (for purposes of this definition)..
        (ii) Exclude Exempt Property – Any property that may be exempt under §522 should be excluded from the Value of the Entity's property (for purposes of this definition).
        (iii) Fair Valuation – The Value of the property shall be calculated at a "fair valuation"
(B)   <u>Partnership</u>
    A Partnership shall be deemed "Insolvent" when the sum of the Partnership's Debts is greater than the aggregate of:
    (i)   Partnership Property – calculated at a Fair Valuation,
PLUS (ii) Partner's Personal Property - equal to:
        a.   Each partner's non-partnership Debt
    less b. Each partner's non-partnership property

(C) <u>Municipality</u>: A Municipality will be deemed Insolvent if it is:
    (i)   Generally not paying its Debts as they become due (except for Debts subject to a bona-fide dispute)

(ii) Unable to pay its Debts as they become due

(35A) "Intellectual Property" includes
(A) Trade secrets
(B) Inventions, process, design, or plant protected under Title 35 (Patents)
(C) Patent Applications
(D) Plant Variety
(E) Work of Authorship protected under Title 17 (Copyrights)
(F) Mask work protected under Chapter 9 of Title 17; to the extent protected by applicable non-bankruptcy law; and

(36) "Judicial Lien" – a Lien obtained by:
A. Judgment
B. Levy
C. Sequestration
D. Other legal or equitable process or proceeding

(37) A "Lien" is any charge against or interest in property to secure payment of a Debt or performance of an obligation.

(41) "Person"
1. The term "Person" includes
   A) An Individual
   B) A Partnership
   C) A Corporation
2. Governmental Units: A Governmental Unit will be deemed a "Person" only for purposes of §1102 (CREDITOR COMMITTEES) and only with respect the following assets:
   (A) An asset from a Person, either:
       i. As a result of the operation of a loan-guarantee agreement
       ii. As a receiver or liquidating agent of a Person
   or (B) A pension, in which it is a guarantor of a pension payable by or on behalf of the Debtor or its Affiliate
   or (C) Legal or beneficial ownership of an asset from:
       i. An Employee Benefit Plan (as defined in §414(d) of the Internal Revenue Code)
       ii. An Eligible Deferred Compensation Plan (as defined in §457(b) of the Internal Revenue Code)
(42) "Petition" – the Petition filed under §301, §302, §303, or §304, commencing a bankruptcy case under this Title.

(43) "Purchaser" means –
    A. A Transferee of a <u>Voluntary Transfer</u>
or B. An immediate or mediate Transferee of such a Transferee

(45) "Relative" means –
    A. An individual related by affinity or consanguinity within the third degree as determined by the common law
    B. An individual in a step or adoptive relationship within the third degree as determined by the common law

(49) "Security"
    (A) <u>Inclusions</u>: The term "Security" includes:
        (i) Note
        (ii) Stock
        (iii) Treasury Stock
        (iv) Bond
        (v) Debenture
        (vi) Collateral Trust Certificate
        (vii) Pre-organization certificate of subscription
        (ix) Voting-Trust Certificate
        (x) Certificate of Deposit
        (xi) Certificate of Deposit for Security
        (xii) Investment Contract or Certificate of Interest - in a Participation in a natural-gas/mineral profit sharing agreement
        (xiii) Limited Partnership Interests
        (xiv) Other Claim or interest commonly known as a "Security"
        (xv) Certificate of interest or participation in or right to subscribe to purchase or sell a Security
    (B) <u>Exclusions</u>: The term "Security" <u>does not</u> include:
        (i) Currency, checks, drafts, letters of credit, bills of exchange
        (ii) leverage transactions
        (iii) Commodity futures contract or Forward Contracts
        (iv) Options, warrants, or rights to subscribe to or purchase or sell a commodity futures contract
        (v) Option to purchase or sell a commodity
        (vi) Debt or evidence of indebtedness for goods sold and delivered, or services rendered.

(50) "Security Agreement" means an agreement that creates or provides for a Security Interest;

(51) "Security Interest" means a Lien created by an agreement;

(51C) "Small Business" – a Person engaged in commercial or business activities if:
1. Its aggregate, non-contingent liquidated Debts (whether secured or unsecured) are <u>not</u> greater than $2,000,000.
and 2. Its primary activity is <u>not</u> the business of owning or operating real estate.

(52) "State" includes each of the United States of America, the District of Columbia and Puerto Rico (except for the purpose of defining who may be a Municipality Debtor under Chapter 9)

(53) "Statutory Lien"
A. A Statutory Lien is either:
1. A Lien arising solely by <u>force of a statute</u> on specified circumstances or conditions
2. <u>Landlord's Lien</u>, created by distress for rent (whether or not statutory in nature)
B. Does not include a Judicial Lien – even if such Lien was derived by a statute.

(54) " Transfer " includes every mode of disposing of or parting with property (or an interest in property) including:
1. A retention of title as a Security Interest
2. Foreclosure of the Debtor's equity of redemption
3. Any direct or indirect, voluntary or involuntary mode of disposition

(55) "United States" includes all locations where the judicial jurisdiction of the United States extends (including territories and possessions of the United States)

CHAPTER 3: CASE ADMINISTRATION

Subchapter I – Commencement of A Case

§301: Commencement of a Voluntary Case:

1. Filing of Petition: To commence a voluntary case under a chapter of the Bankruptcy Code, a <u>Debtor</u> (who is eligible to file under one of the chapters of the Code) must file a Petition under the appropriate chapter with the bankruptcy court.

2. Order for Relief: The entry of an "Order for Relief" in a bankruptcy case happens automatically when a voluntary Petition is filed. The commencement of the case constitutes the "Order for Relief."

§303: Involuntary Cases:

(a) Against Whom an Involuntary Case May Be Commenced:

    1. An involuntary case may only be commenced:
      a. Under chapter 7 or 11 of the Bankruptcy Code (a Chapter 12 or 13 case <u>must be voluntary</u>).
    and b. Against a Person that is "eligible" as a Debtor under the chapter that applies (either Chapter 7 or 11).

    2. An involuntary Petition may not be filed against the following:
      a. A Farmer
      b. A Family Farmer
      c. A Corporation which is <u>not</u>:
        1. A moneyed business
        2. A commercial Corporation (such as a non-profit Corporation)

(b) Who May Commence an Involuntary Case: One of the following may commence an involuntary case against a Person, by filing a Petition (under chapter 7 or 11) with the Bankruptcy Court:

    (1) <u>3 or more creditors</u>, where:
      a. There are <u>12</u> or more creditors.

and   b. Each is either:
          1. A Creditor
    or   2. An Indenture Trustee representing a creditor
and c. The Claim is not:
          1. Contingent as to liability
    or   2. The subject of a bona fide dispute
and d. At least $10,000 of Claims are held in total.

(2) By 1 or more creditors, if:
    a. There are fewer than 12 holders, not including:
       1. Any employee of the Debtor
       2. Any Insider of the Debtor
       3. Anyone who receives a Voidable Transfer (under §§544, 545, 547, 548, 549, or 724(a))
and b. At least $10,000 of Claims are held in total.

(3) General Partner: The following may file if the Debtor is a partnership:
    (A) Less than all of the general partners in the partnership
  or (B) Any of the following, if relief has been ordered under the Code, concerning all of the general partners:
       1. A General Partner in the partnership
       2. The Trustee of a general partner
       3. A Creditor holding a Claim against the partnership

Such action may be taken by fewer than all of the general partners notwithstanding a contrary agreement between the partners or State or local law

(4) Foreign Representative: by a foreign representative of the estate (e.g. trustee, administrator) in a foreign proceeding concerning the Debtor (the Petition is filed to administer the property that's located in the U.S.).

(c) Joining Additional Creditors: A creditor may join in an involuntary Petition after it was filed (with the same effect as if it joined in the original Petition) if:
1. Timing: The court has not dismissed the case or ordered relief yet
2. The Creditor is:
    i. Unsecured
    ii. Holding a non-contingent Claim

iii. The creditor has not already filed under subsection (b) of this section (i.e. the creditor knows that there are at least 12 creditors, but files an involuntary Petition to resolve a dispute, for example).

(d) Filing an Answer: Only the following may file an Answer to an involuntary Petition:
1. The Debtor
or 2. A general partner that did not join in the Petition (in a general partnership Debtor)

(e) Indemnity Bond: The court may require the Petitioning parties (under this §303) to file a bond to indemnify the Debtor for any damages that might be later awarded if the Petition in dismissed (see subsection (i)), provided there is:
1. Notice and a hearing
and 2. Sufficient cause

(f) Debtor's Use and Possession of Property:
1. The Debtor may continue to do the following after the filing of an involuntary Petition but before the entry of an Order for Relief:
   a. The Debtor may continue to operate any business
   b. The Debtor may continue to use, acquire, or dispose of property as if an involuntary case had not been commenced.
2. Exceptions: The Debtor may not do so if:
   a. The court orders otherwise and denies such privileges
   and b. The court appoints an interim trustee
   and c. An Order for Relief is entered

(g) Interim Trustee:
1. Appointment of an Interim Trustee:
   a. The court may order the U. S. Trustee to appoint an Interim Trustee (under section 701) to do the following:
      1. take possession of the Property of the Estate, and
      2. to operate any business of the Debtor
   b. Requirements:
      i. Involuntary Petition under Chapter 7
      ii. Appointment must be made after the commencement case
      iii. An Order for Relief has not been entered
      iv. A Party in Interest has made a request

      v. There has been notice to the Debtor and a hearing about the appointment

     vi. It is necessary to preserve the Property of the Estate or to prevent loss to the estate.

  2. <u>Debtor's Possession</u>: The court may allow the Debtor to retake possession of the property if:

      a. The Debtor files a bond (in an amount set by the court)

and b. An Order for Relief had not been entered

and c. The Debtor accounts for and delivers (to the trustee) the property (or the Value as of the date the Debtor regains possession) of the property, if there is an Order for Relief in the case.

(h) Order for Relief: A court may order relief against a Debtor in an involuntary Petition if either:

      i. The Petition is not answered within <u>20 days</u> after it is served

or ii. Otherwise only if:

     (1) After a trial the court finds that the Debtor is generally not paying his Debts as they become due, and those Debts are not the subject of a bona fide dispute (the court will consider the amount of the Debts and the number of unpaid creditors)

   or (2) After a trial the court finds that within <u>120 days</u> before the Petition was filed a Custodian was appointed or took possession of the Debtor's property.

      • This does not include a trustee, receiver, or agent appointed to take charge of the Debtor's property for the purpose of enforcing a Lien against such property.

The test in section 303(h)(2) authorizes an Order for Relief to be entered in an involuntary case from the <u>later date</u> on which the Custodian was appointed or took possession.

(i) Damages:

      i. <u>A Debtor may be entitled to damages if</u>:

     1. A court dismisses an involuntary Petition

and 2. All of the Petitioning entities did not consent to such dismissal (including the Debtor, where necessary)

and 3. The Debtor does not waive the right to judgment for damages

    ii. The court may award judgment as follows:
        (1) Against the Petitioning parties and in favor of the Debtor for:
           (A) Costs,
    or   (B) Reasonable Attorneys' fee
   or (2) If a court finds that a Petitioning party filed in bad faith damages may be awarded for:
           (A) Any damages proximately caused by the filing
    or   (B) Punitive damages

(j) Dismissal of Involuntary Petition:
    a. Grounds: A court may dismiss an involuntary Petition
       (1) By motion of a Petitioning creditor
   or (2) On consent of all Petitioning creditors and the Debtor
   or (3) For want of prosecution

    b. Notice & Hearing: Before a dismissal, there must first be notice to all creditors and a hearing.

(k) Foreign Banks: An involuntary Petition may be filed against a foreign bank only if:
    1. A similar foreign proceeding is pending with regards to that bank
    2. If the bank is not engaged in business (banking) in the U.S.
    3. The Petition is filed under chapter 7

§307: United States Trustee:

a. The U.S. Trustee has standing to raise on any issue in any bankruptcy case or proceeding
b. The U.S. Trustee may also appear and be heard on such issue raised
c. The U.S. Trustee may not file a plan pursuant to §1121(c).

Subchapter III – Administration

§347: Unclaimed Property:

(a) Property Paid Into Court: The following must take place <u>90 days</u> after a final distribution:
1. The trustee must stop payment on any check remaining unpaid
2. Any remaining Property of the Estate shall be paid into the court and disposed of under 28 U.S.C. Chapter 129.
3. This includes a final distribution under §726, §1226, or §1326 (in a case under chapter 7, 12, or 13, as the case may be).

(b) Property Returned to the Debtor: In a case under chapter 9, 11, or 12:
1. Any Security, money, or other property remaining unclaimed becomes the property of the Debtor or of whoever acquires the Debtor's assets under the plan, at the expiration of the time allowed (as detailed below):
2. <u>Expiration Time</u>:
   i. When the time for presentation of a Security expires
   or ii. When the time for performing any other condition to participating in the distribution under a plan (confirmed under §943(b), §1129, §1173, or §1225) expires.

§348: Effect of Conversion:

(a) Date of Order for Relief in Conversion: The conversion of a case from one chapter to another operates as an "Order for Relief" under the new chapter, but <u>does not</u> change:
1. The date of the filing of the Petition
2. The date of the commencement of the case
3. The date of the Order for Relief (see the exceptions in §348(b) and (c)).

(b) Exception for Standard Order of Relief Date: Unless the court orders otherwise for good cause, the date of the "Order for Relief" is deemed to be the date that the case was converted (under §706, §1112, §1208, or §1307), in the following sections that refer to "the Order for Relief under this chapter": §§701(a), 727(a)(10), 727(b), 728(a), 728(b), 1102(a), 1110(a)(1), 1121(b), 1121(c), 1141(d)(4), 1146(a), 1146(b), 1201(a), 1221, 1228(a), 1301(a), and 1305(a).

(c) Conversion Order as Order for Relief: The Conversion Order in a case that has been converted (under Sec. 706, 1112, 1208, or 1307) is considered to be the "Order for Relief" or the following purposes:
    1. §342, concerning the notice of the Order for Relief
and 2. §365(d), concerning the time allowed for the trustee to assume or reject an executory contract or unexpired lease of the Debtor.

(d) Pre-Conversion Claims:
    1. In a case converted under §1112, §1208, or §1307, a Claim arising against the estate after the Order for Relief but before conversion is treated as a pre-Petition Claim for all purposes.
    2. Exception: A Claim specified in §503(b) (Administrative Expenses)

(e) Effect in Trustee: The service of a trustee or examiner in a case before conversion (under §706, §1112, §1208, or §1307) is terminated by the conversion.

(f) Conversions from Chapter 13:
    (1) When a chapter 13 case is converted to another chapter, the following applies (except as provided in paragraph (2)):
    (A) Property of the Estate – "Property of the Estate" in the converted case consists of all property that:
        1. Is Property of the Estate as of the Petition date
    and 2. Remains in the possession or control of the Debtor on the conversion date
    (B) Valuations of Property (and allowed secured Claims):
        1. Valuations in the chapter 13 case apply in the converted case

2. Allowed secured Claims are reduced in the amount that they have been paid (in accordance with the chapter 13 plan).

(2) If the Debtor converts a chapter 13 case to another chapter in bad faith, the property in the converted case shall consist of the Property of the Estate as of the date of conversion.

Subchapter IV – Administrative Powers

§361: Adequate Protection

A.　Adequate Protection may be provided by:

　　(1)　Cash Payments: Requiring the trustee to make <u>Cash Payments</u> to the extent that the actions by the Trustee (under §362, §363, and §364) result in a decrease in Value of the Creditor's interest in the property

or　(2)　Extra Liens: Providing the Creditor with an <u>Additional or Substituted Security Interest</u> to the extent that actions by the Trustee (under §362, §363, and §364) result in a decrease in Value of the Creditor's interest in the property

or　(3)　Other Relief:　an "indubitable equivalent" of the Creditor's interest (other than giving the Creditor payment as a §503(b)(1) Administrative Expense).

B.　Sections 362 (AUTOMATIC STAY), §363 (USE, SALE, AND LEASE OF PROPERTY), or §364 (OBTAINING CREDIT) may require "Adequate Protection" of a Person's interest in property.

§362: Automatic Stay:

(a)　The Automatic Stay:

　　i)　<u>Creation:</u> Except as provided in <u>§362(b)</u>, filing one of the following Petitions will create an <u>Automatic Stay</u>:
　　　　1)　§301 (VOLUNTARY PETITIONS)
　　　　2)　§302 (JOINT PETITIONS)
　　　　3)　§303 (INVOLUNTARY PETITIONS)
　　　　4)　§5(a)(3) of the Securities Investor Protection Act of 1970

　　ii)　<u>Applicability:</u> The Automatic Stay applies to and affects all entities involved in any of the following:

　　　　(1)　<u>The Commencement or Continuation of an Action</u> against the Debtor, including the issuance or employment of Process of either a
　　　　　　a)　Judicial Action
　　　　or　b)　Administrative Action

178

or c) Other action or proceeding against the Debtor
        which was (or could have been) brought before the
        Bankruptcy Petition was filed

or d) An Action to recover from the Debtor a Claim
        arising before the Bankruptcy Petition was filed

(2) The Enforcement of a Judgment against the Debtor or
    the Estate if the judgement was obtained before the
    Petition was filed.

(3) Any Act to Obtain Possession or Control of property
    belonging to the estate

(4) Any Lien Against the Estate: Any Act to Create,
    Perfect, or Enforce a Lien against any Property of the
    Estate

(5) Any Liens Against the Debtor: Any Act to Create,
    Perfect, or Enforce a Lien against any property of the
    Debtor to the extent that the Lien secures a Claim
    arising before the Petition was filed.

(6) Any Act to Collect, Assess, or Recover from the Debtor
    a Claim which arose before the Petition was filed

(7) A Setoff of a Debt to the Debtor for any Claim against
    the Debtor for any obligation to the Debtor which arose
    before the Petition was filed.

(8) A Tax Proceedings: The Commencement or
    Continuation of a proceeding concerning the Debtor,
    before the U.S. Tax Court.

(b) Exceptions To The Automatic Stay - The following are not
    subject to the Automatic Stay in §362(a):

    (1) Criminal Actions: The Commencement or Continuation
        of a Criminal Action

    (2) Family Actions:
        (A) The Commencement or Continuation of an Action
            to:
            (i) Establish Paternity
        or (ii) Establish or Modify an order for Alimony,
                 Maintenance, or Support
        (B) The Commencement or Continuation of an action
            for the Collection of Alimony, Maintenance or
            Support, from property that is not Property of the
            Estate

    (3) Perfecting, Maintaining, or Continuing Liens: An act to
        Perfect, Maintain or Continue the perfection of an

interest in property will be exempt from the Automatic
Stay to the extent that:
a)   The Trustee is subject to such perfection under
     §546(b) (EXCEPTIONS TO TRUSTEE'S AVOIDING
     POWERS)
or   b)   The act to perfect or maintain or continue the
     perfection takes place within 10 days after property
     is Transferred (under §547(e)(2)(A))
(4) Government Actions: against the Debtor are exempt
     from the Automatic Stay under §362(a)(1)
(5) Government Judgements: against the Debtor are exempt
     from the Automatic Stay under §362(a)(2) if obtained
     in an action by a government unit, and the action is
     brought to enforce the government agency's regulatory
     or police power.
(6) Securities Setoffs: Debts will not be subject to the
     Automatic Stay for purposes of Setoff if the obligor is
     a:
     a)   Commodity Broker
     b)   Forward Contract Merchant
     c)   Stock Broker
     d)   Financial Institutions
     e)   Security Clearinghouse Agency * * * *
(7) Setoffs by Repo Participants: (repurchase agreements,
     margin, or settlement payment)
* * * *
(8) Foreclosure Action by Secretary of Housing and Urban
     Development * * * *
(9) Tax Matters: The following tax matters will not be
     subject to the Automatic Stay:
     (A) An audit by a Governmental Unit to determine Tax
         Liability
or   (B) The issuance to the Debtor of a Notice of Tax
         Deficiency (by a Government Unit)
or   (C) A demand for tax returns
or   (D) A tax assessment Tax Liens that would attach to
         Estate Property because of the assessment shall
         only be effective if:
         i)   The tax liability will not be discharged
     and ii) The property/proceeds are Transferred out of
              the Bankrupt Estate to the Debtor, itself.

(10) <u>Non-Residential Leases:</u> Acts by the Lessor to obtain possession of his property will not be subject to   the Automatic Stay if:
     a.   The lease is for non-residential property
     b.   The lease term expires before or during the Bankruptcy Petition

(11) <u>Negotiable Instruments</u> - The Automatic Stay will not effect:
     a)   Presentment of the instrument
     b)   Giving Notice of Dishonor of the instrument
     c)   Protesting the Dishonor of the instrument

(12) <u>Chapter 11 Foreclosures on Ships by the Secretary of Transportation</u> (for Bankruptcy Petitions filed on or before 12/31/89)* * * *

(13) <u>Chapter 11 Foreclosures on Ships by the Secretary of Commerce</u> (for Bankruptcy Petitions filed on or before 12/31/89)* * *

(14) <u>Actions by an Accrediting Agency:</u> An agency accrediting the Debtor as an education institution may continue to do so, without being subject to the Automatic Stay

(15) <u>Actions by State Licensing Division for Education</u> – regarding licensing of the Debtor as an educational institution.

(16) <u>Action by a Guaranty Agency for Higher Education</u> - regarding the Debtor's eligibility to participate in Higher Education programs.

(17) Swap Agreement Setoffs: * * * *

(18) <u>Tax Liens:</u> The <u>Creation</u> or <u>Perfection</u> of a statutory tax if:
     a.   The tax becomes due after the filing of the Petition
and b.   The tax is an ad valorum property tax
and c.   The tax is imposed by a State or domicile.

(c)   Duration of Automatic Stay:
     (1)   <u>Stay on Actions:</u> The Automatic Stay (under §362(a)) of actions against property will continue until the property is no longer Property of the Estate.
     (2)   <u>Stay on Other Acts:</u> The stay of other acts in §362(a) remains until the <u>earlier</u> of:
         (A) The time the bankruptcy case is <u>closed</u>
         (B) The time the case is <u>dismissed</u>
         (C) The time <u>discharge is granted or denied</u> (in a Chapter 7 case concerning an individual or a case under Chapters 9, 11, 12 or 13)

(d) Relief From The Automatic Stay:

    i. <u>When Relief is Granted</u> - The court must grant relief from the Automatic Stay (by terminating, annulling, modifying or conditioning the stay) if:

        (1) <u>Cause if Shown</u> - including lack of <u>Adequate Protection</u> of a party's interest (as per $361).

or (2) For stays affecting actions against property:

        (A) Equity Test: The Debtor does not have an <u>Equity</u> in the property

   and (B) Necessity Test: The property is not necessary for an effective reorganization

or (3) For stays of acts affecting <u>Single Asset Real Estate</u>: If the creditor's Claim is secured by the real estate, he may be given relief from the Stay, unless:

        (A) The Debtor has filed a Reorganization plan within 90 days of the Order for Relief (this can be changed by the Court within the 90 day period) that will probably be confirmed within a reasonable time

    or (B) Within 90 days the Debtor begins paying the secured creditors <u>monthly payments</u> equal to the interest (at a Fair Market Rate) of the creditor's property interest.

    ii. Additional Requirements:

        1. A Party in Interest requests the relief

and 2. There is <u>notice</u> and a <u>hearing</u>

(e) Lifting the Stay:

  1) The Automatic Stay will be terminated (i.e. "lifted") <u>30 days</u> after the Creditor makes the request for relief, unless the court orders otherwise (after notice and hearing).

  2) The hearing may either be a <u>preliminary hearing</u>, or a <u>final hearing</u> (as required under (d)).

  3) If the hearing is a preliminary hearing, the final hearing must take place within 30 days, unless the parties in interest consent or the court has an otherwise compelling reason.

4) The court shall order the Stay to continue until the court makes a final determination that there is a reasonable likelihood that the party opposing the stay will prevail at the final hearing.

(f) Irreparable Damage: The court may lift the Stay (with or without a hearing) if an interest in property would suffer irreparable damage before there is an opportunity for notice and a hearing.

(g) Burden of Proof - In hearings under (d) and (e):
(1) Party Requesting Relief: Burden on issues of Debtor's equity in property
(2) Party Opposing Relief: Burden on all other issues

(h) Recovery of Actual Damages: An individual injured by any willful violation of the Stay shall recover:
1. Actual Damages
and 2. Costs and Attorney Fees
and 3. Punitive Damages (in appropriate circumstances)

§363: Use, Sale, or Lease of Property:

(a) "Cash Collateral" - In this section, "Cash Collateral" means:
   1. Cash
   2. Negotiable Instruments
   3. Documents of Title
   4. Securities
   5. Deposit Accounts
   6. Other cash equivalents subject to a Security Interest under §552(b) that the estate and an Entity other than the estate have an interest in, including:
      a) Proceeds
      b) Products
      c) Offspring
      d) Rents
      e) Profits for lodging properties (including fees, charges, Accounts or other payments for rooms/facilities at a hotel, motel or other lodging facility)

(b) Not in the Ordinary Course of Business:
   (1) Notice and Hearing Required: The trustee may use, sell, or lease Property of the Estate other than in the Ordinary Course of Business, only after notice and a hearing.
   (2) Cases Where Notification is Required by §7A of the Clayton Act * * * *

(c) In The Ordinary Course of Business:
   (1) The Trustee may Use, Sell or Lease estate property in the Ordinary Course of Business, without notice and a hearing if:
      a) The business of the Debtor is authorized to continue (under §§721, 1108, 1203, 1204, or 1304)
      b) The Court does not order otherwise
   (2) Cash Collateral - The Trustee may not Use, Sell or Lease Cash Collateral (under §363(1)) unless:
      (A) Everyone with an interest in the Cash Collateral consents.
   or (B) The court authorizes such Use, Sale or Lease after otice and a hearing.
   (3) Hearings Under §363(c)(2)(B):

    a. These hearings may be preliminary hearings or consolidated with a §363(e) hearing.

    b. Either way, the hearing must be scheduled in accordance with the Debtor's needs.

    c. If the hearing is a preliminary hearing, the court may authorize the use, sale or lease only if there is a reasonable likelihood that the Trustee will prevail at the final hearing (§363(c)).

    d. The court shall act quickly on a request for authorization for the Trustee to use, sell or lease property (under §363(2)(b)).

(4) Trustee's Duty Not to Commingle Funds: The Trustee shall segregate (and account for) any Cash Collateral in its Possession, Custody, or Control (except as provided in §363(2)).

(d) Limitations on Use: The Trustee may only use, sell or lease property to the extent not inconsistent with other relief granted under §362(c), §362(d), §362(e) or §362(f).

(e) Adequate Protection: Notwithstanding any other provision, the court shall prohibit or condition the Use, Sale or Lease of estate property (and property that is subject to any unexpired lease of personal property) to the extent that it is necessary to provide Adequate Protection of any parties' interests in the property (and Adequate Protection cannot otherwise be provided).

(f) Sale of Property: The Trustee may sell property (under (b) and (c) above) free and clear of any interest in such property only if:

    (1) Law Permits - applicable non-bankruptcy law permits the sale free and clear of the interest

or   (2) Consent - The Creditor consents

or   (3) Beneficial Sale:

        a) The Creditor's interest is a Lien

and   b) The property will be sold for a Value greater than the aggregate Value of all Liens on the property

or   (4) Bona-fide Dispute - The Creditor's interest in the property is in dispute

or   (5) Entitled only to Monetary Interest - The Creditor could be compelled to accept a money satisfaction of its interest in a legal or equitable proceeding.

(g) Sale of Right in Dowery: The Trustee may sell property under §363(b) or (c) free and clear of any dowery or courtesy right (vested or contingent).

(h) Sale of Co-Owned Property:
The Trustee may sell both the estate's interest <u>and</u> the interest of any co-owner of property, if:
(1) Splitting ("partition of") the interests in the property is <u>impracticable</u>
and (2) The Sale of the estate's interest would yield significantly less than the sale of the property free and clear of the co-owner's interest.
and (3) The benefit to the Estate outweighs the detriment to the co-owners
and (4) The property is not used to assist public utilities (heat, light, power)
and (5) At the time of the Petition, the Debtor had an undivided interest as either a:
  a) Tenant in Common
  b) Joint Tenant
  c) Tenant by the Entirety

(i) Purchase of Property By Spouse/Co-owner:
The spouse or co-owner of the property of a Debtor has the first right to purchase the following estate property if a sale is about to take place:
1. Property being sold under §363(g) (COURTESY AND DOWER)
2. Property under sold under §363(h) (TENANT IN COMMON, JOINT TENANT, TENANT BY THE ENTIRETY)
3. Property that was community property immediately before the commencement of the case.

(j) Distribution of Proceeds to Co-Owners: Upon sale of co-owned property under (g) or (h), the Trustee shall distribute the proceeds of the sale to the co-owner (or spouse) less the costs and expenses of the sale (but not the trustee's compensation since it is paid by the Bankruptcy Estate).

(k) Purchase By Lien-holder: The holder of a Lien on property to be sold under (b) (above) may bid at a sale for the property, and may offset the Value of the Lien-holder's Claim from the sale price of the property.

(l) "Ipso Facto" Clauses Not Effective: The Trustee will maintain its right to use, sell or lease property (under §363(b) or (c) or under a bankruptcy plan) even if the contract contains an "Ipso Facto" provision, which is a provision that requires the Debtor's interest in the property to be terminated, modified or forfeited by any of the following events:

            1. The Debtor's insolvency or financial condition

or   2. The filing of a bankruptcy Petition

or   3. On a Bankruptcy Trustee's appointment or taking possession

or   4. On a non-bankruptcy Custodian's taking possession

(m) Reversal on Appeal - If the authorization to sell or lease property is later reversed or modified on appeal, the sale or lease is not affected if:

            1. The Purchaser acted in good faith, regardless of whether or not he knew of the appeal.

and 2. The authorization to sell or lease was not stayed (pending the decision of the appeal).

(n) Voiding "Rigged" Sales:

            1. The Trustee may "avoid" a sale of the property if the bidders planned together to bid for property at a certain price.

            2. The Trustee may recover damages (Value of property – price paid), all costs, fees and expenses, and punitive damages in certain cases (ex: in cases of willfulness).

(o) Burdens of Proof: In hearings under this section for use, sale and lease of property:

            (1) Trustee's Burden: To prove that a Creditor has Adequate Protection

            (2) Creditor's Burden: To prove the validity and priority of its interest

§364: Obtaining Credit:

(a) In the Ordinary Course of Business:
1. A trustee that is authorized to operate the business of the Debtor (under §721, §1108, §1203, §1204, or §1304) may obtain <u>unsecured credit</u> and incur <u>unsecured Debt</u> in the ordinary course of business unless the court orders otherwise.
2. Such credit or Debt is allowable and will have the same priority as an Administrative Expense (under §503(b)(1)).

(b) Out of the Ordinary Course of Business:
1. After notice and a hearing, a court may allow the trustee to obtain <u>unsecured credit</u> or to incur <u>unsecured Debt</u> out of the ordinary course of business.
2. Such credit or Debt is allowable and will have the same priority as an Administrative Expense (under §503(b)(1)).

(c) Secured or Super-Priority Credit: If the trustee is not able to obtain unsecured credit without offering the creditor more than an Administrative Expense priority (under §503(b)(1)), the court, after notice and a hearing, may authorize the trustee to obtain credit or incur Debt as follows:
   (1) <u>Super-Priority</u>: With "super-priority" over all Administrative Expenses specified in §503(b) or §507(b) (super-priority Administrative Expense Claims resulting from the failure of Adequate Protection)
or (2) <u>First Priority Lien</u>: Secured by a Lien on Property of the Estate that is not subject to a Lien
or (3) <u>Junior Lien</u>: Secured by a junior Lien on Property of the Estate that is already subject to a Lien.

(d) First Priority Lien on Previously Encumbered Property:
   (1) The court may authorize the trustee to <u>obtain credit</u> or <u>incur Debt</u> that will be secured by a senior or equal Lien on Property of the Estate that is already subject to a Lien if:
      (A) The trustee is unable to obtain credit on any other basis.
   and (B) Adequate Protection is provided to the original Lienholder (The trustee has the burden of proving Adequate Protection.).
   and (C) There is Notice and a Hearing

(2) <u>Burden of Proof</u>: The trustee has the burden of proof on the issue of Adequate Protection (for purposes of this subsection).

(e) Effect of Appeal: The validity of any Debt incurred or any priority or Lien granted is not affected by the reversal or modification on appeal of the trustee's authorization, if:
1. The lender acted in good faith, whether or not that lender knew of the pendency of the appeal.
2. The authorization and the incurring Debt (or the granting of the priority or Lien) were stayed pending appeal.

(f) Effect on T.I.A.: **The Trust Indenture Act of 1939** (and any State or local law requiring either registration for offer or sale of a Security or registration or licensing of an issuer, underwriter, or broker or dealer in a Security) **only applies to the offer or sale of a Security** (under §364) **that is an <u>equity Security</u>, except with respect to a party that is an "underwriter"** (as defined in Securities Act of 1933, §5, 1145(b)).

§365: Executory Contracts and Unexpired Leases:

(a) Trustee's Strong-Arm Power: The Trustee may <u>assume</u> or <u>reject</u> any Executory contract or Unexpired lease of the Debtor, subject to:
1. The Court's Approval
2. Reasonable notice and a hearing
3. §365(b), (c), and (d)
4. §765-§766 (CUSTOMER PROPERTY)

(b) Executory contracts Defaulted by Debtor:

(1) If the Debtor previously defaulted on an Executory contract/Unexpired lease, the Trustee may only assume it if he:
(A) <u>Cures the Default</u>, or provides <u>Adequate Assurance</u> that he will cure soon
and (B) <u>Compensates</u> the other party for any actual monetary loss arising from the default or provides <u>Adequate Assurance</u> that the Trustee will compensate.

and (C) Provides <u>Adequate Assurance</u> of future performance under the contract/lease

(2) <u>Exceptions</u>: §365(b)(1) does not apply if the default is a breach of an ipso facto provision relating to:

    (A) The <u>Insolvency or Financial Condition</u> of the Debtor (at any time before the closing of the Bankruptcy case)

or (B) The Commencement of a Bankruptcy case

or (C) The <u>Appointment of a Trustee</u> under Bankruptcy (or the taking of possession by a non-bankruptcy Custodian.)

or (D) The <u>Satisfaction of any Penalty Rate/Provision</u> relating to a default from the Debtor for non-performance of a <u>non-monetary obligation</u> under the executory contract

(3) Definition of "Adequate Assurance" (as used in §365(b)(1) and (f)(2)(b)) for future performance of a real property lease in a <u>shopping center</u> ***

(4) <u>Supplies and Services Incidental to Unassumed Lease</u>: If there is an unexpired lease in default (but not one described in (b)(2) (OBLIGATIONS UNDER IPSO FACTO PROVISIONS)), the lessor <u>does not</u> have to give services or supplies incidental to the lease unless the Trustee pays (by the terms of the lease) for services or supplies given before the lease is assumed.

(c) Restrictions - When Trustee May Not Assume or Assign - The trustee may not Assume or Assign an executory contract/unexpired lease (whether or not the contract prohibits/restricts assignment of rights), if:

(1) Applicable Law Excuses Performance:

    (A) Applicable law excuses the other party from performing the contract with an Entity other than the Debtor .

and (B) The party does not consent to an Assumption or Assignment.

or (2) <u>Contracts to Make Loans</u>: The contract is a commitment to loan money to the Debtor or to issue a Security of the Debtor.

or (3) <u>Commercial Leases</u> - The lease is a non-residential lease which has been <u>terminated</u> under applicable non-bankruptcy law before the Order for Relief was filed.

or (4) Airport Terminal Leases * * *

(d) Time Limit:

(1) <u>Residential Real/Personal Property in Chapter 7</u>: If the Trustee in a Chapter 7 case does not assume a contract/lease within <u>60 days</u> after the Petition (may be extended by Court within the 60 days), the contract/lease is presumed <u>rejected</u>.

(2) Residential Real/Personal Property in Chapters 9,11,12, or 13:

    a. The Trustee may assume the contract at any time <u>before</u> Confirmation of the Plan.

    b. Upon motion, a court may require the Trustee to make a determination by a specific time.

(3) Trustee's Obligations under Unexpired lease of Non-Residential Real Property:

    a. After the Order for Relief, the Trustee must perform all obligations under an unexpired lease of non-residential real property until the lease is Assumed or Rejected.

    b. <u>Duties Excluded</u>: Duties under §365(b)(2) (OBLIGATIONS UNDER IPSO FACTO PROVISIONS).

(4) <u>Non-Residential Real Property Leases</u> (any Chapter): If the Trustee does not Assume or Reject the lease within <u>60 days</u> of the Order for Relief, the lease is deemed Rejected (the property must be surrendered to the Lessor)

(5) Leases of Aircraft Terminals or Gates * * *

(6) Leases of Aircraft Terminals or Gates * * *

(7) Leases of Aircraft Terminals or Gates * * *

(8) Leases of Aircraft Terminals or Gates * * *

(9) Aircraft * * *

(10) Trustee's Obligations under Unexpired lease of Personal Property - Chapter 11:

    a. The Trustee must perform all obligations arising after <u>60 days</u> of the Order for Relief until the lease is Assumed or Rejected

    b. The Court may order otherwise (regarding the timing or the obligations themselves), if:

        1. There is <u>notice</u> and a <u>hearing</u>.

and 2. The equities of the case favor a modification.

    c. <u>Duties Excluded</u>: Duties under §365(b)(2) (OBLIGATIONS UNDER IPSO FACTO PROVISIONS).

    d. The Lessor <u>does not</u> waive his rights under the lease or under the Code by accepting performance of the Debtor's obligations by the Trustee.

(e) Modifications Not Allowed:

(1) The Debtor may not modify or terminate an executory
     contract/unexpired lease (including contracts for personal
     property, but not property that was relieved from the
     Automatic Stay of §362) based soley on an Ipso Facto
     provision relating to:
     (A) The Insolvency or Financial Condition of the Debtor (at
          any time before the closing of the Bankruptcy case)
or   (B) The Commencement of a Bankruptcy case
or   (C) The Appointment of a Trustee under Bankruptcy (or the
          taking of possession by a non-bankruptcy Custodian).

(2) Exception: §365(e)(1) does not apply (i.e. ipso facto clauses
     will be effective) to the following types of Contracts/Leases:
     (A) Non-assignable Contract/Lease – if:
          (i) Applicable law excuses a party from accepting/
               rendering performance to a Trustee or Assignee
      and (ii) The party does not consent to an Assumption or
               Assignment
or   (B) Contracts to Make Loans – if the contract is a
          commitment to loan money to the Debtor or to issue a
          Security of the Debtor.

(f) When Trustee May Assign:
     (1) The Trustee may assign an executory contract or unexpired
          lease (regardless of a restriction clause or prohibiting law).[28]
     (2) Requirements for Assignment:
          (A) The Trustee assumes the contract/lease
          (B) The Assignee gives Adequate Assurance of Future
               Performance (whether or not there is a default)
     (3) The Contract/Lease terms cannot be terminated or modified
          because of the assumption or assignment by the Trustee
          (regardless of a termination or modification clause or
          applicable law).

(g) Time of Breach: The rejection of an executory
     contract/unexpired lease of the Debtor will be considered a
     breach as of the following dates:

     (1) Unassumed Contract/Lease – The breach is deemed to have
          occurred immediately before Petition date if the
          contract/lease has not been assumed either:

---

[28] With the exception of leases of airport terminals and gates.

a) under §365

or b) under a Chapter 9, 11, 12 or 13 Plan

(2) Assumed Contract/Lease -
   (A) NON-CONVERTED CASE: The breach is deemed to have occurred <u>at the time of rejection</u> if the lease case not been converted to a Chapter 7 proceeding (under §1112, 1208 or 1307).

and (B) CONVERTED CASES:
   (i) Immediately before the time of Conversion if:
      a) It was assumed before the Conversion
   and b) It was rejected after the Conversion
   or (ii) At The Time Of Rejection if:
      a) It was assumed after the Conversion
   and b) It was rejected after the Conversion

(h) Debtor as Lessor of Real Property Lease:
   (1) Real Property Leases:
      (A) Lessee's Rights in Rejected Lease:
         (i) If the Trustee's Rejection of the Unexpired Real Property Lease would allow the Lessee to treat the lease as terminated (under the lease itself, applicable law or an agreement), the Lessee may treat the lease as terminated.
         (ii) If the lease term has begun, the Lessee may retain its leasehold rights[29] for the remainder of the lease term to the extent they are enforceable under applicable non-bankruptcy law
      (B) <u>Lessee's Right to Setoff</u>: If the Lessee elects to retain control of the property, it may setoff any damages from Debtor's non-performance before it pays its rent (but only rent reserved for the remainder of the term after the date of rejection).
      (C) Rejection of a Lease of Real Property in a Shopping Center * * *

   (2) Rejection of Timeshares * * * *

      (i) Executory Contract to Sell Real Estate:
         (1) <u>Purchaser's Possessory Rights:</u> If the trustee rejects an executory contract to sell real estate, and the

---

[29] Includes rights relating to the amount of rent and the timing of payments; rights of use, possession, quiet enjoyment, subletting, assignment, hypothecation.

Purchaser <u>remains in possession</u> of the property, the Purchaser may either:
- a) Treat the contract as terminated

or b) Remain in Possession of the Property

   (2) <u>Purchasers Retaining Possession</u>: If the Purchaser retains possession of the property then the parties will have the following duties:

A) The Purchaser's Duty to Pay:
1. He shall continue to make all payments to the Estate
2. He may offset any damages occurring after the date of rejection from nonperformance by the Trustee

(B) The Trustee's Duty to Deliver Title:
1. The Trustee must deliver title to the Purchaser, as per the contract
2. The Trustee is <u>not</u> required to perform all other obligations of the contract

(j) Purchaser's Lien:
1. Applicability - Purchasers not electing §365(i)(2): This section applies to:
   a) A Purchaser whose executory contract is rejected and who treats it as terminated under §365(i).
   b) A Purchaser whose executory contract is rejected and he is not in <u>possession</u> of the property.
2. Rights: The above Purchasers will maintain a <u>Lien</u> on the property for the portion of the purchase price already paid.

(k) Automatic Novation: An assignment of an executory contract or unexpired lease by the Trustee will relieve the Trustee and the Estate from any liability for a breach occurring after the assignment.

(l) Lessor's Right to Security: If the Debtor is a <u>lessee,</u> the landlord may require the same deposit or Security from the Assignee as the one he would have obtained from a similar tenant at the beginning of the lease term.

(m) Rental Agreements: Leases of real property shall include any rental agreement to use real property (for purposes of,

§541(b)(2) (PROPERTY OF THE ESTATE), §362(b)(10)
(EXCEPTIONS TO AUTOMATIC STAY), and this section).

(n) Intellectual Property

(1) If the Debtor is a Licensor of an Intellectual Property right
under an executory contract, and the Trustee rejects the
contract, the Licensee may either:
(A) Treat the contract as terminated – If the Trustee's
rejection is the equivalent of a breach that would allow
the Licensee to treat the contract as terminated by:
    1. Its own terms
or 2. Applicable non-bankruptcy law
or 3. An agreement made by the Licensee with another
      party
(B) Retain its Rights:
    1. The Licensee may retain its rights under the
      contract (and any supplementary agreement) to the
      Intellectual Property as they existed before the case
      commenced.
    2. Rights Included:
      a. Right to enforce exclusivity provisions in the
        contract.
      b. The rights retained do not include the right to
        specific performance.
    3. Time for Retention of Rights:
      (i) Until the end of the contract period
or (ii) Until any period that the contract is extended
         as of right by applicable non-bankruptcy law
(2) Licensee's Rights: If the Licensee chooses to retain its rights
(under (1)(B)):
(A) The Trustee must allow the Licensee to exercise its
rights.
and (B) The Licensee must make any royalty payments due
under the contract for the entire time the Licensee
retains its rights.
and (C) The Licensee is deemed to waive:
    (i) Any setoff right it might have with respect to the
       contract (under the Bankruptcy Code or under
       applicable non-bankruptcy law).
or (ii) Any Claim allowable under §503(b) arising from
       performance of the contract.

(3) <u>Trustee's Responsibilities</u>: If the Licensee chooses to retain its rights (under (1)(B)), and the Licensee makes a <u>written</u> request, then the Trustee must:
(A) Provide the Intellectual Property (and any embodiment) held by the Trustee.
and (B) Not interfere with the Licensee's rights, including the right to obtain the property from a third party.
(4) So long as the Trustee does not reject the contract, and the Licensee makes a <u>written</u> request, the Trustee must:
(A) To the extent provided in the contract:
(i) Perform the contract.
and (ii) Provide the Intellectual Property (and any embodiment) held by the Trustee.
and (B) Not interfere with the Licensee's rights, including the right to obtain the property from a third party.

(o) Commitments to Federal Depositories Assumed

1. In a Chapter 11 case, the Trustee is deemed to have assumed any commitment by the Debtor to an agency regulating federal depository institutions to maintain the capital of an insured depository institution.
2. The Trustee shall immediately cure any deficiency under any such commitment.
3. Any Claim for a later breach of the Debtor's obligations is entitled to priority under §507 (PRIORITIES).
4. This subsection <u>does not</u> extend any commitment that would otherwise be terminated by an act of the regulatory agency.

CHAPTER 5: CREDITORS, DEBTOR, AND THE ESTATE

Subchapter I – CREDITORS AND CLAIMS

§501: Filing Proofs of Claims and Interests:

(a) Who May File:
1. The following may file a Proof of Claim:
   a. A Creditor
   b. An Indenture Trustee
2. A Proof of Interest may be filed by an Equity Security Holder.

(b) Alternate Filers: If a Creditor does not timely file a Proof of Claim, the following may file a Proof of Claim in his place:
1. An Entity liable to the Creditor with the Debtor (i.e. a Guarantor)

or 2. An Entity that has Secured the Creditor

(c) Debtor's Filing: The Debtor or Trustee may file a Proof of Claim for the Creditor if the Creditor does not timely file.

(d) Special "Relation Back" Claims: The following Claims may be filed under this section, as if they were Claims against the Debtor arising before the Petition is filed:
1. Claims for Reimbursement or Contribution (§502(e)(2))
2. Claims for Ordinary Course Payments in an Involuntary Case (§502(f))
3. Claims for Damages from Rejected Contracts/Leases (§502(g))
4. Claims for Damages resulting from Recovered Property (§502(h))
5. Claims for §507(a)(8) Priority Tax Claims (§502(i))

197

§502: Allowance of Claims or Interests:

(a) Presumption that Claim is Allowed:
   1. A Claim filed under §501 will be presumed allowed unless a Party in Interest objects.
   2. A Party in Interest includes the Creditor of a general partner, where the partnership is a Debtor in a Chapter 7 case.

(b) Procedure Upon Objection:
   i) Valuation by Hearing:
      a) The Court shall determine the admissible dollar Value of the Claim (if any).
      b) There must be notice and a hearing.
   ii) Inadmissible Claims: The Court shall not allow the Claim to the extent the Claim is:
     (1) Unenforceable against the Debtor under any agreement or applicable law (ex: State law exemptions) (for reasons other than the fact that the Claim is contingent or unmatured)
     (2) For Unmatured Interest
     (3) For Property Taxes which exceed the Estate's interest in the property
     (4) For Services of an Insider or Attorney which exceed the reasonable Value of the services
     (5) For Unmatured Debts (as of filing date) which are exempt from discharge under §523(a)(5).
     (6) For a Lessor's Damages from early termination of a real property lease, which exceeds:
       (A) The greater of the following:
          1. 1 year's rent, after the earlier of:
             (i) The Petition Date
         or (ii) The Date the Lessee surrendered the property
       or 2. 15% of Rent for the remaining term of the lease (up to 3 years' rent), after the earlier of:
             (i) The Petition Date
         or (ii) The Date the Lessee surrendered the property
     Plus (B) Any Unpaid Rent (without acceleration) due on the earlier of:
       1. The Petition Date
     or 2. The Date the Lessee surrendered the property

(7) For Damages of <u>employee</u> resulting from termination of an employment contract which exceed:
  (A) <u>1 Year's Compensation</u> provided for under the contract (without acceleration), from the <u>earlier</u> of the following:
    (i) The Petition Date
  or (ii) The date the employee was terminated
  Plus(B) Any <u>Unpaid Compensation</u> due under the contract by the <u>earlier</u> of:
    1. The Petition Date
  or 2. The date the employee was terminated
(8) Resulting from a <u>reduction</u> of a federal employment tax credit caused by late payment of tax
(9) Proof of Claim Untimely:
  a. Claims where the Proof of Claim is <u>not timely filed</u>, unless:
    1. Excused under §726(a)
    2. Excused under Federal Rules of Bankruptcy Procedure
  b. For Governmental Units – filed within 180 days after the Order for Relief (that is considered "timely")

iii) <u>Exceptions</u>: This section is subject to the "Relation Back" provisions of §502:
  1. Claims for Reimbursement or Contribution (§502(e)(2))
  2. Claims for Ordinary Course Payments in an Involuntary Case (§502(f))
  3. Claims for Damages from Rejected Contracts/Leases (§502(g))
  4. Claims for Damages resulting from Recovered Property (§502(h))
  5. Claims for §507(a)(8) Priority Tax Claims (§502(I))

(c) Estimations: For purposes of this section, the court shall estimate the Value of:
  (1) <u>Any Contingent or Unliquidated Claim</u> - if the fixing of the amount would cause undue delay to the administration of the case.
  (2) <u>Any Right to Payment</u> arising from a right to an <u>equitable remedy</u> for breach of performance.

(d) Other Disallowed Claims: The Court shall disallow the
following Claims unless the Claimant returns the property or
pays the Value of the property:
1. Property recoverable under a Turnover Order (under §542
and §543).
2. Property recoverable for a Voidable Preference (under §544,
§545, §547, §548, §549, and §550).
3. Property recoverable due to a Setoff (under §553).
4. The Transfer is exempt (under §522(i)).
5. The Property is subject to a Tax Lien (under §724(a)).

(e) Claims for Contribution or Reimbursement:

(1) Disallowed Claims: The Court shall disallow Claims for
Reimbursement or Contribution to an Entity that is a co-
Debtor, surety or guarantor, to the extent that:
(A) The Principal Creditor's Claim is disallowed.
or (B) The Claim for Reimbursement is contingent as of the
time of allowance or disallowance of the Claim (i.e. the
surety has not paid the Creditor).
or (C) The Surety chooses Subrogation to the rights of the
Creditor (under §509) (i.e. the Creditor can either Claim
Reimbursement for a Claim paid or a Right of
Subrogation).

(2) Relation Back for Fixed Claims: If the Claim for
Reimbursement or Contribution was fixed after the Petition
was filed, the Claim is considered to have been fixed as of
the Petition date for purposes of allowing or disallowing the
Claim (i.e. it becomes a pre-Petition Claim).

(f) Claims Arising Out of the Ordinary Course:
1. Relation Back: Claims arising out of the Ordinary Course of
the Debtor's Business Affairs are considered pre-Petition
Claims if:
a) The Claim arises out of the Ordinary Course of the
Debtor's Business Affairs
and b) The case is an Involuntary Proceeding
and c) The Claim arose:
1. After the filing, but before the earlier of:
a) A Trustee's appointment
and b) An Order for Relief

and 2.   The Claim shall be determined as of the date the
Claim arose, as if it arose before the Petition date
2.   Although the Claim will "date back" to Petition date, the
Value of the Claim will be determined as of the date the
Claim actually arose.

(g)   Claims Resulting From Rejected Contracts and Leases: A Claim
arising from the Trustee's Rejection of an executory contract or
unexpired lease (under §365 or pursuant to a Reorganization
Plan) is considered a pre-Petition Claim.

(h)   Claims Resulting From Recovered Property: A Claim arising out
of the following recovered property shall be considered to have
arisen before the Petition was filed for purposes of allowing or
disallowing the Claim:
    a)   Exempt Property (as per §522)
or b)   Voidable Preference Property (as per §550)
or c)   Setoff Property (as per §553)

(i)   Claims Arising From Post-Petition Tax Assessment: A Claim for
a tax entitled to §507(a)(8) priority which arises after the
commencement of the case is considered a pre-Petition Claim.

(j)   Reconsideration of Allowed/Disallowed Claims:
1.   A Claim that has been allowed/disallowed may be
reconsidered for cause.
2.   Grounds for Changing Decision: A reconsidered Claim may
be allowed/disallowed based on the equities of the case.
3.   Treatment of Priority to Distribution: If an allowed Claim is
reconsidered, the validity of any payment or Transfer from
the estate made to the Claim holder (of the allowed Claim)
will not be affected.
4.   Creditors will also not be entitled to further payments until
the Creditor with the newly allowed Claim is paid in the
same proportion that the other Creditors of the class are
paid.
5.   This subsection does not change the Trustee's right to
recover any excess payment or Transfer made to the
Creditor.

§503: Allowance Of Administrative Expenses:

(a) Filing for Administrative Expenses:[30]
   1. Timely Claims: Entities holding Claims for Administrative
       Expenses may timely file a request for payment.
   2. Untimely Claims: An Entity may only file a late Claim if:
       a)   It shows cause
   and b)   The court grants permission to do so.

(b) Kinds of Administrative Expenses Allowed:
   i)   The following are various Administrative Expenses (in
        addition to those under §502(f)) allowed after notice and a
        hearing:
        (1) Expenses:
             (A) Costs of Preserving the Estate: The actual and
                 necessary costs of preserving the estate, including:
                 1.   wages
             and 2.   salaries
             and 3.   commissions for services rendered after the
                      commencement of the case (e.g. Attorney's
                      fees)
             and 4.   Payment to an individual Debtor for services
                      rendered to the estate (ex: When the individual
                      was a sole proprietor and was employed by the
                      estate to run the business after the
                      commencement of the case. (Local Loan v.
                      Hunt, 292 U.S. 234, 243 (1943)).
             (B) Taxes - Either:
                 (i)   Post-Petition taxes - incurred by the estate,
                       except those specified in §507(a)(8)
                       (Note: This includes taxes on capital gains
                       from sales of property by the trustee and taxes
                       on income earned by the estate during the
                       case).
             or (ii) Taxes due as a result of an excessive carryover
                       allowance - which the Estate benefited from,
                       regardless of whether the taxes related to a

---

[30] Note: The Rules of Bankruptcy Procedure will specify the time, the form, and the
method of the filing

202

year ending before or after the Petition was filed.[31]

(C) Fines & Penalties (or reduction in credit) - relating to a tax specified in §503(B) (including interest on tax liabilities and certain tax penalties incurred by the trustee.)

(2) Compensation and Reimbursement - awarded under §330(a) (to a trustee, examiner, Debtor's Attorney, and other professionals)

(3) The actual and necessary expenses – incurred by any of the following (other than compensation and reimbursement specified in (4)) :

    (A) A creditor that files an involuntary Petition (§303).

or (B) A creditor who (with the court's approval) recovers property for the benefit of the estate that the Debtor Transferred or concealed.

or (C) A creditor who incurred expenses in a criminal prosecution related to the bankruptcy case or the Debtor's business or property.

or (D) Any of the following who incur expenses in making a substantial contribution to a Chapter 9 or 11 case:

    1. A creditor

or 2. An Indenture trustee

or 3. An equity Security holder

or 4. A committee representing creditors or equity Security holders (other than an "official committee" appointed under §1102)

or (E) A Custodian superseded under §543 (and in addition to actual and necessary expenses, compensation for the Custodian's services which benefit the estate)

---

31 Background: The tax code allows the trustee of an estate which suffers a net operating loss to carry back the loss against an earlier profit year of the estate/Debtor and to get a tentative refund for the earlier year. This is subject, however, to a later full audit of the loss which led to the refund. The IRS is required to issue a tentative refund to the trustee (whether the refund was applied for by the Debtor or by the trustee), but if the refund amount later proves to have been wrong, the IRS can request that the tax due because of the error be payable by the estate as an Administrative Expense.

or (F) A <u>member of a committee</u> appointed under §1102, if the expenses are incurred in the performance of the committee's duties.

(4) Compensation for Professionals – allowed if:
1. <u>Compensation is reasonable, based on the:</u>
      a. Time of the services
and b. Nature of the services
and c. Extent of the services
and d. Value of the services
and e. Cost of comparable services in a non-bankruptcy case
and 2. Services are of an <u>Attorney</u> or an <u>accountant.</u>
and 3. The Entity incurring the Professional expenses is one listed in paragraph (3) above (i.e. an Entity for which necessary and actual expenses are allowed)
and 4. Compensation represents reimbursement for <u>actual, necessary expenses</u> incurred by the Attorney or accountant

(5) Indenture Trustees:
1. <u>Reasonable Compensation</u> for the service of an Indenture trustee making a substantial contribution in a Chapter 9 or 11 case
2. The reasonableness of the compensation shall be based on the :
      a. Time of the services
and b. Nature of the services
and c. Extent of the services
and d. Value of the services
and e. Cost of comparable services in a non-bankruptcy case

(6) Fees and Mileage are payable pursuant to Title 28, Ch. 119 (§2041 et seq.).

ii) None of the above Claims will be allowed if they are Claims or expenses allowed under §502(f), which include:
a) Claims that arise in the o<u>rdinary course</u> of the Debtor's business
and b) Claims that arise between the <u>commencement</u> of an <u>involuntary</u> case and
    1. The <u>appointment </u>of a Trustee

or   2.   The <u>Order for Relief</u>

§504: Sharing Of Compensation:

(a) Sharing Prohibited: It is prohibited to share <u>compensation</u> or <u>fees</u> (reimbursed under §503(b)(2) or §503(b)(4)):

     (1)   With Attorneys, other professionals or trustees

or   (2)   From Attorneys, other professionals or trustees

(b) Exceptions: Compensation may be shared in the following 2 cases:

     (1)   Members of Same Firm: Compensation or reimbursement may be shared with another member, partner or associate of the same professional association, Corporation, or partnership.

     (2)   Contributing Attorney: An Attorney for a creditor may share compensation and reimbursement (received under 503(b)(4)) with any other Attorney if:

         1.   <u>Contribution:</u> the other Attorney contributed to the Attorney's services or expenses

     or   2.   <u>Involuntary Case:</u> the case involves an involuntary Petition (filed under §303)

§506: Determination of Secured Status:

(a) Bifurcation:
1. An "Allowed Secured Claim" is a claim secured by a Lien on estate property or subject to a setoff, and is secured only to the extent of:
     a)   The Value of the Creditor's interest in the property (i.e. collateral)
     b)   The Value of the Creditor's setoff (under §553)
2. An "Unsecured Claim/Non-Allowed Secured Claim" is the part of the claim that exceeds the Value of the collateral or setoff.
3. The Value of the collateral and claim is determined at a hearing, taking into account the purpose of the valuation and the intended use/disposition of the collateral.

(b) Allowable Interest to Oversecured Creditors:
1. If the Value of the Creditor's interest is greater than the Creditor's original claim together with the Trustee's fees (under (c) below), he is an "Oversecured Creditor."
2. Oversecured Creditors are allowed to take, in addition to the amount of their original claim:
     a)   Post-Petition Interest
     b)   Reasonable fees, costs or charges provided for under the Security Agreement

(c) Trustee's Recoverable Fees: The Trustee may recover the reasonable and necessary costs and expenses incurred to preserve or dispose of the property, to the extent the Secured Party benefits.

(d) Unsecured Claims: Unsecured Claims are void (for purposes of surviving Bankruptcy), unless:
     (1) The claim was only disallowed under §502(b)(5) (UNMATURED CLAIMS) or §502(e) (REIMBURSEMENT CLAIMS)
or   (2) The only reason the claim is not an Allowed Secured Claim is because the Creditor neglected to file a proof of claim (under §501).

§507: Priorities:

(a) Expenses and Claims: The following <u>expenses</u> and <u>claims</u> have priority of distribution in the following order after the Secured Creditors have been paid (as per §725/§726: DISPOSITION/DISTRIBUTION OF PROPERTY):

(1) Administrative Expenses:
    a. Allowed under §503(b), including the following (Note: If there are competing claims, they get divided pro-rata):
        1. Actual and necessary costs and expenses of <u>Preserving the Estate</u> (§503(b)(1)(A))
        2. Wages, salaries, or commission for <u>Post-Petition Services</u> (§503(b)(1)(A))
        3. <u>Taxes</u> incurred by the estate (§503(b)(1)(B))
        4. Reimbursement and Compensation to the <u>Trustee</u> (§503(b)(2) and §330(a))
        5. Allowable Attorneys' and Accountants' <u>Fees</u> (§503(b)(4))
    b. Fees and Charges assessed against the estate (under 28 USC Ch. 123).

(2) §502(f) Post-Petition Unsecured Claims:
    a. The case is an Involuntary Case
    b. The claim arises out of the ordinary course of the Debtor's business or financial affairs
    c. The claims occur <u>after</u> the Petition is filed, but <u>before</u> the earlier of:
        1) The appointment of a Trustee
  or 2) The Determination of the Order for Relief

(3) Up To $4,000[32] of Compensation Claims - to each entity if:
    i) It is earned by the earlier of:
        1. <u>90 days</u> before the Petition was filed
  or 2. The date the business ceased to operate
and ii) The claim was for either:
        (A) <u>Wages, Salaries or Commissions</u> - including vacation, sick, and severance pay earned by an individual

---

[32] $4,300 as of April 1, 1998.

    or (B) <u>Sales Commissions</u> - earned by a corporation with only 1 employee acting as an Independent Contractor, as long as:
- 1. The Sales Person sold goods/services for the Debtor in the ordinary course of business.
- and 2. The Sales Person earned 75% of his income from the Debtor in the last year.

(4) Allowed Unsecured Claims For Contributions to Employee Benefit Plans:

(A) Benefits must arise from services rendered within <u>6 months</u> before the Petition was filed.

(B) Allowable Amount:

$$((\text{No. of Employees}) * (\$4,000)^{33}) - \text{Total Distributions}$$
under (3) + Distributions to other Employee Benefit Plans

(5) $4,000[34] of Unsecured Claims of Fishermen and Farmers:

(6) <u>$1,800[35] of Deposits on Consumer Goods/Services</u> - Up to $1,800[36] for each individual who gave the Debtor a deposit for consumer goods/services that were never tendered.

(7) Alimony and Child Support

(8) Taxes:

(A) Income Tax for returns due within past <u>3 years</u>

(B) Property Tax payable within <u>1 year</u> of Petition

(C) Trust fund Tax

(D) Employment Taxes within <u>3 years</u> before Petition

(E) Excise Taxes within <u>3 years</u>

(F) Custom Duties

(G) Tax Penalties

(9) <u>Unsecured Claims by Insurance Companies</u> - in which the Debtor promised to make regular installment payments

(b) Secured Party's Attorneys' Fees:

---

[33] $4,300 as of April 1, 1998.
[34] $4,300 as of April 1, 1998.
[35] $1,950 as of April 1, 1998.
[36] $1,950 as of April 1, 1998.

The Secured Party's claim for Attorneys' Fees has priority over all other claims in this section if:
1) The Secured Party is secured by a Lien on the Debtor's property
and 2) The Trustee provides Adequate Protection for the Secured Party
and 3) The Creditor has a claim under §507(a)(1) for reimbursement of Attorneys' fees arising from lifting the Automatic Stay (under §362) or preventing the <u>use, sale,</u> or <u>lease</u> of property (under §363)

(c) Erroneous Tax Refund or Credit: The IRS has the same priority over regaining the erroneously made refund/credit as it did in the original taxed amount.

(d) Subrogation Rights: An entity that is subrogated to the rights of the holder of a claim specified in (a)(3)-(9) is <u>not</u> subrogated to the right of that claim holder to priority under that subsection.

§509: Claims of Co-Debtors:

(a) Right of Subrogation:[37] A surety or co-Debtor is subrogated to the rights of a creditor (except as provided in (b) and (c)) to the extent that:
1. Any payments are made by the surety or co-Debtor to the creditor
or 2. The Surety or co-Debtor secured any Claim of the creditor

(b) Exceptions to Subrogation: A co-Debtor may <u>not</u> be subrogated to the extent that:
(1) The co-Debtor's Claim for reimbursement or contribution (already paid to the primary creditor) is:
(A) allowed under §502
or (B) disallowed other than under §502(e)
or (C) subordinated under §510
or (2) The co-Debtor, rather than the Debtor, actually received the consideration for the Claim held by the creditor (i.e. a

---

37 Note: Whether the creditor's Claim was filed under § 501(a) or 501(b) is irrelevant. The right of subrogation will exist even if the primary creditor's Claim is allowed by being listed under proposed 11 U.S.C. 924 or 1111, and not by reason of a proof of Claim.

Debtor that is ultimately liable on the Debt cannot recover from a surety or co-Debtor).

(c) Subordination Allowed Claims of Co-Debtor:
1. A co-Debtor's allowed Claims will be subordinated to the principal creditor's Claim until that Claim is paid in full.
2. The principal creditor's Claim may be paid in full either:
   a. Through payments under the Bankruptcy Code
or b. Otherwise
3. The co-Debtor's Claim which are subordinated under this section may arise either:
   a. By way of subrogation under §509
or b. For reimbursement or contribution

§510: Subordination:

(a) Subordination Agreements Enforceable: A subordination agreement is enforceable in a Bankruptcy case to the same extent that it would be enforceable under applicable non-bankruptcy law (ex: contract law).

(b) Subordination of Security Holder's Claim:
1. Any of the following Claims arising from the purchase or sale of the Debtor's (or an Affiliate's) Security are subordinated to all Claims that are senior (or equal) to a Claim represented by the Security, for purposes of distribution:
   i. A Claim arising from rescission of a purchase or sale of the Debtor's (or one of its Affiliate's) Security
or ii. A Claim for damages arising from the purchase or sale of the Security
or iii. A Claim for reimbursement or contribution allowed under §502 on account of the Claim
2. Common Stock Exception: If the Security is common stock, the above Claims have the same priority as the common stock would.

(c) Other Subordination of Claims: In addition to (a) and (b), the court may (after notice and a hearing):
(1) Subordinate Allowed Claims: Subordinate an allowed Claim (or interest) for purposes of distribution to another allowed

Claim (or interest), under principles of equitable subordination.[38]

and (2) Transfer <u>Liens</u>: Order that any Lien securing such a subordinated Claim be Transferred to the estate.

---

38 Note: The legislature intended that the "principles of equitable subordination" follow case law and leave the development of the principle to the courts. Under existing law, a Claim is generally subordinated only if its holder is guilty of inequitable conduct, or the Claim itself is susceptible to subordination, such as a penalty or a Claim for damages arising from the purchase or sale of a Security of the Debtor. The fact that the Claim may be secured has no effect on the issue of subordination. However, it is rare that because a Claim is a secured Claim, that itself justifies equitable subordination.

Subchapter II – Debtor's Duties and Benefits

§522: Exemptions:

(a) Definitions:
  (1) "Dependent" includes spouse (whether or not actually dependent)
  (2) "Value" = Fair Market Value as of:
     a. The date of the Petition
  or b. The date property became part of the estate if after the Petition is filed

(b) Available Exemptions:
  i) An Individual Debtor may choose to exempt property either under §522(b)(1) or §522(b)(2).
  ii) In cases where the proceeding is for Joint Debtors (filed under §302) or Husband and Wife (filed under §301 or §303), both Debtors must choose to exempt property under the same subsection. If they cannot agree, they are deemed to have chosen §522(b)(1) (unless not permitted by local law)
  iii) Exemptions Choices: A Debtor may choose to exempt the following property under either of the two sections:
     (1) Property specified in §522(d), unless applicable State law specifically does not authorize the exemption
     (2) Other Exempt Property:
       (A) Any property exempt under both:
         1. State or Local law where the Debtor was domiciled in the 180 days (or for most of the 180 days) immediately preceding the Petition date (the law applicable on the Petition date governs).
        or 2. Federal Law (other than §522(d))
       and (B) Any property where the Debtor has an interest as a Tenant by the Entirety or Joint Tenant exempt from process under non-bankruptcy law

(c) Effect of Exemption: Exempt property will not be subject to any Pre-Petition Debt (including "Relation Back" Claims under §502) unless:

(1) The Debt falls under §523(a)(1) or §523(a)(5) and is <u>not</u> discharged.

or (2) The Debt is secured by:
    (A) A Lien that is not void:
        (i) Under Voidable Preference Law (§544, §545, §547, §548, §549, or §724(a))
        (ii) After Bifurcation Lien (not void under §506(d))
    or (B) A <u>Tax Lien</u>

or (3) The Debt is non-dischargeable under §523(a)(4) or §523(a)(6) because it is owed by an institution-affiliated party of an insured depository institution to a regulatory agency (for Federal depository institutions) acting as a conservator, receiver or liquidating agent for the institution.

or (4) The case is dismissed.

(d) §522(b)(1) Exemptions: The following property will be exempt from the Bankruptcy Estate if the Debtor elects the §522(b)(1) exemption:

  (1) <u>Homestead</u>: The Debtor's aggregate interest in Real or Personal Property used as a Residence (including co-op stock) or the Debtor's interest in a Burial Plot (for the Debtor or a dependent) up to <u>$15,000</u>[39]

  (2) The Debtor's interest in a <u>motor vehicle</u> up to <u>$2,400</u>[40]

  (3) <u>Personal Goods</u> - up to <u>$8,000</u>[41] total (and no more than <u>$400</u>,[42] per item), in goods which are used primarily for the personal, family, or household use of the Debtor (or a dependent), which includes:
    a. Household Furniture/Household Goods
    b. Clothing
    c. Appliances
    d. Books
    e. Animals
    f. Crops
    g. Musical Instruments

  (4) <u>Jewelry</u> - the Debtor's aggregate interest in personal jewelry, up to <u>$1,000</u>[43]

---

[39] $16,150 as of April 1, 1998.
[40] $2,575 as of April 1, 1998.
[41] $8,625 as of April 1, 1998.
[42] $425 as of April 1, 1998.
[43] $1,075 as of April 1, 1998.

(5) Miscellaneous Exemption:

    a) $800[44] in any other property

and b) $7,500[45] of any <u>unused</u> Homestead exemption amount (exempt under §522(d)(1))

(6) Debtor's interest in his <u>Tools of Trade</u> up to $1,500[46] (i.e. professional books, tools)

(7) <u>Unmatured Life Insurance</u> contracts (unless it is a credit Life Insurance Contract)

(8) Debtor's interest in a dividend from an Unmatured Insurance Interest up to $8,000[47] - <u>Value of Turnover Property Recovered</u>

(9) Medically Prescribed Medicine or Health Aids

(10) The Debtor's Right to Receive:

    (A) Social Security Benefits, Unemployment, and other Government Assistance

    (B) Veteran's Benefits

    (C) Disability or Unemployment Benefits

    (D) Alimony, Child Support reasonably necessary for the Debtor's support

(11) Payment under a Stock Pension/Profit-sharing plan, unless:
* * * *

(12) The Debtor's Right to Receive property traceable to:

    (A) An Award under a Crime Victim's reparation Law

    (B) Payment on account for Wrongful Death Action

    (C) Payment under a Life Insurance Contract from deceased family member

    (D) Up to $15,000[48] of a personal injury claim (not including Pain, Suffering, or Pecuniary Loss)

    (E) Compensation for Loss of Future Earnings from a dependent

(e) Waivers Unenforceable: The following actions will be unenforceable:

    1) The Debtor waives an exemption of §522(d) property in order to satisfy an <u>unsecured Creditor's</u> claim (because the unsecured Creditor would be better off than others. In such a case, the property will be a Debt to the Estate.)

---

[44] $850 as of April 1, 1998.
[45] $8,075 as of April 1, 1998.
[46] $1,625 as of April 1, 1998.
[47] $8,625 as of April 1, 1998.
[48] $16,150 as of April 1, 1998.

2) The Debtor waived the right to avoid a Transfer of exempt property (under §522(g) and (i)).

3) The Debtor waived the right to recover property (under §522(g) and (i)).

(f) Avoiding Liens on Exempt Property:

(1) The Debtor may avoid fixing a Lien on property he has an interest in to the extent the Lien will impair his right to a §522(b) exemption, if the Lien is:

(A) An unassigned <u>Judicial Lien</u> that:
  1. Was not made to secure a debt
  2. Was based on Alimony or Child Support
  * * *

(B) <u>Property Subject to §522(f)</u>: A non-possessory, non-Purchase Money Security Interest in any:
  (i) Household/personal consumer goods (under §522(d)(3) and (4))
  (ii) Professional books/ tools of the trade (under §522(d)(6))
  (iii) Health aids/medicines (under §522(d)(9))

(2) When Lien Impairs Exemption:

(A) A Lien "<u>impairs an exemption</u>" to the extent the Debtor's interest in the property plus all Liens on the property is less than the sum of:
  (i) The Lien
  Plus(ii) All other Liens on the Property
  Plus (iii) The amount of the exemption the Debtor could claim (as per §522(b))

(B) <u>Calculations when more than 1 Lien exists</u>: Any avoided Liens are <u>not</u> considered in calculating the above equation.

(C) §522(f) shall not apply with respect to a judgement arising out of a <u>Mortgage Foreclosure</u>.

(3) Cases Where State Law Applies to Debtor:

i) The Debtor may <u>not</u> avoid fixing a Lien (i.e. the Lien will survive) on property exempt under State law if:

(A) State law either permits a Person to voluntarily waive a right to claim exemptions under §522(d) or prohibits the Debtor to claim exemptions under §522(d).

and (B) <u>Either</u>:

215

1. State law permits the Debtor to claim exemptions under without monetary limitations (except to the extent the Debtor has allowed the property to be encumbered by a consensual Lien).

or 2. State law prohibits the Debtor to avoid a consensual Lien on property which would otherwise be exempt.

and (C) The Lien is a non-possessory, non-purchase money Security Interest in §522(d)(3) or (6) property.

ii) The Trustee may recover $5,000 from the Lien Value.

(g) Exempting Recovered Property: The Trustee may exempt property recovered (under §510(c)(2), §542, §543, §550, §551, §553, etc.) to the extent it would have been exempt if the Transfer were never made if either:

(1) Both:
(A) The Transfer was not a voluntary Transfer by the Debtor (ex: a Judicial Lien).
and (B) The Debtor did not conceal the property.

or (2) The Debtor could have avoided the Transfer under §522(f)(2) (WHEN LIEN IMPAIRS EXEMPTION).

(h) Avoiding Exempted Property: The Debtor may avoid a Transfer or recover a setoff to the extent they would have been exempt under §522(g)(1) had the Trustee avoided the Transfer , so long as:

(1) The Transfer is avoidable by the Trustee (under Voidable Preference Law).
(2) The Trustee does not attempt to avoid the Transfer .

(i) Exempting Property Recovered From Setoffs:
(1) The Debtor may recover voidable preferences and setoffs (under §522(f) or (h)) and exempt such property.
(2) An avoided Transfer may be preserved for the benefit of the Debtor to the extent it would have been exempt under §522(g) or §522(i)(1).

(j) Exempting Other Property: The Debtor may exempt a particular type of property under §522(g) or (i), but only to the extent the Debtor has exempted less property (in Value) than the type of property that the Debtor is allowed under §522(b)(AVAILABLE EXEMPTIONS).

(k) Administrative Expenses: Property exempt under this section is not subject to payment of any Administrative Expenses, except:
    (1) The proportional share of unpaid costs and expenses of:
        a. Avoiding a Transfer of property that the Debtor exempts under §522(g)
  or b. Recovering property that the Debtor exempts under §522(g)
and (2) Any unpaid costs and expenses of:
        a. Avoiding a Transfer under §522(f) or (h)
  or b. Recovering property under §522(i)(1)

(l) Debtor's Filing:
    1. The Debtor (or dependent) shall file a list of property it claims as exempt under §522(b).
    2. Unless a Party in Interest objects, any property claimed as exempt on the list will be exempt (regardless of its allowance under law).

(m) Joint Exemptions: In a joint case, this section shall apply separately with respect to each Debtor (subject to the limitation in §522(b)(2)).

§523: Exceptions to Discharge:

(a) Debts that are Excepted from Discharge: The following Debts
     survive a bankruptcy discharge under §727, §1141, §1228(a),
     §1228(b), or §1328(b):

  (1) TAXES - Any of the following taxes or customs duties:
       (A) Taxes specified in one of the following sections,
            whether or not a Claim for the tax was filed or allowed:
            i.   §507(a)(2) (unsecured tax Claims arising in the
                 Debtor's ordinary course of business between the
                 Petition date and the appointment of a trustee or an
                 Order for Relief)
       or   ii. §507(a)(8) (various unsecured pre-Petition tax
                 Claims)

       (B) Taxes for which a tax return (if required) was either:
            (i)   Not filed
       or   (ii) Filed late, and within 2 years before the Petition
                 date
       (C) Taxes concerning which the Debtor filed a fraudulent
            return (or entry or invoice) or attempted intentionally to
            evade or defeat the tax

  (2) DEBTS FOR PROPERTY RECEIVED UNDER FALSE
       PRETENSES OR BY CONSUMERS: Debts for money,
       property, services, or an extension, renewal, or refinancing
       of credit, if obtained in the following ways:

       (A) By false pretenses, a false representation, or actual
            fraud (not fraud implied in law), other than a statement
            respecting the Debtor's or an Insider's financial
            condition

       (B) By use of a statement in writing:
            (i)   That is materially false (Note: A discharge is not
                 allowed, but only as to that part of a loan
                 concerning which a false financial statement is
                 materially false)
       and (ii) That describes the Debtor's or an Insider's financial
                 condition

218

and (iii) That the creditor (giving the money, property, services, or credit) reasonably relied upon

and (iv) That the Debtor made or published with intent to deceive

(C) <u>Consumer Debts</u> Presumed Dischargeable:
1. For purposes of (A), the following Consumer Debts are presumed <u>non-dischargeable</u>:
   a. <u>Consumer Debts</u> that:
     i. Are incurred by an individual Debtor on or within <u>60 days</u> before the Order for Relief

  and ii. Are owed to a single creditor

  and iii. Total more than $1,000 for "<u>luxury goods or services</u>"'

  or b. <u>Consumer Cash advances</u> that:
     i. Total more than $1,000

  and ii. Are extensions of consumer credit under an "<u>open end credit plan.</u>"

  and iii. The plan was obtained by an individual Debtor on or within <u>60 days</u> before the Order for Relief

2. "<u>Luxury goods or services</u>" - do not include goods or services that a Debtor reasonably needs for support or maintenance (of himself or a dependent).

3. "<u>An extension of consumer credit under an open end credit plan</u>" is defined in the Consumer Credit Protection Act (P.L. 90-321, May 29, 1968, 82 Stat. 146, as amended (See 15 U.S.C §1601 et seq.))

(3) <u>UNSCHEDULED DEBTS</u>: Debts that are not listed nor scheduled (as required by §521(1)), with the name of the creditor (if the Debtor knows) will not be discharged in the following circumstances:

(A) <u>Debts Not specified in §523(2), (4), or (6)</u>: If the Debt was not listed in time to allow a creditor to timely file a Proof of Claim (i.e. the Creditor was without notice or actual knowledge of the case in time to file a Claim).

or (B) <u>Debts specified in §523(2), (4), or (6)</u>: If the Debt was not listed in time to allow a creditor to:

1. Timely file a proof of Claim (i.e. the Creditor was without notice or actual knowledge of the case in time)

or 2. Timely request the determination of dischargeability of the Debt (under in §523(2), (4), or (6))

(4) FRAUD OR THEFT - Debts arising from Debtor's:
    a. Fraud or defalcation (while acting in a fiduciary capacity)
or b. Embezzlement
or c. Larceny

(5) ALIMONY, MAINTENANCE OR CHILD SUPPORT:
    i) Non-dischargeable Claims: Debts owed for alimony, maintenance, or child support (to the Debtor's spouse, former spouse or child) will not be discharged if they arose in connection with a:
        A. Separation agreement
or B. Divorce decree
or C. Another order of a court of record
or D. Determination made in accordance with State or territorial law by a Governmental Unit
or E. Property settlement agreement

    ii) Dischargeable Clams: The following are dischargeable:
        (A) Assigned Claims: A Debt for alimony, maintenance or child support, to the extent it is assigned (voluntarily, by operation of law, or otherwise) to any other Entity (but not the government) including:
            1. Debts assigned pursuant to §402(a)(26) of the Social Security Act (42 U.S.C. §602(a)(26))
        or 2. Any Debt which has been assigned to the Federal Government or to a State or any political subdivision of that State
    or (B) Other Related Claims: A Debt that is not actually in the nature of alimony, maintenance or child support.

(6) **WILLFUL AND MALICIOUS INJURY**: Debts for willful and malicious injury caused by the Debtor to another Entity or its property.[49]

(7) **FINES AND PENALTIES**: Debts for fines, penalties, or forfeitures owed to a Governmental Unit, is nondischargeable unless it is compensation for actual pecuniary loss, with the exception of Tax Penalties:
(A) A Non-Compensatory Tax Penalty – (not specified in §523(1)) is not dischargeable (i.e. a penalty relating to a tax cannot be dischargeable unless the tax itself is dischargeable).
(B) Old Tax Penalties: A tax penalty concerning a transaction or event that took place more than 3 years before the Petition date is not dischargeable.

(8) **STUDENT LOANS**:
a. Debts for an educational loan (or benefit overpayment) that was:
1. Made by a Governmental Unit
or 2. Insured or guaranteed by a Governmental Unit
or 3. Made under any program funded (in whole or in part) by a Governmental Unit or nonprofit institution

or b. Debts for funds received as an educational benefit, scholarship or stipend, unless:
(A) The loan, benefit, scholarship, or stipend overpayment first became due more than 7 years (regardless of any suspension of the repayment period) before the Petition date.
or (B) There will be an undue hardship on the Debtor and his dependents if the Debt is not discharged.

(9) **DRUNK OR DRUGGED DRIVING**: Debts for death or personal injury caused by the Debtor's use of a motor vehicle while unlawfully intoxicated from using alcohol, a drug, or another substance.

---

[49] Note: "Willful" means deliberate or intentional.

(10) **PRIOR BANKRUPTCY**: A Debt that was (or could have been) listed or scheduled by the Debtor in a prior bankruptcy case, where the Debtor either:

    a.   Waived discharge

or b.   Was denied a discharge under §727(a)(2), (3), (4), (5), (6), or (7) (or under §14c(1), (2), (3), (4), (6), or (7) of the Bankruptcy Act - (July 1, 1898, Ch. 541, 30 Stat. 544, as amended and codified in former Title 11))

(11) **FRAUD OR DEFALCATION TO AN INSURED BANK**:

    A.   Debts arising from any act of fraud or defalcation (while acting in a fiduciary capacity) committed with respect to any depository institution or insured credit union will not be discharged.

    B.   This includes liability provided in any final judgment, non-reviewable order or consent order/decree:

        i.   Entered in any court of the United States

or ii.   Entered in any State court

or iii. Issued by a government agency that regulates Federal depository institutions

or iv. Contained in any settlement agreement entered into by the Debtor

(12) **FAILURE TO MAINTAIN COMMITMENT WITH INSURED BANK**:

    a.   Debts for malicious or reckless failure to maintain the capital of an insured depository institution (pursuant to any commitment by the Debtor to a government agency that regulates Federal depository institutions) are non-dischargeable.

    b.   Exception: This Rule shall not extend any commitment which would otherwise be terminated because of any act of the regulatory agency.

(13) **DEBTS FOR ORDERS OF REINSTITUION**: Debts for any payment of an order of restitution issued (under Title 18, United States Code) are not dischargeable.

(14) **DEBTS TO PAY TAXES**: Debts incurred to pay a tax to the U.S. are not dischargeable if the tax is nondischargeable under §523(1).

(15) DEBTS INCURRED IN DIVORCE/SEPARATION PROCEEDINGS:

i. Non-Dischargeable Claims: Debts not described in §523(5) are non-dischargeable anyway if they are incurred by the Debtor:
   A. In the course of: a divorce or separation
or B. In connection with a separation agreement, divorce decree or other order of a court of record, by a determination made in accordance with State or territorial law by a Governmental Unit.
ii. Dischargeable Claims: The above rule will not apply if:

(A) Debtor is Unable to Pay: The Debtor is unable to pay the Debt from his income or property not reasonably necessary for:
   1. The Debtor's (or a dependent's) maintenance or support
and 2. If the Debtor is engaged in a business: For the payment of expenses needed for the continuation, preservation, and operation of the business.
(B) Benefit Outweighs Costs: Discharging the Debt would result in a benefit to the Debtor that outweighs the detrimental consequences to the Debtor's spouse, former spouse or child.

(16) CO-OP AND CONDOMINIUM MEMBERSHIP FEE:

i) Debts for membership fees to an association concerning the Debtor's interest in a condominium or share of a cooperative housing Corporation that becomes due after the Order for Relief, but only if the fee is payable for a period during which:
(A) The Debtor physically occupied a dwelling unit in the condominium or cooperative project
or (B) The Debtor rented the dwelling unit to a tenant and received payments from the tenant for that period.
ii) The Debt of a Debtor for a membership association fee or assessment for a period arising before entry of the Order for Relief in a pending or subsequent bankruptcy case is dischargeable.

(b) Debts Discharged in Prior Bankruptcy: Notwithstanding
subsection (a), a Debt that was excepted from discharge under
any of the following in a prior bankruptcy case, is <u>dischargeable</u>
in a current bankruptcy case unless, by the terms of (a), the Debt
is not dischargeable in the current case:

  1. Debts non-dischargeable under §523(a)(1), (a)(3), or (a)(8)

or 2. Debts non-dischargeable under §17a(1), 17a(3), or 17a(5) of
the Bankruptcy Act (July 1, 1898, Ch. 541, 30 Stat. 544, as
amended and codified in former Title 11)

or 3. Debts non-dischargeable under §439A of the Higher
Education Act of 1965 (20 U.S.C. §1087-3; repealed by
Pub. L. 95-598, title III, §317, Nov. 6, 1978, 92 Stat. 2678)

or 4. Debts non-dischargeable under §733(g) of the Public Health
Service Act (repealed by Pub. L. 95-598, title III, §327,
Nov. 6, 1978, 92 Stat. 2679. See P.L. 97-35, title XXVII, §
2730, Aug. 13, 1981, 95 Stat. 919)

(c) Notice and Hearing:

  (1) <u>Court's Exclusive Jurisdiction to Determine
  Dischargeability</u>:

    a. Except as provided in §523(a)(3)(B), a creditor who is
    owed a dischargeable Debt under §523(a) (2), (4), (6)
    or (15) (dealing with false statements, defalcation or
    larceny; misappropriation, willful and malicious injury;
    Debts concerning a divorce decree) must request a
    determination of dischargeability by the court.

    b. The Debt will not be discharged if the court so decides,
    upon <u>notice</u> and a <u>hearing.</u>

    c. If the creditor does not act, the Debt will be discharged
    (see Rules of Bankruptcy Procedure, Rule 4007(c) for
    time limits).

  (2) <u>Exception</u>: In the case of a government agency that
  regulates <u>Federal depository institutions</u> if:

    a. The Agency is seeking (as conservator, receiver, or
    liquidating agent for an insured depository institution)
    to recover a Debt

  and b. The Debt is one described in §523(a)(2), (4), (6), or
    (11)

  and c. The Debt is owed to the institution by an institution-
    Affiliated party

  and d. The agency was not appointed in time to reasonably
    comply with §523(a)(3)(B), as a <u>Creditor of the</u>

Institution-Affiliated party, which would be required if the agency is acting:

1. As a receiver, conservator, or liquidating agency

or 2. In its corporate capacity as a successor to the receiver, conservator, or liquidating agent

(d) Protection to Honest Consumer Debtors: [50]

1. The bankruptcy court shall grant judgment in favor of the Debtor for the costs (and reasonable Attorney's fees) of a proceeding to declare a consumer Debt non-dischargeable (a §523 (a)(2) proceeding), if:

   a. The creditor requested such a determination with respect to a Consumer Debt.

   and b. The Debt is discharged, and the Creditor is unsuccessful.

   and c. The court finds that the position of the creditor was not substantially justified. (Note: The Rules of Bankruptcy Procedure specify who may request determinations of dischargeability, subject to 11 U.S.C. 523(c), and when such a request may be made. See §523(c).)

2. Exception: The court shall not award costs and fees if special circumstances would make the award unjust.

---

[50] This provides protection to a Consumer Debtor that dealt honestly with a Creditor who tried to have a Debt excepted from discharge on the ground of falsity in the incurring of the Debt. The Debtor may be awarded costs and a reasonable Attorney's fee for the proceeding to determine the dischargeability of a Debt under subsection (a)(2), if the court finds that the proceeding was frivolous or not brought by the Creditor in good faith.

The purpose of the provision is to discourage Creditors from initiating proceedings to obtaining a "false financial statement" exception to discharge in the hope of obtaining a settlement from an honest Debtor anxious to save Attorney's fees. These practices hurt the Debtor's fresh start and are against the spirit of the bankruptcy laws.

(e) Fiduciary Status: Any institution-affiliated party of an insured depository institution is considered a fiduciary for the purposes of (a)(4) and (11).

§524: Effect of Discharge:

(a) Effects of Discharge:
(1) Judgments Void: Discharge voids any judgment (obtained at any time), to the extent that the judgment is for the Debtor's personal liability for any Debt (defined in 101(12)) discharged under §§727, 944, 1141, 1228, or 1328, whether or not discharge of the Debt is waived.
and (2) Injunction Against Action:
i.   Discharge also operates as an injunction prohibiting Creditors (whether or not discharge of the Debt is waived) from trying to collect, recover or offset any of the Debtor's personal liabilities that were discharged.
ii. The Creditors may not:
a.   Take any action
or   b.   File any lawsuit
or   c.   Continue any lawsuit
or   d.   Employ any process
and (3) Community Property: Discharge operates as constitutes an injunction prohibiting the creditor from trying to collect, recover or offset an allowable community Claim from the Debtor's community property (specified in §541(a)(2)) that was acquired by the Debtor after the Petition date (whether or not discharge of the Debt is waived).
a.   Actions Prohibited by Creditor:
1.   Starting a lawsuit
2.   Continuing a lawsuit
3.   Employing any process
4.   Taking any action
b.   Exceptions - The following are not affected by the injunction:
1.   A community Claim that is non-dischargeable under §523, §1228(a)(1), or §1328(a)(1)
or   2.   A community Claim that would be non-dischargeable (under §523(c) and §523(d)), in a case concerning the Debtor's spouse that was filed on the Debtor's Petition date.

(b) Exception to §524(a)(3): Subsection 524(a)(3) does not apply if:
   (1) <u>Debtor's Spouse in prior Bankruptcy</u>:
      (A) The Debtor's spouse is a Debtor in a bankruptcy case (or a bankrupt or a Debtor in a case under the Bankruptcy Act) that was started within <u>6 years</u> of the Debtor's Petition date
   and (B) The court does not grant the Debtor's spouse a discharge in the spouse's case

or (2) <u>Debtor's Spouse in Current Bankruptcy</u>:
      (A) The court would not grant the Debtor's spouse a discharge in a Chapter 7 case of the spouse that was started on the Debtor's Petition date
   and (B) The Bankruptcy Court decides not to grant a discharge within the time (and in the manner) required to make a decision under §727 (which discusses when the court must determine when a Debt is discharged).

(c) Reaffirmation Agreements:
   1. <u>Definition</u>: A "Reaffirmation Agreement" is a contract (based at least in part on a dischargeable Claim) between the Debtor and a Claim-holder, where the Debtor agrees to repay a discharged Claim to a Creditor after bankruptcy.
   2. <u>Basic Requirement</u>: To be enforceable, the contract must be enforceable under non-bankruptcy law (regardless of whether or not discharge is waived).
   3. <u>Other Requirements</u>:
      (1) Time of Agreement: The agreement was made before the granting of the discharge (under §§727, 1141, 1228, or 1328)
   and (2) Clear and Conspicuous Statement:
      (A) The agreement has a clear and conspicuous statement which advises the Debtor that the agreement may be rescinded by giving notice to the Claim-holder by the later of:
         1. Any time before discharge
      or 2. Within 60 days after the agreement is filed with the court
   and (B) The agreement has a clear and conspicuous statement which advises the Debtor that the <u>agreement is not required</u> under any law (bankruptcy or non-bankruptcy), or under any other

type of agreement that is not a Reaffirmation Agreement.

and (3) Filing with the Court:
  i)   The agreement must be filed with the court to be enforceable.
  and ii) The agreement must be accompanied by an Attorney's declaration or an affidavit (of the Attorney that represented the Debtor in negotiating the Reaffirmation Agreement), stating:
      (A) The agreement is a fully informed and voluntary agreement by the Debtor
      and (B) The agreement does not impose an undue hardship on the Debtor or a dependent
      and (C) The Attorney fully advised the Debtor of the legal effect and consequences of both:
          (i) A Reaffirmation Agreement
          and (ii) Any default under a Reaffirmation Agreement.

and (4) The Debtor has not rescinded the agreement (pursuant to (2)(A) above).
and (5) Subsection (d) has been complied with
and (6) Unrepresented Debtors:
      (A) If there is no Attorney who negotiated the agreement, the court approves that the agreement:
          1. Does not impose an undue hardship on the Debtor or a dependent
          and 2. Is in the best interest of the Debtor
      (B) Subparagraph (A) does not apply if the underlying Debt is:
          1. A Consumer Debt
          and 2. It is also secured by real property

(d) Discharge Hearing:
  1. When the Court may hold a "Discharge Hearing":
      a. In a case concerning an individual
      b. Where the court has determined whether or not to grant a discharge (under Sec. 727, 1141, 1228, or 1328).

  2. Conduct of Hearing:
      a. The Debtor must appear in Person
      b. The court must inform the Debtor that:

        i.   A discharge has been granted

or ii.   The reason why a discharge has not been granted

 c.   If a discharge has been granted and the Debtor wants to make a Reaffirmation Agreement (specified in (c)) and did not have an Attorney when the agreement was negotiated, then the court shall:

    (1) Inform the Debtor:

        (A) That the agreement is not required under any law (bankruptcy or nonbankruptcy), or under any agreement that is not a Reaffirmation Agreement

    and (B) The legal effect and consequences of:

           (i)   A Reaffirmation Agreement

      and (ii) A default under a Reaffirmation Agreement

   and (2) Check Compliance with (c)(6): If the agreement is based on an underlying Debt that is:

        1.   A consumer Debt

    and 2.   Not secured by real property of the Debtor

(e) Liability of Other Entities: Discharge of a Debt of the Debtor does not affect (except as provided in (a)(3) for Community Property) the liability on that Debt owed to a Creditor by any other Entity (e.g. co-Debtor, guarantor) or their property.

(f) Voluntary Repayment: Nothing in (c) or (d) prevents a Debtor from voluntarily repaying any Debt.

(g) Other Injunctions:

   (1) <u>Chapter 11 Reorganization Cases</u>:

     (A) A court may issue an injunction (in accordance with this subsection) to supplement §524 injunctive effects (DISCHARGE) if:

       1.   The court enters an order confirming a Chapter 11 Reorganization Plan and the injunction is in connection with that order

    and 2.   There is notice and a hearing

     (B) Actions Prohibited and Permitted:

       1.   Legal Action Prohibited: An injunction may be issued under subparagraph (g)(1)(A) to prohibit legal action to (directly or indirectly) collect,

recover, or receive payment or recovery for any Claim or demand that is to be paid (in whole or in part (under a reorganization plan)) by a trust described in (2)(B)(i)).

2. Legal Actions Permitted: Legal actions are permitted if expressly allowed by:
   a. The injunction
   or b. The confirmation order
   or c. The reorganization plan

(2) Jurisdiction for Actions under Injunction:

(A) Court and Proceedings:
   1. Permitted Proceedings: If the requirements of (g)(1)(B) are met when an injunction (described in (g)(1)) is entered, then after it is entered, any of the following may be commenced:
      a. Proceedings that involve the validity of the injunction
      or b. Proceedings that involve the application, construction, or modification of the injunction
      or c. Proceedings that involve the application, construction, or modification of an injunction under this section.
   2. Jurisdiction: The district court where the injunction was entered has exclusive jurisdiction over any of these proceedings regardless of the amount in controversy.
   3. This subsection is subject to (h).

(B) Requirements:
   (i) A Trust: The injunction must be implemented with a trust that (pursuant to the reorganization plan) will do the following:
      (I) Assume Liabilities: If the Debtor is a defendant (at the time of entry of the Order for Relief) in personal injury, wrongful death, or property-damage actions seeking recovery for damages allegedly caused by asbestos or asbestos-containing products, the trust must assume the liabilities of the Debtor
      and (II) Funding: The trust is to be funded (in whole or in part) by:

230

      a. The securities of 1 or more Debtors
          involved in the plan
and b. The obligation of the Debtor(s) to make
          future payments, including dividends
and (III) Ownership: The trust is to own (or would be
          entitled to own by rights granted under the
          plan if specific contingencies occur) a majority
          of the voting shares of:
          (aa) each Debtor
  or (bb) the parent Corporation of each Debtor
  or (cc) a subsidiary of each Debtor that is also a
          Debtor.

and (IV) Use of Proceeds: The trust is to use its assets
          or income to pay Claims and demands.

and (ii) Debtor Subject to Demands for Payment: The court
      determines that (subject to subsection (h)):
      (I) Substantial Future Demands for Payment: The
          Debtor is likely to face substantial future
          demands for payment arising out of the same
          events that gave rise to the Claims that the
          injunction deals with
    and (II) Undeterminable Amount: The actual amounts,
          numbers, and timing of those future demands
          cannot be determined
    and (III) Demands Threaten Plan's Purpose: Pursuit of
          those demands outside the plan's procedures is
          likely to threaten the plan's purpose (to "deal
          equitably with Claims and future demands")
    and (IV) Terms Stated: As part of the process of
          seeking confirmation of the plan:
          (aa) The terms of the injunction proposed
              (under (1)(A)) (including any provisions
              barring actions against third parties
              pursuant to (4)(A)) are set out in:
          1. The plan
        and 2. In any disclosure statement supporting
             the plan
    and (bb) Class of Claimants Established:
          1. A separate class (or classes) of the
              Claimants who are to be dealt with by

the trust (described in clause (i)) is established.

and 2. The class(es) votes in favor of the plan by at least 75% of those voting.

and (V) Operation of the Trust:

    1. The trust will operate through mechanisms that provide reasonable assurance that the trust will be in a financial position to pay present and future Claims that involve similar Claims in substantially the same manner. Such mechanisms may include:

        a. Structured, periodic, or supplemental payments

        b. Pro rata distributions, matrices, or periodic review of estimates of the numbers and Values of present Claims and future demands

or c. Other comparable mechanisms

    2. The mechanisms are employed pursuant to court orders or otherwise.

    3. This subsection is subject to (h).

(3) Transferees and Successors

(A) Modification and Transferees of Debtor or Trust:

    1. Effects of Requirements Being Met: If the requirements below are met, then:

      (i) Revocable Only by Appeal: The injunction becomes valid and enforceable and may not be revoked or modified by any court except through appeal (in accordance with paragraph (6))

      (ii) Transferee Not Liable for any Claim: A Transferee (of a Debtor or trust that is the subject of the injunction pursuant to the plan or thereafter) or Successor (to any assets of a Debtor or trust) is not liable for any Claim or demand made against him because of his status as a Transferee or successor.

        (iii) <u>Lender Not Liable for any Claim</u>:
- a. No one making a loan (under the plan or after) to the Debtor or trust (or to a successor or Transferee) is, because of making the loan, liable for any Claim or demand made against him.
- b. No pledge of assets made in connection with the loan shall be impaired for that reason.

2. <u>Requirements</u>:
- a. The requirements of paragraph (2)(B) are met
- and b. The time for appeal of the order that issues or affirms the plan has passed
- and c. The order confirming the reorganization plan was issued or affirmed by the district court that has jurisdiction over the reorganization case

(B) Subparagraph (A) <u>shall not</u> be construed to mean:
- (i) That someone described in (A)(ii) or (iii) would be liable for any of the acts described in (A) if this paragraph (3) did not apply
- or (ii) That someone described in (A)(ii) or (iii) is exempt from compliance with or liability under any Federal or State law dealing with the making of a fraudulent conveyance in a transaction described in (A)(ii) or (iii)
- or (iii) <u>Compliance With a Reorganization Plan</u>:
  - a. That a Debtor has no obligation to comply with the terms of the reorganization plan
  - or b. That a court does not have the power to exercise its authority under §§1141 and 1142 to compel the Debtor to comply with the plan.

(4) <u>Parties Affected by Injunction</u>

(A) Third Parties
- (i) An injunction described in paragraph (1) is enforceable (subject to (B) below) against all parties that it addresses.
- (ii) The injunction may bar any action against that third party if:

1. The third party is identifiable from the terms of the injunction (by name or as part of a group)

and 2. The third party is allegedly liable (directly or indirectly) for the Debts or conduct of a Debtor

and 3. The liability arises from - one of the following reasons (notwithstanding §524(e)):

　　(I)　Financial Interest - The third party owns a financial interest in:

　　　　a.　The Debtor company

or　　b.　A past Affiliate of the Debtor

or　　c.　A present Affiliate of the Debtor

or　　d.　A predecessor in interest of the Debtor

or　(II)　Manager or Officer - The third party is:

　　　　a.　A manager of the Debtor or a predecessor in interest of the Debtor

or　　b.　Is an officer, director or employee of the Debtor or a Related Party

or　(III)　Insurer - The third party provides insurance to the Debtor or a Related Party

or　(IV)　Financial Transactions - The third party is involved in:

　　　　a.　A transaction changing the corporate structure of the Debtor or a Related Party

or　　b.　In a loan or other financial transaction affecting the financial condition of the Debtor or a Related Party, including (but not limited to):

　　　　(aa) Providing financing (Debt or equity), or advice to a party to the transaction

or　　(bb) Acquiring or selling a financial interest in a party as part of the transaction

(iii) "Related Party" - Definition of "Related Party" in this paragraph:

　　(I)　A past or present Affiliate of the Debtor

or　(II)　A predecessor in interest of the Debtor

or (III) Any Entity that owned a financial interest in either:
    (aa) the Debtor
   or (bb) A past or present Affiliate of the Debtor
   or (cc) A predecessor in interest of the Debtor

(B) Demand Described in Reorganization Plan
  1. If a demand described in a reorganization plan is to be paid (in whole or in part) by a §524(2)(B)(I) trust where there is an injunction (described in paragraph (1)), then after the plan is confirmed the injunction will be enforceable against the Debtor or Debtors involved in the demand, or against a third party described in (A)(ii), if:
   (i) The court (as part of the proceedings issuing of the injunction) appoints a legal representative to protect the rights of people that might later assert similar demands
  and (ii) The court determines, before entering the order confirming the plan, that identifying the Debtor(s) or the third party in the injunction (by name or as part of a group) for purposes of this subparagraph is <u>fair and equitable</u> with respect to those who might later assert similar demands, in light of the benefits provided (or to be provided) to the trust on behalf of the Debtor(s) or the third party.
  2. This §524(g)(4) is subject to §524(h).

(5) "Demand" - In this subsection, "Demand'" means a demand for present or future payment that:
  (A) <u>Was not a Claim during the proceedings</u> leading to the confirmation of a plan of reorganization
  and (B) <u>Arises out of the same (or similar) events that gave rise to the Claims</u> - addressed by the injunction issued under paragraph (1)
  and (C) <u>Is to be paid by a trust</u> - described in paragraph (2)(B)(i) pursuant to the plan
   (6) Appealable Injunctions: §524(g) (3)(A)(i) does not bar an action taken by (or at the direction of) an appellate court on appeal of:

        1.   An injunction issued under paragraph (1)
        2.   The confirmation order that relates to the
             injunction
  (7) This subsection does not affect the operation of Sec. 1144
      (i.e. revocation of an Order of Confirmation) or the power
      of the district court to refer a proceeding under 28 U.S.C.
      §157 or any reference of a proceeding made before this
      subsection was enacted.

(h) Application to Existing Injunctions under Chapter 11: For
     purposes of subsection (g):

  (1) The injunction is considered to meet the requirements of
      §543(g)(2)(B) (i.e. the requirements to bar a third party
      action under §543(g)(2)(A)), and to satisfy
      §543(g)(4)(A)(ii), if:

      (A) The court determined at the time the plan was
           confirmed that the plan was fair and equitable in
           accordance with §1129(b).
and   (B) The court (as part of the proceedings issuing of the
           injunction) appoints a legal representative to protect the
           rights of people that might later assert similar demands.
and   (C) The legal representative did not object to
           confirmation of the plan or issuance of the injunction.
and (D) The injunction (described in (g)(1)(B)) was:
           1.   Issued before this Act was enacted as part of a plan
              of reorganization
      and 2.   Confirmed by an order entered before that date

  (2) For purposes of paragraph (1), if a trust (described in
      (g)(2)(B)(i)) is subject to a court order on the date this Act
      was enacted staying the trust from settling or paying further
      Claims, then:
      (A) The requirements of (g)(2)(B)(ii)(V) shall not apply to
           that trust until the stay is lifted or dissolved
and (B) If the trust meets the requirements on the date the stay
           is lifted or dissolved, the trust is considered to have met
           the requirements as of the date this Act was enacted.

Subchapter III – The Estate

§541: Property of the Estate:

(a) The Estate: The Bankruptcy Estate (created by the commencement of the case under §301, §302 or §303) is comprised of all of the following property (regardless of where it is located or who holds it):

    (1) All Legal or Equitable interests in property of the Debtor as of the commencement of the Petition (subject to §541(b) and (c)(2) below).

    (2) All interests of the Debtor and his spouse in Community Property that is:

        (A) Under the Debtor's control (sole or joint)

    or (B) Liable for a claim against the Debtor or for both a claim against the Debtor and the Debtor's spouse

    (3) Any interest in property which the Trustee recovers (under §329(b), §363(n), §543, §550, §553 or §723)

    (4) Any Interest in property which is either:

        a) Preserved for the benefit of the estate (under §510(c))

    or b) Ordered Transferred to the Estate under §551

    (5) Any interest that would have been Property of the Estate if:

        a) The Debtor would have had an interest in it on the date of filing

    or b) The Debtor acquired/became entitled to the property within 6 months after the filing, and the property was acquired:

        1) By devise, bequest, or inheritance

        or 2) As a result of a Property Settlement Agreement (with the Debtor's spouse)

        or 3) As a Beneficiary of a Life Insurance plan

    (6) Proceeds, Product, Offspring, Rents, or Profits from Estate property, unless earned by an individual debtor after the Petition (Personal Services).

    (7) Any interest in property acquired by the Estate (not the Debtor) after the Petition was filed.

(b) Exclusions from Estate:

    (1) Any Power which the Debtor may exercise solely for the benefit of another Person or entity.

    (2) Any interest as a lessee under an expired non-residential real property lease, where the lease has terminated by its terms

before the Petition date (or interest in a lease that terminated during the case – that ceases to be included)

(3)　Any eligibility for Debtor to participate in higher Education Act of 1965.

(4)　Any Interest of Debtor in liquid or gaseous hydrocarbons. *
　　* *

(5)　Cash Proceeds - Any interest in Cash or cash equivalents which are proceeds from the sale of a Money Order that is made:

(A)　On or after the date 14 days before the Petition date

and (B)　Under an agreement with a money order issuer that prohibits commingling such proceeds with the Debtor's property (even if the proceeds were commingled anyway, contrary to the agreement)

(c)　Superceding Contract Clauses:

(1)　This section applies (subject to §541(c)(2)) regardless of contractual restrictions that:

(A)　Restrict or condition the Transfer of the Debtor's interest by the Debtor

or　(B)　Require the Debtor to return property or terminate its interest in its property in the case of bankruptcy or insolvency, before giving it to the Bankruptcy Estate.

(2)　Pension Plans/Spendthrift Trust: A restriction on a Transfer of a trust for the benefit of the Debtor is enforceable under the Bankruptcy Code, if the Spendthrift Trust/ERISA Plan is enforceable under non-Bankruptcy law.

(d)　Debtor's Legal Title in Trust Property:

1)　If the Debtor only holds the legal title to property and no equitable interest (ex: he is the Trustee of a trust), only the legal interest will become Property of the Estate (and not the equitable interest).

2)　Note: This section does not apply to Real Property held in Trust (because §541(a)(3) makes property recoverable under §544(a)(3): REAL PROPERTY OF THE ESTATE)

§542: Turnover of Property of the Estate:

(a) Return of Property to the Estate: The Trustee may order property to be returned to the estate if it falls under §363 (SALE/USE OF PROPERTY) or §522 (EXEMPT PROPERTY) unless the property is of inconsequential Value or benefit to the estate.

(b) Debts to the Estate: Entities that owe money to the estate must pay their debts when they are due (either matured, or they are debts payable in demand or order) less any setoffs (under §553: SETOFF)

(c) Property Not Subject to Turnover: Property will not be subject to Turnover if the Creditor:
   1. Had no actual notice or actual knowledge of the commencement of the case
   2. Transferred the property in Good Faith
   3. Transferred to an entity other than the Trustee

(d) Life Insurance Companies may receive property of the Debtor under particular circumstances, as when the property is used to pay premiums under a life insurance contract that was entered into before the Petition date.

(e) Books and Records:
   1. The Court may order records and documents relating to the Debtor's property to be turned over or disclosed to the Trustee.
   2. Privileges that may apply remain intact.
   3. There must be notice and a hearing.

§543: Turnover of Property by A Custodian:

(a) Actions Prohibited by Custodian:
   1. A Custodian (defined in §101(11)) who knows that a bankruptcy case was started may not disburse or administer any of the following property in the Custodian's estate:
      a. Property of the Debtor
      b. Proceeds, product, offspring, rents, or profits of the property
      c. Property of the Estate
   2. Exception: The Custodian may administer property if necessary to preserve it.

(b) Turnover by Custodian - A Custodian must:

239

(1) <u>Turnover</u>: Deliver to the trustee any of the above-listed property held by the Custodian or Transferred to the Custodian that is in the Custodian's custody control on the date that the Custodian first knew of the starting of the case

and   (2)   <u>Accounting</u>: File an accounting of any of the above-listed property of the Debtor that the Custodian controlled at any time

(c) Disbursements: After notice and a hearing, the court shall:
   (1) Protect all parties that the Custodian has become obligated to with respect to the Debtor's such property
   (2) Award the Custodian reasonable compensation for services and expenses incurred
   (3) <u>Custodian Liable for Wrongful Disbursements</u>:
      a.   The court shall hold the Custodian liable for any improper or excessive disbursement
      b.   <u>Exceptions</u>:
         1.   If the Custodian is an assignee for the benefit of the creditors that was appointed or took possession more than 120 days before the Petition date.
         2.   The disbursement was made in accordance with applicable law.
         3.   The disbursement was approved:
            a.   By a court of competent jurisdiction
      and   b.   After notice and a hearing
      and   c.   Before the start of the bankruptcy case

(d) Exceptions to Turnover: After notice and a hearing, the bankruptcy court:
   (1) <u>May</u> excuse the Custodian from subsection (a), (b), or (c) in the best interests of <u>creditors</u> and equity <u>Security holders</u> (if the Debtor is not Insolvent).
   (2) <u>Must</u> excuse the Custodian from subsections (a) and (b)(1) if:
      a.   The Custodian is an assignee for the benefit of the Debtor's creditors.
      and   b.   The Custodian was appointed or took possession more than <u>120 days</u> before the Petition date.
      and   c. Compliance is not necessary to prevent fraud or injustice.

§544: Avoiding Powers:

"The Strong-Arm Statute"
(a) Trustee's Avoidance Powers:
  i) At the commencement of the case, the Trustee shall have the
      1. Rights and powers of any Creditor
      2. Right to avoid any Transfer of Debtor's property
      3. Right to avoid any obligation incurred by the Debtor
  ii) These powers are received regardless of the Trustee or any
      Creditor knowledge
  iii) Scope of Avoidance Powers: Avoidance powers apply to
      obligations/ Transfers that are voidable by:
      (1) A Creditor that:
          a) Extends credit to Debtor by Petition date
      and b) Obtains a Judicial Lien with respect to such credit
              1. At Petition date
          and 2. On all property on which a Creditor on a
                  simple contract could have obtained such a
                  Judicial Lien, regardless of whether a Creditor
                  actually exists (i.e. a "Hypothetical Lien
                  Creditor")
      or (2) A Creditor that:
          a) Extends credit to the Debtor by the Petition date
      and b) Obtains an execution against the Debtor that is
              returned unsatisfied, regardless of its actual
              existence (i.e. "Hypothetical Lien Creditor")
      or (3) A Bona-Fide Purchaser of Real Property (other than
              fixtures) that buys from a Debtor:
          a) Against whom applicable law permits such
              Transfer to be perfected
          b) That obtains the status of Bona-Fide Purchaser
          c) Who has a perfected such Transfer by the Petition
              date, regardless of whether or not such a Purchaser
              actually exists (i.e. "Hypothetical Lien Creditor")

(b) Property and Interests the Trustee May Avoid:
    The Trustee may avoid any Transfer of interest of the Debtor in
    property/any obligation or Debt incurred by the Debtor that is:
    a. Voidable (under applicable law) by an unsecured Creditor
        who has an allowable claim under §502 (ALLOWANCE OF
        CLAIMS OF INTERESTS)

or　b.　Not allowable only under §502(e) (CLAIMS FOR
　　　　CONTRIBUTION OR REIMBURSEMENT)

§545: Statutory Liens:

The Trustee may avoid the fixing of a Statutory Lien on the Debtor's
property if:

(1)　The Statutory Lien became effective against the debtor:
　　　(A)　When the Bankruptcy Petition was filed
　　　(B)　When an Insolvency (other than under this Title) proceeding
　　　　　　against the debtor was commenced
　　　(C)　When a Custodian is Appointed or Authorized to take (or
　　　　　　actually takes) possession of Debtor's property
　　　(D)　When the Debtor becomes Insolvent
　　　(E)　At the execution of the property which was levied by
　　　　　　another Lien-holder

or (2)　Unperfected Liens: The Lien is not Perfected or Enforceable
　　　　　against a Bona Fide Purchaser at the time the Bankruptcy
　　　　　Petition is filed.

or (3)　Rents: It is for rent

or　(4)　It is a Lien of Distress for Rent

§546: Exceptions To Avoiding Powers:

(a)　Time Limitation: An action (under §544, §545, §547, §548, or
　　　§553) must be commenced after the earlier of:
　　　(1)　2 Years after Trustee's appointment
　　　(2)　The time the case is closed or dismissed

(b)　Trustee's avoidance powers are subject to:
　　　1)　Any generally applicable law permitting perfection to relate-
　　　　　back in time (thereby allowing a later Security Interest to be
　　　　　effective against an earlier interest in the same property).
　　　2)　An interest in property shall be perfected by notice if:
　　　　　a)　Such law dictates that perfection can only be
　　　　　　　accomplished by either:
　　　　　　　1.　Seizure of property
　　　　　or　2.　Commencement of an action

242

b) There has been no seizure or commencement by Petition date.
3) Notice must be made within the time fixed by the law requiring seizure or commencement (for perfection).

(c) Reclamation Rights:
The rights and powers of a Trustee (under §544(a), §545, §547, and §549) are subject to any rights (statutory or common law) of a Seller of Goods to reclaim goods sold to Debtor.

   (1) Requirements:
      a. Goods are sold in the Ordinary Course of the Seller's Business
      b. Debtor received goods while Insolvent
      c. Seller makes a written demand within 10 days after the Debtor received the goods

   (2) Seller's Right to Reclamation may be denied if the Court:
      (A) Grants Seller's claim under §503(b)(ADMINISTRATIVE EXPENSES ALLOWED)
  or (B) Secures Seller's claim by a Lien

(d) Crops * * *
(e,f) Trustee Cannot Avoid Margin Payments * * *
(g) Trustee Cannot Avoid "Swap Agreements" * * *

§547: Preferences:

(a) Definitions

   (1) Inventory - Personal Property which is:
      a. Leased or furnished
      b. Held for sale or lease
      c. To be furnished under a contract for service
      d. Raw Materials
      e. Work-in-process
      f. Materials used or consumed in business
      g. Farm products held for lease (such as crops or livestock)
   (2) New Value:
      a) This includes:
         1) Money

or 2) Money's worth in goods, services or new credit
or 3) Release by a Transferee of property (which was
        previously Transferred to it) in a valid transaction
        by the Debtor (or Trustee under applicable law)
        including proceeds of such property.
    b) An obligation substituted for an existing obligation is
        not considered new Value.

(3) Receivable - a right to payment (whether or not such right
     has been earned by performance)

(4) A Debt for a tax is incurred on the day when the tax is last
     payable without penalty (including any extensions).

(b) Voidable Preferences - A Trustee may avoid any Transfer of
     interest of the Debtor, in property which is:
     (1) To or for the benefit of a Creditor
and (2) For/on account of an Antecedent Debt (i.e. a past debt, owed
          by the Debtor before the Transfer was made, and not a
          contemporaneous exchange as in §547(c)(1))
and (3) Made while the Debtor was Insolvent
and (4) Made either:
          (A) Within 90 days of the Petition date
          (B) Within 1 Year of the Petition date for Insiders (as per
               §101)
and (5) A Transfer that enables the Creditor to receive more than he
          would if:
          (A) The case were under Chapter 7 (Liquidation (i.e. not
               over-secured as per §725))
          (B) The Transfer had not been made·
          (C) Creditor received payment of Debt under the
               Bankruptcy Code

(c) Exceptions (Savings Clauses):
     (1) Contemporaneous Exchanges: Transactions will be
          considered "contemporaneous" to the extent they were both:
          (A) Intended to be a Contemporaneous Exchange for new
               Value (ex: A check that is cashed within 30 days is
               considered contemporaneous).
          (B) In fact substantially a Contemporaneous Exchange (see
               §547(e)).

     (2) Ordinary Course of Business - Transfers qualify if:

(A) It was a payment of a Debt that was incurred in the Ordinary Course of Business.

and (B) It was made in the Ordinary Course of Business or financial affairs of the Debtor and the Transferee (ex: regular bond payments, regular installments on a loan).

and (C) Made according to Ordinary Business Terms.

(3) PMSI's - Qualify only if:
   (A) The Security Interest secures new Value that was:
      (i) Given at or after signing a Security Agreement (Security Agreement must contain description of new collateral)
      and (ii) Given by the Secured Party
      and (iii) Given as a PMSI (i.e. to enable Debtor to acquire property)
      and (iv) Was actually used by Debtor to acquire property (i.e. a "true PMSI").
   (B) It was perfected within 10 days after the Debtor receives possession of the property.

(4) New Value: A Transfer given to the Creditor who gave new Value after the Debtor made the Transfer , if:
   (A) The new Value was not secured by an unavoidable Security Interest (i.e. not perfected and, thus, subject to a Judicial Lien or the Trustee's Avoiding Powers under §546)
   (B) The Debtor did not make the Creditor better off than he would have been if the Creditor never gave the Debtor new Value (ex: over-secures, to extend to past debts)

(5) Floating Liens: New Perfected Security Interests in Inventory or Receivables, including their proceeds: As long as the Security Interest does not prejudice unsecured creditors by "over-securing" to cover debts made during the later of:
   (A) Either:
      (i) 90 Days before the Petition date (for a Transfer applying to §547(b)(4)(A)).
      (ii) 1 Year before the Petition date, if the Transfer was made by an "Insider" (as per §547(b)(4)(B)).
   (B) The date that new Value was first given under the Security Agreement (i.e. the Security Agreement which created the Security Interest).

245

(6) Unavoidable Statutory Liens (ex: Tax Liens, pursuant to
     §545) * * * *

(7) Payments to Ex-Spouses: * * * *

(8) Property of a Personal Debtor if:
     a)   The Debtor's debts are primarily Consumer Debts
and b)   The total Value of all affected Transferred property is
          less than $600.

(d) Avoiding Transfers to a Surety
     1)   The Trustee may avoid a Transfer of an interest in the
          Debtor's property which is to or for the benefit of a Surety
          if:
          a)   It is to secure reimbursement of the Surety
          b)   The Surety furnished a bond or other obligation to
               dissolve a Judicial Lien (which the Trustee could have
               avoided under 547(b)).
     2)   The liability of the Surety under such a bond/obligation
          shall be discharged to the extent of either:
          a)   The Value of such property recovered by the Trustee
     or   b)   The amount paid to the Trustee

(e) Time of Transfer (for purposes of this section)
     (1) Perfection:
          (A) Real Property (other than fixtures): Perfection occurs
              when a Bona-Fide Purchaser who buys from the Debtor
              (against whom applicable law permits such a Transfer
              to be perfected) cannot acquire an interest that is
              superior to that of the Secured Party (i.e. Recorded).
          (B) Personal Property (including fixtures): Perfection
              occurs when a Creditor cannot acquire a superior
              Judicial Lien to that of the Secured Party (i.e. Perfected,
              so it has superiority to Judicial Liens under UCC §9-
              301(1)(b)).
     (2) When Transfer is Made:
          (A) When the Transfer is actually made, if it is perfected
              within 10 days of Transfer
     or   (B) Upon perfection, if perfected after 10 days from the
              Transfer
     or   (C) Immediately before Petition is filed if it is not perfected
              by the later of:

(i) The commencement of the case (Petition date)
or (ii) <u>10 days</u> after the Transfer is actually made
(3) Debtor must acquire rights in property for Transfer to be made.

(f) Preference Period: The Debtor is presumed to have been Insolvent within the <u>90 days</u> immediately preceding the Petition date (for purposes of this section).

(g) Burden of Proof - For purposes of this section:
1. The Trustee has the burden of proving avoidability of a Transfer under §547(b).
2. The Creditor (or Party in Interest against whom the Trustee is seeking recovery or avoidance) has the burden of proving non-avoidability under §547(c).

§548: Fraudulent Transfers:

(a) Avoiding Transfers - A Trustee may avoid Transfers made within <u>1 year</u> of the Petition date if:
(1) The Debtor made the Transfer with actual intent to <u>hinder, delay</u> or <u>defraud</u> any other Creditors (including those created after the Transfer).
and (2) Either:
(A) Received <u>less than</u> a reasonable equivalent in exchange (for the Transfer /obligation)
(B) The Debtor was:
(i) Insolvent either:
1) As a result of the Transfer /obligation
or 2) When the Transfer was made
or (ii) Undercapitalized
or (iii) The Creditor knew/should have known that the Debtor could not "afford" the Transfer

(b) Trustee of a Partnership: A Trustee can generally avoid Transfers by an Insolvent partnership to a general partner if the Debtor was Insolvent when the Transfer was made (or became Insolvent as a result of the Transfer).

(c) Exception: Unless a Trustee can avoid the Transfer (under §544, §545, §546, or §547), a Creditor may retain its interest if it takes the Transfer or <u>obligation</u>:

    1)   For New Value
    2)   In Good Faith
    3)   For a "fair" price

(d) Terms of Transfer :
    (1) Time of Transfer (for purposes of this section):
        a)   A Transfer is made when it is so perfected that even a Bona-Fide Purchaser who buys from the Debtor (against whom applicable law permits such a Transfer to be perfected) cannot acquire an interest superior to that of the Transferee.
        b)   If such a Transfer is not so perfected (as indicated above) before the Petition date, then the Transfer will be deemed made immediately before the date of the filing of the Petition.

    (2) <u>Value</u>:
        (A) "<u>Value</u>" – General Definition:
            1.   "Value" means:
                a.   Property
           or   b.   Satisfaction of a present or antecedent debt
           or   c.   Securing of a present or antecedent debt
            2.   "Value" does not include an unfulfilled promise to support the Debtor or the Debtor's family.
        (B) A stock broker or commodity broker take "Value" if they:
            1.   Receive a <u>margin payment</u> (defined in §101, §741 or §761)
          or   2.   Receive a <u>settlement payment</u> (defined in §101 or §741)
        (C) A "Repo" participant takes "Value" if he:
            1.   Receives a <u>margin payment</u> (defined in §101, §741 or §761)
            2.   Receives a <u>settlement payment</u> (defined in §101 or §741)
        (D) A swap participant takes for Value if he receives a Transfer in connection with a Swap Agreement.

§549: Post-Petition Transactions:

(a) General Rule: Except as provided in §549 (b) or (c) below, the trustee may avoid a Transfer of Property of the Estate if:
  (1) It occurs <u>after</u> the filing of the bankruptcy Petition
and (2) <u>The Transaction was Unauthorized</u>
      (A) That is authorized only under §303(f) or §542(c) (which is meant to protect the Transferor only)
      or (B) That is not authorized under the Bankruptcy Code or by the court

(b) Involuntary Cases:
  1. The Trustee's power to avoid <u>post-Petition</u> Transfers (under §549(a)) will not be enforceable to the extent <u>Value</u> was given for such property if:
    a) The post-Petition Transfer was made <u>before</u> the Order for Relief was made (the "gap" period).
    and b) The Proceeding is an Involuntary Case.

  2. "Value" includes services, but not satisfaction or securing of a Debt that arose before the Petition was filed.

  3. Notice or knowledge of the Transferee is irrelevant in determining whether he is protected under this provision.

(c) Good Faith Purchaser Exception:
  1. <u>Real Property Purchased at Fair Value</u>: The trustee may not avoid (under (a)) a post-Petition Transfer of Real Property if:
    a. The Transferee was a good faith Purchaser without knowledge of the case
    and b. The Transferee gave present fair equivalent Value
    and c. A copy or notice of the Petition was not filed:
      i) In the place such a Transfer may be recorded to perfect it
      and ii) Before the Transfer is perfected in such a way that a bona fide Purchaser of the property (against whom the Transfer can be perfected) could not obtain an interest that is superior to the good faith Purchaser's interest.
  2. <u>Purchase for Less than Fair Value</u>: A Good Faith Purchaser without knowledge of the case and for less than present fair equivalent Value has a <u>Lien</u> on the property Transferred in the amount of any Value given, unless a copy or notice of the Petition was filed before the Transfer was perfected.

(d) Statute of Limitations - An action under §549 may not be commenced after the earlier of:
  (1) 2 years after the date of such Transfer
or (2) The date the bankruptcy case is closed or dismissed

§550: Liability of Transferee of Avoided Transfers:

(a) Persons Whom Trustee May Recover From:
  i) To the extent that a Transfer is avoided (under §544, §545, §548, §549, or §724(a)), the Trustee may recover (for the benefit of the estate):
    1) The Transferred property
  or 2) The Value of the property (if the court consents)
  ii) The Trustee may recover such property or Value from:
    (1) Either:
      a) The Initial Transferee
      or b) The Entity for whose benefit the Transfer was made
    or (2) Any Immediate or Intermediate Transferee of the initial Transferee

(b) Persons Whom Trustee May Not Recover From:
  (1) A Transferee (from the initial Transferee) who is a Good Faith Purchaser, taking the property:
    a) For Value (see definition above)
    and b) In Good Faith
    and c) Without knowledge that the Transfer was voidable
  (2) Any immediate or intermediate Good Faith Transferee of the Good Faith Purchaser

(c) Insiders: The Transferee may only recover property (under §550(a)) from an "Insider" if:
  (1) The Transfer was avoided under §547(b).
  and (2) The Transfer was made for the benefit of a Creditor who was an Insider at the time of the Transfer .
  and (3) The Transfer was made within 1 year of the filing, but before the 90 day Preference Period.

(d) Trustee Limited to Loss: The Trustee is only entitled to a single satisfaction under §550(a).

(e) Transferee's Rights in Recovered Property:

(1) Transferee's Lien on Recovered Property:
A Good Faith Transferee (from whom the Trustee may recover property under §550(a)) will obtain a Lien on the recovered property in an amount equal to the lesser of:
  (A) The cost the Transferee incurred in improving the property less any profit realized from it
  (B) Any increase in Value of the property resulting in the improvement
(2) "Improvement" under this section includes:
  (A) Physical additions or changes to the Transferred property
  (B) Repairs
  (C) Payment of any Tax on the property
  (D) Payment of any Debt secured by a Lien on the property (that is superior or equal to the rights of the trustee)
  (E) Preservation of the property

(f) Time Limit: An action or proceeding to recover property under §550 may not be commenced after the earlier of:
  (1) 1 year after the Transfer is avoided
or (2) The time the case is dismissed

§551: Automatic Preservation of Avoided Transfer :

1. The following avoided Transfers or Liens are automatically preserved for the benefit of the estate:
   a. Any Transfer avoided under §522, §544, §545, §547, §548, §549, or §724(a)
   or b. Any Lien void under section 506(d)

2. These Liens are preserved only with respect to Property of the Estate (this prevents the trustee from asserting an avoided tax Lien against after acquired property of the Debtor).

3. If a preserved Lien does not benefit the estate, the trustee may abandon it under §554.

4. The section prevents junior Lienholders from improving their position at the expense of the estate when a senior Lien is avoided.

§552: Post-Petition Effect of Security Interest:[51]

(a) After-Acquired Property: Property acquired by the Debtor or the estate <u>after</u> the bankruptcy Petition was filed will <u>not</u> become subject to a pre-Petition Security Interest or Lien covering after-acquired property.

(b) Exception - Post-Petition Proceeds:

(1) <u>When Security Interest Includes Post-Petition Proceeds</u>: If a pre-Petition Security Agreement covers <u>proceeds</u> or profits from collateral, then, even if such proceeds (or profits) are acquired <u>after</u> the Petition was filed.

(2) <u>When Security Interest Includes Post-Petition Rents, Fees and Charges</u>: If a pre-Petition Security Agreement covers <u>rents</u> from collateral, then, even if such rents (or other income from the property) are acquired <u>after</u> the Petition was filed.

(3) <u>Exceptions</u>: The above rules do not apply if:
  a. A court orders otherwise, after notice and a hearing and based on the equities of the case (the court may consider the expenses of the estate relating to proceeds and any related improvement in the secured party's position (like where raw materials are converted into inventory, or inventory into Accounts, at some expense to the estate, thus depleting the fund available for general unsecured creditors)).
  b. Except as provided in §§363, 506(c), 522, 544, 545, 547, and 548 (e.g., the trustee or Debtor in possession may use, sell, or lease proceeds, product, offspring, rents or profits under §363).

§553: Setoff:

(a) Right to Setoff:

---

51 Note: §552 applies to all Security Interests as defined in §101(51) of the bankruptcy code, not only to U.C.C. Security Interests

i) The rights of a Creditor to offset are not affected by Bankruptcy Provisions (except the Automatic Stay (§362) and §363) if:
   1) The Debt is a <u>Mutual Debt</u>.
   And 2) The Debt arose <u>before</u> the commencement of the case

ii) <u>Exceptions:</u> Setoffs may not be made to the extent that:
   (1) <u>Disallowed Claim:</u> The Creditor's claim is disallowed
   (2) <u>Assignment:</u> The Claim was <u>Transferred to the Creditor</u> by another entity, either:
      (A) After the Commencement of the Case
   or (B) During Insolvency:
         (i) Within the <u>90 day</u> Preference Period
      or (ii) While the Debtor was Insolvent
   (3) <u>Bad Intent:</u> The Creditor incurred its obligation to the Debtor:
      (A) Within the <u>90 day</u> Preference Period
      (B) While the Debtor was Insolvent
      (C) <u>Intent:</u> For the purpose of obtaining a right of setoff against the Debtor

(b) Limitation for Setoff: The Creditor may be no better than he would have been without having taken the Setoff:
   (1) If the Creditor made the Setoff during the <u>Preference Period,</u> the Trustee may recover from the setoff amount the difference between:
      1. The Insufficiency on the <u>later</u> of:
         (A) <u>90 Days</u> before Petition Date
      and (B) The first day (during the Preference Period) in which there is an insufficiency
   and 2. The Insufficiency on the date of the Setoff

   (2) "Insufficiency" is the amount Debtor owes the Creditor less that amount the Creditor owes the Debtor

(c) Presumption of Insolvency: The Debtor is presumed to be Insolvent during the <u>90-day</u> Preference Period.

§554: Abandonment of Property

(a) Grounds for Abandonment: The Trustee may abandon estate property (after a hearing and notice) if:

       1.   The property is <u>burdensome</u> to the estate.

or   2.   The property is of <u>inconsequential Value</u>.

(b) Court Ordered Abandonment: The court may order that the Trustee abandon estate property (for the same reasons indicated above):

       1.   After <u>notice</u> and a <u>hearing</u>

and 2.   Upon a Creditor's request

(c) Administered Property: Any property scheduled under §521(1) (DEBTOR'S DUTIES) and not otherwise administered when a case is closed is abandoned to the Debtor and administered for the purposes of §350 (CLOSING AND REOPENING CASES), unless the court orders otherwise.

(d) Property Not Abandoned: Property not <u>abandoned</u> or <u>administered</u> remains with the estate, unless the court orders otherwise.

Chapter 7: LIQUIDATION

§706: Conversion:

(a) Conversion by Debtor:
  1. <u>One Time Right to Convert</u>: The Debtor may convert a Chapter 7 case to a Chapter 11, 12, or 13 case at any time, if the case has not already been converted from another Chapter (under §1112, §1208, or §1307) (i.e. this is a one-time right) (Rationale: The Debtor should always be given the opportunity to repay his Debts).
  2. <u>Waivers Unenforceable</u>: Any waiver of the right to convert a case under §706(a) is unenforceable.

(b) Conversion to Chapter 11 by Court: After notice and hearing, the court may convert a Chapter 7 case to a Chapter 11 case at any time on request of a Party in Interest (the decision is in the court's discretion and is based on what will most be to the benefit of all parties in interest).

(c) Conversion to Chapter 12 or 13 by Court: The court <u>may not</u> convert a Chapter 7 to a Chapter 12 or 13 case without the Debtor's consent.

(d) Eligibility Requirement: A case <u>may not</u> be converted to another chapter unless the Debtor is eligible to be a Debtor under that chapter (regardless of the previous subsections).

Subchapter II – Collection, Liquidation, And Distribution of The Estate

§721: Authorization to Operate Business:

The court may authorize the trustee to operate the business of the Debtor for a limited period if it is:

    1. In the best interest of the estate

and 2. Is consistent with the orderly liquidation of the estate (ex: The operation of a watch company to convert watch movements and cases into completed watches which will bring much higher prices than the component parts would have brought.)

§722: Redemption:

a) Redeemable Property: An individual Debtor may redeem tangible personal property if:
    1) It is intended for <u>personal</u>, <u>family</u>, or <u>household</u> use
and 2) It was secured by a Lien securing a dischargeable consumer debt
and 3) It has either been:
        a. Exempt (under §522)
    or b. Abandonment (under §554)

b) Method of Redemption: Property may be redeemed when the Debtor pays the holder of the Lien the amount that the holder is secured by the Lien.

§724: Treatment of Certain Liens:

(a) Fines and Penalties: The Trustee may avoid a Lien that secures a claim for any fine or penalty arising before the Trustee was appointed (as specified in §726(a)(4)).

(b) Tax Liens - Allowable, unavoidable secured claims subject to a tax Lien, (or proceeds of such property), shall be distributed as follows:
    (1) To any holder of an allowed secured claim (as per §725) which is:
        a) Not avoidable under the Bankruptcy Code

and   b)   Senior to the tax Lien
(2) To holders of claims under §507(a)(1)-(7) claims (i.e. not tax claims) to the extent the tax claim is secured by the Lien
(3) To the holder of the Tax Lien, in the amount exceeding the distribution of (2) above
(4) To secured parties junior to the tax Lien
(5) The balance of the tax Lien holder's claim (not paid under (3) above)
(6) To the estate (under §727)

(c) Competing Claimants: If two claimants would be entitled to distribution under the same section in §724(b) above, then the distribution would be divided up as if the claim were not governed by this section.

(d) Statutory Liens shall be treated as tax Liens if their priority is to be determined under Internal Revenue Code §6323.

§725: Distribution of Certain Property:

Before property is to be distributed under §726 (and after the Petition has been filed), the Trustee must dispose of any estate property if:

a)   A Creditor has an interet in it (i.e. it is the collateral of a Secured Party).
And b)   The property has not been disposed of under another Bankruptcy Code section.
And c)   There was notice and a hearing.

§726: Distribution of Property of the Estate

(a) Priority of Distribution: Property of the Estate (left over after paying Secured Parties, Administrative Expenses, and Tax Liens) shall be distributed as follows (subject to §510's subrogation rights):
(1) Payments of §507 claims (distributed as per §507)
(2) Payment of any Allowed Unsecured Claim (not falling under other subsections of §726) if:
(A) It is timely filed under §501(a)
(B) It is timely Filed under §501(b)
(C) It is filed late, and:

(i) The Creditor holding the claim did not have <u>notice</u> or <u>actual knowledge</u> of the Bankruptcy in time to file timely;

and (ii) The Proof of Claim is filed in time to permit payment

(3) Allowable Unsecured Claims which were filed late (and not excused under §726(a)(2)(C)).

(4) Payment of any Secured or Unsecured Fine, Penalty, Forfeiture, or Punitive Damage if:

    a) They arose before the <u>earlier</u> of:

       1. The time the Trustee was appointed

  or 2. The time the Order of Relief was granted

and b) The damages or money was not compensation for actual monetary losses suffered by the claim holder

(5) Payment of Interest of all of the above claims (at Legal Rate form date of filing)

(6) To the Debtor

(b) Claimants Under The Same Distribution Class: If there is not enough money to cover the entire class, they shall receive a pro rata payment for their share of claims in their class. * * * *

(c) Distribution of Community Property * * * *

§727: Discharge:

(a) <u>The court must grant the Debtor a discharge</u> after assets have been distributed, <u>unless</u> one of the following 10 scenarios occurs:

(1) <u>Debtor Not an Individual</u> - The Debtor is not an individual (i.e. Corporations and partnerships may not be discharged in liquidation cases).[52]

OR (2) Transfer <u>of Property with Intent to Defraud</u> - The Debtor has Transferred, removed, destroyed, mutilated, or concealed (or has permitted) any of the following property with intent to hinder, delay, or defraud a creditor (or an officer of the estate entitled to possession of the property):

---

52 Rationale: This is to avoid trafficking in corporate shells and in bankrupt partnerships.

Note: "Individual" includes a deceased individual, so if the Debtor dies during the bankruptcy case, he will still be released from his Debts and his estate will not be liable for them. Creditors will be entitled to only satisfaction from the bankruptcy estate and not from the probate estate.

(A) Property of the Debtor - within 1 year before the
Petition date
or (B) Property of the Estate - after the Petition date

or (3) Unjustified Destruction or Concealment of Books and
Records - The Debtor has concealed, destroyed, mutilated,
falsified, or failed to keep or preserve any recorded
information, including books, documents, records, and
papers, that might reveal the Debtor's financial condition or
business transactions, unless the act (or failure to act) was
justified under all of the circumstances of the case.

or (4) Commission of Crime - The Debtor knowingly and
fraudulently commits one of the following crimes in
connection with the bankruptcy[53]:
(A) Made a false oath or account
or (B) Presented or used a false Claim
or (C) Gave, offered, received, or attempted to obtain money,
property, or advantage, or a promise of money,
property, or advantage, for acting or forbearing to act
or (D) Withheld any recorded information (including books,
documents, records, and papers) relating to the Debtor's
property or financial affairs from an officer of the estate
entitled to possession

or (5) Failure to Account for Loss of Assets - The Debtor has
failed to explain any loss of assets or deficiency of assets to
meet his liabilities.

or (6) Refusal to Obey Court Order - The Debtor has refused to do
any of the following:
(A) Obey any lawful court order, other than an order to
respond to a material question or to testify
or (B) Self-Incrimination:
1. The Debtor wishes to exercise the privilege against
self-incrimination
2. The Debtor has been granted immunity concerning
the matter

---

[53] Note: The standard of proof for these crimes is preponderance of the evidence rather
than proof beyond a reasonable doubt

3. The Debtor still refuses to respond to a material
question (approved by the court) or to testify

or (C) Respond to a material question (approved by the court)
or to testify (on a ground other than the privilege
against self-incrimination).

or (7) <u>Insider Cases</u> - The Debtor has committed any act
specified in grounds (2), (3), (4), (5), or (6), within <u>1</u>
<u>year</u> before the Petition date (or during the case), in
connection with another case concerning an Insider

or (8) <u>Prior Discharge - Chapter 7 or 11</u> - The Debtor was
granted a discharge (under this section, §1141, or §14,
§371, or §476 of the Bankruptcy Act) in a case filed
within <u>6 years</u> before the Petition date.

or (9) <u>Prior Discharge - Chapter 12 or 13</u> - The Debtor was
granted a discharge (under §1228 or §1328, or under
§660 or §661 of the Bankruptcy Act) in a case filed
within <u>6 years</u> before the Petition date, <u>unless</u> payments
under the plan in that case totaled at least:
(A) 100% of the allowed unsecured Claims in the case
(B) <u>Both</u>:
    (i) 70% of the allowed unsecured Claims in the
         case
and (ii) The plan was proposed by the Debtor in good
         faith, and was the Debtor's best effort.

or (10) <u>Waiver</u> - The court approves a written waiver of
discharge executed by the Debtor after the Chapter 7
Order for Relief.

(b) Effect of Discharge:
1. A discharge under subsection (a) discharges the Debtor
    from all Debts that arose before the date of the Order for
    Relief (except as provided in §523).
2. Any liability on a Claim that is considered to be a Claim
    that arose before the Petition date (under §502), whether or
    not:
    i) A proof of Claim based on any such Debt or liability is
        filed under §501
or ii) A Claim based on any such Debt or liability is allowed
        under §502.

(c) Objection to Discharge:
    (1) Any of the following may object to the granting of a discharge under subsection (a):
        a. The trustee
or b. A creditor
or c. The United States trustee
    (2) On request of a Party in Interest, the court may order the trustee to investigate the acts of the Debtor to determine whether there is a ground to deny discharge.

(d) Revocation of Discharge:
    1. Revocation of Discharge - The court must revoke a discharge granted under subsection (a) if:
        a. One of the grounds below exist
and b. The trustee, a creditor, or the United States Trustee requests
and c. There is notice and a hearing
    2. Grounds:
        (1) Fraud:
            a. The Debtor obtained the discharge through fraud
        and b. The requesting party did not know of the fraud until after the discharge was granted
or (2) Failure to Report Acquisition of Property:
        1. The Debtor either:
            a. Acquired property that is Property of the Estate
        or b. Became entitled property that would constitute Property of the Estate
        and 2. The Debtor either:
            a. Knowingly and fraudulently failed to report the acquisition of or entitlement to the property
        or b. Failed to deliver or surrender the property to the trustee
or (3) The Debtor committed one of the acts described in (a)(6).

(e) Limit for Revocation of Discharge - The trustee, a creditor, or the United States trustee may request a revocation of a discharge:
    (1) For discharges under (d)(1): Within 1 year after the discharge is granted
or (2) For discharges under (d)(2) or (d)(3): Before the later of:

    (A) <u>1 year</u> after the discharge is granted
and (B) The date the case is closed

CHAPTER 11: REORGANIZATION

Subchapter II – The Plan

§1121: Who May File A Plan:

(a) The Debtor
    1. The Debtor may file a reorganization plan.
    2. Time for Filing:
        a. Voluntary Case: At any time or with the Petition that commenced the case
        b. Involuntary Case: At any time after the Petition is filed

(b) 120-Day Rule - Debtor's Exclusive Right to File:
    1. Only the Debtor may file a plan during the first <u>120 days</u> after the Order for Relief is made.
    2. <u>Exceptions</u>: See §1121(c).

(c) When Any Party in Interest Files Plan:
    i) Any Party in Interest may file a plan before the <u>120-day</u> waiting period (in §1121(b)) if:
        (1) A Trustee has been appointed
    or (2) The Debtor does not file a plan within <u>120 days</u> after the Order for Relief
    or (3) The Debtor fails to file an plan that was accepted within <u>180 days</u> of the Order for Relief by each class of Claims or interests that is impaired under the plan.
    ii) "Party in Interest" includes:[54]
        a. The Debtor
        b. The Trustee
        c. A creditors committee
        d. An equity Security holders committee
        e. A creditor
        f. An equity Security holder
        g. Any Indenture trustee

(d) Extension of Deadlines: The court may increase or reduce the 120-day and 180-day periods if:

---

[54] This list is not exhaustive (ex: In the case of a public company, a Trustee is appointed within 10 days of the Petition; then, for most purposes any Party in Interest may file a plan).

    i.   A "Party in Interest" makes a request within the periods and ii.   There is <u>notice</u> and a <u>hearing</u>[55]

(e) Small Business Exception: If the Debtor elects to be considered a Small Business:
    (1) The Debtor may file a plan until <u>100 days</u> after the Order for Relief is filed.
    (2) All plans must be filed within the first <u>160 days</u> after the Order for Relief is filed.
    (3) Extensions and Reductions:
        i.   The court may:
           (A) <u>Reduce</u> the <u>100-day</u> period ((e)(1)) or the 160-day period ((e)(2)) for cause
       and (B) <u>Increase</u> the <u>100-day</u> period ((e)(1)), only if the Debtor shows that the extension is needed because of circumstances which he did not cause.
        ii. Requirements:
           A. A "Party in Interest" makes a request within the period.
       And   B. There is notice and a hearing.

§1122: Classification of Claims or Interests:

(a) Interests and Claims in Same Class: A Claim or an interest may be placed in the same class if it is "substantially similar" to the other Claims or interests in that class.

(b) Exception: The plan may designate a separate class of Claims for unsecured Claims which are not "substantially similar" if:
    1. Each Claim in the class is <u>less than</u> (or reduced to) a certain "approved amount."
    2. The "approved amount" is found by the court to be <u>reasonable and necessary</u> for administrative convenience.

---

[55] Note: Under §1121(a) the Debtor has an exclusive privilege for 6 months to file a plan. Therefore, the legislative notes to §1121 State that an extension should be based on a showing of probable success; an extension should not be used as a tactical device to put pressure on parties in interest to yield to a plan they might not agree with.

§1123: Contents of Plan:

(a) Requirements for the Contents of a Plan – The following is required in a Reorganization Plan (regardless of any other applicable non-bankruptcy law):

   (1) Designation of Classes:
      i. The plan must designate classes of Claims and interests (subject to §1122).
      ii. Priority Claims Exception: Priority Claims (specified in §507(a)(1), §507(a)(2), or §507(a)(8)) are not required to be classified (since they may not have arisen when the plan is filed).

   (2) Unimpaired Claims: The plan must specify Claims or interests that are unimpaired by the plan (ex: Secured Claims).

   (3) Impaired Claims:
      i. The plan must specify the treatment of any class of Claims or interests that is impaired under the plan.
      ii. This paragraph applies to Claims, not creditors.[56]

   (4) Equal Treatment Within a Class:
      i. The plan must provide the same treatment for each Claim or interest in a particular class.
      ii. Exception: The holder of a particular Claim or interest can agree to a different treatment of that Claim, so long as it is not better.

   (5) Execution of the Plan:
      i. The plan must provide adequate means for its execution.
      ii. These means may include the following:
        (A) Retain Property: The Debtor retains all (or any part of) the estate's property.
        (B) Transfer Property: The estate's property is Transferred (all or any part) to 1 or more entities, whether organized before or after the plan is confirmed.
        (C) Merger or Consolidation: The Debtor merges or consolidates with 1 or more Persons.

---

[56] Therefore, if a creditor is under-secured, and so has both a secured Claim and an unsecured Claim, this paragraph will be applied to each of his Claims.

(D) <u>Sale of Property</u>: The Property of the Estate (all or any part) is sold. The sale is either subject to or free of:
    1. Any Lien
or 2. The distribution of the estate's property (all or any part) among "interested parties"
(E) Satisfaction or modification of any Lien.
(F) Cancellation or modification of any Indenture or similar instrument (This might include a deposit with an agent for distribution (not an Indenture trustee)).
(G) Any default is cured or waived.
(H) Changing Terms of Outstanding Securities - For example:
    1. An extension of a maturity date
or 2. A change in an interest rate
or 3. A change in some other term
(I) The Debtor's charter is amended.
(J) The securities of the Debtor (or any other Entity referred to in (B) or (C)) are issued for:
    1. Cash
    2. Property
    3. Existing securities
    4. In exchange for Claims or interests
    5. For any other appropriate purpose

(6) Voting Power for Classes of Securities:
    i. The plan must prohibit the issuing of non-voting equity securities, by requiring a provision to this effect in the Debtor's charter (if the Debtor if a Corporation; otherwise, in the charter of any Corporation referred to in (5)(B) or (5)(C)).
    ii. The plan must provide for an appropriate distribution of voting power among the various classes of equity securities (ex: if one class has a preference over another with respect to dividends, the plan would have to provide for the election of directors representing the preferred class in the event of default in the payment of such dividends).

(7) <u>Selection of Officers, Directors, Trustees</u>: The plan's provisions for the selection of officers, directors and trustees (and their successors) <u>must be</u> consistent with:

i. The interests of creditors and equity Security holders
and ii. Public policy

(b) Matters That a Plan May Propose (subject to (a)):
(1) The plan may impair or leave unimpaired any class of Claims (secured or unsecured) or interests.

and (2) Executory Contracts: The plan may provide that any executory contract or unexpired lease of the Debtor that was not previously rejected under §365, be:
a. assumed
or b. rejected
or c. assigned.

and (3) Pursuing Claims and Interests - The plan may provide for:
(A) the settlement or adjustment of any of the Debtor's or the estate's Claims or interests
or (B) the retention and enforcement of any Claim or interest by:
1. The Debtor
2. The Trustee
3. A representative of the estate appointed for that purpose

and (4) Sale of Property (This would be a "liquidating plan") - The plan may provide for:
a. The sale of (all or substantially all) of the estate's property
and b. The distribution of the sale proceeds among Claim holders

and (5) Modification of Rights of Claim Holders:
a. The plan may modify the rights of holders of secured Claims.
b. This does not include a Claim secured only by a Security Interest in the Debtor's principal residence.
c. The plan may also leave the rights of holders of any class of Claims unaffected

and (6) Other Provisions: The plan may include any other appropriate provision not inconsistent with the Bankruptcy Code.

(c) Cases Concerning Individuals: To protect individual Debtors, a plan may not provide for the use, sale, or lease of property exempted under §522, unless:
1. The plan is proposed by the Debtor

267

or   2.   The Debtor consents

(d) Curing Defaults: If a plan proposes to cure a default, the amount
     necessary to cure the default is to be determined by:
     1.   The underlying agreement
and 2.   Applicable non-bankruptcy law (regardless of subsection (a)
          and §506(b), 1129(a)(7), and 1129(b))

§1124: Impairment of Claims or Interests:[57]

a)   Definition of "Impaired" Claim - A class of Claims or interests
     is "impaired" under a plan unless:
     (1) The plan does not change the rights (legal, equitable, and
          contractual) that each Claim in a class entitles its holder.
or   (2) Defaults:
          (A) The plan cures any default (other than those described
              in §365(b)(2), i.e. a default under an ipso facto or
              bankruptcy clause) that occurred before or after the
              commencement of the case.
          And(B) The plan reinstates the original maturity date of a Claim
              or interest.
          And(C) The plan pays the Claim holder for any damages
              resulting from his reasonable reliance on a contractual
              provision or law that would entitle him to accelerate
              payment after the default.
          and (D) The plan does not otherwise change the rights (legal,
              equitable, and contractual) of the Claim holder.

b)   Exception: Consent to less-favorable treatment under
     §1123(a)(4) is not an "impairment."

§1125: Post-Petition Disclosure and Solicitation:

(a) Definitions for this Section:

---

[57] Note: This section does not include payment "in property" other than cash. Except
for a rare case, Claims payable in property (by their terms), but a plan may provide
that and any affected Persons may accept or reject the proposed plan. They may not be
forced to accept a plan declaring the holders' Claims or interests to be "unimpaired."

(1) "Adequate Information"

  a.   <u>Definition</u>: Information that would enable (by its type and detail) a hypothetical reasonable investor (typical of Claim holders of the relevant class) to make an informed judgment about the plan.

  b.   Both the kind and form of information are left to the court's discretion, guided by what is reasonably practicable, taking into account:
   1.   The nature and history of the Debtor
and 2.   The condition of the Debtor's books and records

  c.   "Adequate Information" <u>does not</u> have to include similar information about other possible or proposed plans

(2) "Investor typical of holders of Claims or interests of the relevant class" is an investor that has:
  (A)   A Claim or interest of the relevant class
and (B)   A relationship with the Debtor that is similar to all other Claim holders of the class.
and (C)   The ability to obtain information (other than the disclosure required by this section) from sources that the other Claim holders of the class generally have.

(b)   Solicitations for Plan: An acceptance or rejection of a plan may <u>only</u> be solicited from a Claim holder if:
  1.   The solicitation is made after the commencement of the case
and 2.   The following is sent to the solicited Claim holder either during or before the solicitation:
   a.   The plan or a summary of the plan
and b.   A written disclosure statement containing "Adequate Information," as approved by the court:
    i.   The court determines "Adequate Information" in a <u>hearing</u> with <u>notice</u>.
    ii.   The court may approve a disclosure statement without a valuation of the Debtor or an appraisal of the Debtor's assets (Note that in some cases, a valuation or appraisal will be necessary to develop Adequate Information).

(c) Similarity of Disclosure Statements:
  1. The same disclosure statement shall be transmitted to each Claim holder of the same class.
  2. Different classes may be sent different disclosure statements (i.e. differing in amount, detail, or kind of information).

(d) Determining the Adequacy of a Disclosure Statement:
  1. The court does not have to follow any otherwise applicable Federal or State law in determining if there is "Adequate Information" in the submitted disclosure statement.
  2. An agency or official who administers or enforces such a law <u>may</u> be heard on the issue of whether a disclosure statement has "Adequate Information."
  3. The agency or official <u>may not</u> appeal an order approving a disclosure statement.

(e) "Safe Harbor" Provision for Good Faith Solicitation
  1. <u>General Rule</u>: A Person that solicits or participates in the <u>offer, issuance, sale</u> or <u>purchase</u> of securities in good faith is not responsible for violating any law governing such solicitation or offers, issuances, sales, or purchases of securities (anti-fraud laws), if:
      a. <u>Good Faith Requirement</u>: The Person that solicits acceptance or rejection of a plan, or participates in the securities dealings must do so in good faith
   and b. In compliance with the provisions of the Bankruptcy Code
   and c. Securities in Offer, Issuance, Sale or Purchase belonged to:
          i. The Debtor
       or ii. An Affiliate participating in a joint plan with the Debtor
       or iii. A successor to the Debtor newly organized under the plan
  2. <u>Note</u>: §1125(e) does not affect civil or criminal liability for defects and inadequacies that are beyond the limits of good faith.

(f) Small Businesses:
  i. A "Small Business" is a Debtor who has elected under §1121(e) to be considered a Small Business

ii. <u>Special Rules for Small Businesses</u> (notwithstanding subsection (b)):
   (1) The court may conditionally approve a disclosure statement (subject to final approval after notice and a hearing).
   (2) A conditionally approved disclosure statement may be used to solicit acceptances and rejections of a plan, <u>as long as</u>:
      a. The Debtor provides Adequate Information to each solicited Claim holder.
      b. The conditionally approved disclosure statement is mailed at least <u>10 days</u> before the hearing on confirmation of the plan.
   (3) A hearing on the <u>disclosure statement</u> may be combined with a hearing on <u>confirmation of a plan</u>.

§1126: Acceptance of Plan:

(a) Who May Accept:
   1. The holder of a Claim (allowed under §502) may <u>accept</u> or <u>reject</u> a plan.
   2. The Secretary of the Treasury may <u>accept</u> or <u>reject</u> the plan on behalf of the United States if the U.S. is a creditor or equity Security holder.

(b) Pre-Petition Solicitation: For the purposes of §1126(c) and (d), a Claim holder that has accepted or rejected the plan before the commencement of the case is deemed to have accepted or rejected the plan (as the case may be) if:
   (1) <u>Applicable Non-Bankruptcy Law</u>: The solicitation was in compliance with any applicable non-bankruptcy law that governs whether disclosure in connection with the solicitation is adequate.
or (2) <u>If there is no Law or Rule</u>: The solicitation occurred after disclosure of "Adequate Information" (defined in §1125(a)) to the holder.

(c) Acceptances by An Entire Class of Claimants: A plan is "accepted" by a class of Claims if:

   1. The plan has been accepted by creditors holding at least 2/3 <u>the amount</u> of the allowed Claims of the class that are voted.

and 2.   The plan has been accepted by creditors holding at least ½ the number of the allowed Claims of the class that are voted.

and 3.   The creditors are not entities discounted under

§1126(e) (ACCEPTANCE OR REJECTION IN BAD FAITH).

(d) Required Amount of Acceptances for a Class of Interests: A plan is "accepted" by a class of interests if:
1.   The plan has been accepted by creditors holding at least 2/3 the amount of the allowed interests of the class that are voted.
and 2.   The plan has been accepted by creditors holding at least ½ the number of the allowed interests of the class that are voted.
and 3.   The creditors are not entities designated under §1126(e).

(e) Exclusions from Calculations for Acceptance or Rejection in Bad Faith:
1.   The following Claims are excluded from the calculations in (c) and (d):
   a.   Claims not voted in good faith
and b.   Claims procured or solicited not in good faith
and c.   Claims procured or solicited not in accordance with the Bankruptcy Code
2.   Requirements for Such an Exclusion:
   a.   A Party in Interest makes a request
and b.   Notice and a hearing

(f) Presumed Acceptance of Plan – Unimpaired Classes:
1.   A class (and each Claim holder in the class) that is not impaired under a plan is conclusively presumed to have accepted the plan (regardless of any other provision in §1126).
2.   Acceptances from the Claim holders of the class therefore do not have to be solicited.

(g) No Presumed Acceptance of Plan – Classes With No Priority: A class of Claim holders that is not entitled under the plan to receive (or retain) any property under the plan on account of their Claims is deemed <u>not</u> to have accepted a plan (regardless of any other provision in §1126).

§1127: Modification of Plan:

(a) Modification Prior to Confirmation:
   1. <u>Who May Modify</u>: Only the proponent of a plan may modify the plan <u>at any time</u> before confirmation.
   2. <u>Requirements</u>: The modification is subject to the requirements of §1122 and §1123 (CLASSIFICATION AND CONTENTS OF A PLAN).
   3. <u>Effect of Modification</u>: After the proponent of a plan files a modification of the plan with the court, the plan as modified becomes the plan, and is to be treated the same as an original plan.

(b) Modification After Confirmation:
   1. Who May Modify:
      a. The proponent of the plan
   or b. The reorganized Debtor

   2. Requirements:
      a. The modification must be proposed before substantial consummation of the original plan.
   and b. The requirements of §1122 and §1123 (CLASSIFICATION AND CONTENTS OF A PLAN) continue to apply.
   3. <u>Confirmation</u> - The plan as modified under this subsection becomes the plan only if:
      a. The court, after notice and a hearing, confirms the plan as modified under §1129 (CONFIRMATION OF A PLAN).
   and b. The circumstances warrant the modification.

(c) Compliance with §1125: The proponent of a modification shall comply with §1125 (DISCLOSURE REQUIREMENTS) with respect to the modified plan (Note that if the modifications were minor enough, the court under the circumstances might not require additional disclosure).

(d) Presumed Acceptance of Modification: Any Claim holder that has accepted/rejected a plan is deemed to have accepted or rejected (as the case may be) the modification, <u>unless</u>, within the time fixed by the court, the holder changes his previous acceptance or rejection.

§1128: Confirmation Hearing:

(a) After notice, the court shall hold a hearing on confirmation of a plan.
(b) Only a "Party in Interest" may object to confirmation of a plan.[58]

§1129: Confirmation of Plan:

(a) Requirements: The court <u>must</u> confirm a plan if:

    (1) The plan complies with the applicable provisions of the Bankruptcy Code (ex: §§1122 and 1123: CLASSIFICATION AND CONTENTS OF A PLAN).

and (2) The proponent of the plan complies with the applicable provisions of the Bankruptcy Code (ex: §1125: DISCLOSURE).

and (3) The plan has been proposed in good faith and not by any unlawful means.

and (4) Payments Made are Reasonable:

    a. Any payment made (or to be made) in connection with the case have been approved by (or is subject to approval by) the court as reasonable.
    b. Payments include payments made for:
        1. Services or costs/expenses in connection with the case
        2. Services or costs/expenses in connection with the plan and incident to the case
    c. Payments include those made by:
        1. The proponent of the plan
        2. The Debtor
        3. A Person issuing securities or acquiring property under the plan

---

[58] Note: The Securities and Exchange Commission and Indenture trustees, as parties in interest under §1109, may object to confirmation of the plan.

and (5) Disclosures - Identity of Officers, Directors and Insiders

    (A) Individuals in Office
        (i) The plan must disclose the identity and affiliations of any individual proposed to serve as any of the following after confirmation:
               a. Director of the reorganized Debtor
        or b. Officer of the reorganized Debtor
        or c. Voting trustee of the reorganized Debtor
        or d. An Affiliate of the Debtor participating in a joint plan with the Debtor
        or e. A successor to the Debtor under the plan

    and (ii) The appointment to (or continuance in) one of these offices by the individual must be consistent with:
               a. The interests of creditors and equity Security holders
       and b. Public policy

and (B) Insiders - The plan must also disclose:
        1. The identity of any Insider that will be employed/retained by the reorganized Debtor
    and 2. The nature of any compensation to be paid to the Insider

(6) Approval of Governmental Agency:
    a. Any governmental regulatory commission that will have jurisdiction over the Debtor after confirmation of the plan (i.e. the Debtor's rates are regulated by the government) must approve any rate change provided for in the plan.
    b. The rate change may be conditioned on the agency's approval instead.

(7) Impaired Classes of Claims - The court must confirm the plan if it finds:

    (A) Unsecured Claims:
        (i) That there is unanimous consent of all affected Claim holders.
    or (ii) Each Claim holder will get (or retain) property equal to or greater than what the creditor would get

if the Debtor were liquidated under Chapter 7 on the plan's effective date.

Note: This standard adapts the test of "best interest of creditors." It is given broad application in Chapter 11 since a Chapter 11 plan may affect not only unsecured Claims but also secured Claims and stock.

or   (B) Secured Claims (Claim holder makes an election under §1111(b)(2)): That each Claim holder will get (or retain) property equal to or greater than the creditor's share of the estate's interest in the collateral on the plan's effective date.

(8) Other Classes:
    (A) The class has accepted the plan; OR
    (B) The class is not impaired under the plan.

(9) Priority Claims Must be Paid in Full - The plan provides that (unless the Claim holder agrees otherwise):

    (A) Administrative Expense and Certain Unsecured Claims (specified in §507(a)(1) or §507(a)(2)): The Claim holder will get (on the plan's effective date) cash equal to the allowed amount of the Claim.
    (B) Other Claims (specified in §507(a)(3), §507(a)(4), §507(a)(5), §507(a)(6), or §507(a)(7)) - Each Claim holder of the class will get:
       (i) If the class has accepted the plan - Deferred cash payments that would equal the allowed amount of the Claim on the plan's effective date; OR
       (ii) If the class has not accepted the plan - Cash that would equal the allowed amount of the Claim on the plan's effective date.

    (C) Claims for Alimony or Child Support (specified in §507(a)(8)):
       i.   The Claim holder will get deferred cash payments that would equal the allowed amount of the Claim on the plan's effective date.
       ii. The payments may not extend over a period exceeding 6 years after the date of assessment of the Claim.

(10) <u>Impaired Classes</u>: At least one class of Claims that is impaired (not including Insiders) under the plan has accepted the plan (if there are any impaired classes).

(11) Liquidation Is Not Likely:
    a. The plan's confirmation is <u>not likely</u> to be followed by either:
       i. Liquidation of the Debtor (or any successor under the plan)
    or ii. The need for further financial reorganization of the Debtor (or successor)
    b. <u>Exception</u>: If the liquidation or reorganization is proposed in the plan.

(12) Bankruptcy Fees:
    a. Payment:
       i. All fees payable under 28 USC §1930 (BANKRUPTCY FEES) have been paid
    or ii. The plan provides for the payment of all such fees on its effective date.
    b. Whether Bankruptcy Fees are payable is determined by the court at the hearing on the plan's confirmation.

(13) Retiree Benefits:
    a. The plan provides that all retiree benefits are continued after its effective date until the end of the period the Debtor has obligated itself to provide those benefits.
    b. "Retiree Benefits" is defined in §1114.
    c. The level of benefits is established by §1114(e)(1)(B) or (g), at any time prior to the plan's confirmation.

(b) The "Cram-Down": Alternatives for Confirmation of a Plan:[59]

(1) Requirements for a "Cram Down":
    a. The plan must not discriminate unfairly, and must be "Fair and Equitable," with respect to each class of Claims or interests that is impaired under the plan and has not been accepted.

---

[59] Note: Together with §1111(b) and §1129(a)(7)(C), this section provides when a plan may be confirmed, notwithstanding the failure of an impaired class to accept the plan under §1129(a)(8). This alternative confirmation standard is called "cram down."

and b.   All of the applicable requirements of §1129(a) must be met, with the exception of (a)(8).

and c.   A "cram down" will only be used at the request of the plan's proponent.

(2)   Definition of "Fair and Equitable" - For the purpose of this §1129(b), a plan is "Fair and Equitable" if it meets the following requirements:

     (A) For a Class of Secured Claims:

         (i)   Claim Holders Retain Security Interest and Receive Cash Payments - The plan provides that:

             (I)   The Claim holders retain the Liens securing their Claims (to the extent of the allowed amount of the Claims) whether the Debtor retains the secured property or Transfers it.

       and (II)   Each Claim holder in the class receive deferred cash payments totaling at least the allowed amount of his Claim, equal to (as of the plan's effective date) at least the creditor's share of the estate's interest in the property.

   or   (ii)   Sale of Property:

         a.   The plan provides for a sale (subject to §363(k)) of any property that is subject to the Liens securing the Claims.

         b.   The sale is to occur free and clear of those Liens.

         c.   The Liens are to attach to the proceeds of the sale.

         d.   The treatment of those Liens on the proceeds are to be in accordance with (i) or (iii).

   or   (iii)   "Indubitable Equivalent" - The plan provides the "indubitable equivalent" of the Claim holders' Claims.

     (B) For a Class of Unsecured Claims:

         (i)   The plan provides that each Claim holder in the class get (or retain) property whose Value is equal to the allowed amount of the Claim on the plan's effective date.

or (ii) A holder whose Claim is junior to the Claims of the class does not receive (or retain) any property for his Claim.

(C) For a Class of Interests:

(i) The plan provides that each interest holder in the class receive (or retain) property equal to (Value as of the plan's effective date) the greater of:
  a. The allowed amount of any fixed liquidation preference that the holder is entitled to
or b. The allowed amount of any fixed redemption price that the holder is entitled to
or c. The allowed amount of the interest

or (ii) A holder whose interest is junior to the interests of the class does not receive (or retain) any property for his interest.

(c) Multiple Plan Meeting Requirements – Confirmation of Best Plan:

1. The court may only confirm 1 plan, unless the order of confirmation in the case has been revoked under §1144 (REVOCATION OF AN ORDER FOR CONFIRMATION).
2. If the requirements for confirmation (§1129(a) and (b)) are met by more than 1 plan, the court must consider what the creditors and equity Security holders prefer in deciding which plan to confirm.
3. Exception: As provided in §1127(b) (MODIFICATION AFTER CONFIRMATION)

(d) Denial of Confirmation

1. The court may deny confirmation of a plan if its principal purpose is:
  a. To avoid taxes (through use of §346 and §1146, and applicable provisions of State law or the Internal Revenue Code (Title 26) governing bankruptcy reorganizations)
or b. To avoid §5 of the Securities Act of 1933 (15 U.S.C. §77e: COMMUNICATIONS GUIDELINES FOR SELLING SECURITIES) (through use of §1145).

2. Requirements:
    a. <u>Request by Government</u>: A "Party in Interest" that is a
        Governmental Unit makes a request.
    b. <u>Burden of Proof</u>: The Governmental Unit has the
        burden of proof on the issue of avoidance.

Subchapter III – Postconfirmation Matters

§1141: Effect of Confirmation:

(a) Persons Bound By Plan:
    1. The provisions of a confirmed plan are binding on:
        a. The Debtor
        b. Any Entity issuing securities under the plan
        c. Any Entity acquiring property under the plan
        d. Any creditor
        e. Any equity Security holder
        f. Any general partner in the Debtor

    2. Creditors, Shareholders and General Partners are bound
        regardless of:
        a. Whether their Claim is impaired under the plan.
   and b. Whether they have accepted the plan.

    3. <u>Exceptions</u>: See (d)(2) and (d)(3) below (EXCEPTIONS TO
        DISCHARGE: TAXES; EXCEPTIONS FOR DEBTOR'S NON-
        COOPERATION).

(b) Vesting of Property - The confirmation of a plan vests all of the
     estate's property in the Debtor, unless otherwise provided in:
    1. The plan
   or 2. The order confirming the plan

(c) Property Free and Clear of Claims and Interests:
    1. After confirmation, the property dealt with by the plan is
        <u>free and clear</u> of all Claims and interests of:
        a. Creditors
   and b. Equity Security holders
   and c. General partners in the Debtor
    2. Exceptions - If otherwise provided in:
        a. The plan

or b. The order confirming the plan

or c. Subsections (d)(2) and (d)(3) below (EXCEPTIONS TO DISCHARGE: TAXES; EXCEPTIONS FOR DEBTOR'S NON-COOPERATION).

(d) Discharge for Reorganized Debtor:

(1) Discharge of Debts

    i. Debts That Are Discharged:
    (A) The following Debts are discharged upon confirmation of the plan:
      1. Debts that arose before the date of the confirmation.

and 2. Any Debt specified in §502(g), 502(h), or 502(i), regardless of:

    (i) Whether a proof of the Claim based on the Debt is filed (or deemed filed) under §501

or (ii) Whether the Claim is allowed under §502

or (iii) Whether the Claim holder has accepted the plan

and (B) The confirmation also terminates all rights and interests of equity Security holders and general partners provided for by the plan.

    ii. Exceptions - If otherwise provided in:
    a. This subsection

or b. The plan

or c. The order confirming the plan

(2) Exceptions to Discharge: Taxes - The confirmation of a plan does not discharge an individual Debtor from any Debt falling under §523 (EXCEPTIONS TO DISCHARGE).[60]

---

[60] Note: Non-dischargeable taxes are the priority taxes (under §507) and tax payments which come due during and after the proceeding under a deferred or part-payment agreement which the Debtor had entered into with the tax authority before the bankruptcy proceedings began.

A Corporation which is taken over by its creditors through a plan of reorganization will not continue to be liable for non-priority taxes arising from the Corporation's (a) pre-Petition fraud, (b) failure to file a return, or (c) failure to file a timely return, since the creditors who take over the reorganized company should not bear the burden of acts for which the creditors were not at fault.

(3) Exceptions for Debtor's Non-Cooperation:
The Debtor is <u>not</u> discharged by confirmation if:
(A) The plan is a liquidating plan (it provides for the liquidation of all (or substantially all) of the estate's property).
And(B) The Debtor does not engage in business after consummation of the plan.
And (C) The Debtor would be denied a discharge under §727(a) if the case were a Chapter 7 case.

(4) Waiver of Discharge - The court may approve a written waiver of discharge executed by the Debtor after the Order for Relief.

§1142: Implementation of Plan:

(a) Carrying Out Plan
1. The Debtor and any Entity organized (or to be organized) to carry out the plan must carry out the plan and must comply with any court orders.
2. This applies regardless of any otherwise applicable non-bankruptcy law, rule, or regulation relating to financial condition.

(b) Acts Necessary to Consummate Plan: The court may direct the Debtor (and any other necessary party) to:
1. <u>Execute any instrument</u> (or join in its execution) that is needed to Transfer property included in a plan.
2. <u>Deliver any instrument</u> (or join in its delivery) that is needed to Transfer property included in a plan.
3. <u>Perform any other act</u> (including satisfying any Lien) that is necessary for the consummation of the plan.

§1143: Distribution:

1. 5-Year Limitation on Presentment or Surrender of Securities - The following actions must be done within 5 years:
a. Presentment or surrender of a Security (if the plan so requires)
or b. Performing any other act as a condition to participation in distribution under the plan

2. The 5 years runs from the date the order of confirmation is entered.
3. Any Entity that does not take the appropriate action with the 5-year period is barred from participating in the distribution under the plan.

§1144: Revocation of an Order of Confirmation:

a. When a Court May Revoke - The court may revoke an order of confirmation order only if the order was procured by fraud.

b. Requirements:
    1. Request: Request of a Party in Interest
    2. Time: The request must be made at any time before 180 days after the date the order of confirmation is entered.
    3. Notice: There must be notice and a hearing

c. Contents of Order of Revocation - An order revoking an Order of Confirmation must:
    (1) Contain the provisions that are necessary to protect any Entity acquiring rights in good faith reliance on the order of confirmation;
and (2) Revoke the discharge of the Debtor.

§1145: Exemption From Securities Laws:

(a) Exemption From Securities Laws:
    i. Securities offered or sold by the Debtor (see list below) are exempt from the following registration requirements:
        a. §5 of the Securities Act of 1933 (15 U.S.C. §77e: COMMUNICATIONS GUIDELINES FOR SELLING SECURITIES); AND
        b. Any State or local law requiring registration or licensing of:
            1. An issuer of a Security
            2. Underwriter of a Security
            3. Securities broker or dealer

    ii. Exception: An Entity that is an "underwriter" (as defined in subsection (b)) is not exempt.
    iii. Securities Exempted:

283

(1)　The offer or sale of any Security of the Debtor (or an
　　　Affiliate in a joint plan with the Debtor or a successor
　　　to the Debtor under the plan)
　　(A)　In exchange for any of the following:
　　　　1.　A Claim against the Debtor or Affiliate
　　　　2.　An interest in the Debtor or Affiliate
　　　　3.　A Claim for an Administrative Expense in the
　　　　　　case concerning the Debtor or Affiliate; OR
　　(B)　Principally in exchange for any of the above and in
　　　　part for cash or property;　OR
(2)　Subscription Rights and Conversion Privileges:
　　a.　The offer of a Security through any of the
　　　　following, so long as they were sold in the manner
　　　　specified in paragraph (1):
　　　　1.　Warrant
　　　　2.　Option
　　　　3.　Right to subscribe
　　　　4.　Conversion privilege; OR
　　b.　The sale of a Security upon the exercise of the
　　　　warrant, option, right, or privilege[61]

(3)　The offer or sale (other than under a plan) of a Security
　　　of an issuer other than the Debtor or an Affiliate, if:
　　(A)　The Security was owned by the Debtor on the
　　　　Petition date; AND
　　(B)　The issuer of such Security is:
　　　　(i)　Required to file reports under §13 or 15(d) of
　　　　　　the Securities Exchange Act of 1934 (15
　　　　　　U.S.C.§78m)[62]; AND
　　　　(ii)　In compliance with the disclosure and
　　　　　　reporting provision of the applicable section;
　　　　　　AND
　　(C)　Relaxation of the Resale Rules for Debtors in
　　　　Holding Restricted Securities - The offer or sale is
　　　　of no more than:
　　　　(i)　4% of the securities of such class outstanding -
　　　　　　during the first 2-years after the filing of the
　　　　　　Petition; AND

---

[61] Note: This exemption is necessary in order to enhance the marketability of
subscription rights or conversion privileges, including warrants, offered or sold under
a plan.
[62] Note: This limitation effectively prevents selling into the market "cats and dogs" of
a non-reporting company.

(ii) 1% of the securities outstanding at the beginning of a particular 180-day period - during any 180-day period after the 2-year period[63]; OR

(4) Stockbrokers or Dealers
   a. Scope of this Exception:
     1. The transaction was made by a stockbroker.
     2. The Security must be executed after a transaction of the type described in (1) or (2) in the Security.
     3. The transaction takes place before the end of 40 days after the first date on which the Security was bona fide offered to the public by the issuer (or by or through an underwriter).
   b. Requirements:
     1. The stockbroker must provide a disclosure statement approved under §1125 (POST-PETITION DISCLOSURE).
     2. The stockbroker must also provide information supplementing the disclosure statement, if the court orders.
     3. The stockbroker must do so at the time of or before the transaction.
     4. No prospectus is required of the stockbroker.

(b) When a Creditor or Equity Security Holder May Resell Securities Received by the Plan:

(1) "Real Underwriters":
   i. Definition: An Entity is an "Underwriter" under §2(11) of the Securities Act of 1933, if it:
   (A) Purchases any of the following with an intent to distribute the Security received or to be received in exchange:
     1. A Claim against the Debtor
     2. An interest in the Debtor
     3. A Claim for an Administrative Expense in the case; OR

---

[63] Note: The purpose of this exemption is to allow the Debtor or trustee to sell or distribute, without allowing manipulation schemes, restricted portfolio securities held or acquired by the Debtor.

(B) Offers to sell securities offered or sold under the plan for the holders; OR

(C) Offers to buy securities offered or sold under the plan from the holders, if that offer is:
    (i) With a view to distribute the securities; AND
    (ii) Under an agreement made:
        a. In connection with the plan; OR
        b. With the consummation of the plan; OR
        c. With the offer or sale of securities under the plan; OR

(D) Is an issuer (as used in §2(11)) with respect to the securities.

  ii. Exceptions:
     1. As provided in paragraph (2) below; AND
     2. With respect to ordinary trading transactions of an Entity that is not an issuer.

(2) Where Agreement is Limited to Matching or Combining Fractional Shares - An Entity is not an "underwriter" under §2(11) of the Securities Act of 1933 (15 U.S.C. §77b(11)) or under paragraph (1) if the agreement provides only for:

(A) Either:
    (i) The matching or combining of fractional interests in securities offered or sold under the plan into whole interests; OR
    (ii) The purchase or sale of those fractional interests from or to entities getting the fractional interests under the plan; OR

(B) The purchase or sale (for the entities) of the fractional or whole interests that are needed to adjust for any fractional interests remaining after the matching.

(3) An Entity other than an Entity specified in (a)(1) is not an "underwriter" under §2(11) of the Securities Act of 1933 (15 U.S.C. §77b(11)) with respect to any securities offered or sold to the Entity in the manner specified in (a)(1).

(c) Offer or Sale Deemed Public Offering: An offer or sale of securities specified under (a)(1) is deemed a public offering.

(d) Applicability of The Trust Indenture Act: The Trust Indenture Act of 1939 (15 U.S.C. §77aaa et seq.) does not apply to a note issued under the plan that matures within 1 year after the effective date of the plan.

§1146: Special Tax Provisions:

(a) Termination of Taxable Period
   1. The taxable period of an individual Debtor (for the purposes of any State or local law imposing an income tax) terminates on the date of the Order for Relief.
   2. Exception: Where the case has been converted into a reorganization (under §706) from a liquidation proceeding.
(b) Filing of Tax Returns
   1. Individual Debtors: The Trustee of the estate in a reorganization must file a (State or local) tax return for each taxable period while the case is pending after the Order for Relief.
   2. Corporations: For Corporations in Chapter 11, the Trustee is required to file the tax returns due while the case is pending (§346(c)(2)).
(c) Exemptions From Tax
   1. The following are exempt from Federal, State, or local stamp taxes:
      a. The issuance, Transfer , or exchange of a Security
      b. The making or delivery of an instrument of Transfer under a plan (confirmed under §1129)
(d) Advance Rulings from the IRS
   1. The court may authorize the proponent of a reorganization plan to request an advance ruling on the tax effects of the proposed plan (under §346) from the Internal Revenue Service (or State or local tax authority).
   2. The bankruptcy court may resolve disputes and determine the tax effects of the proposed plan if:
      (1) A ruling is obtained but the proponent of the plan disagrees with it.
   or (2) A ruling is requested but not obtained within 270 days.

Chapter 13: ADJUSTMENT OF DEBTS OF AN INDIVIDUAL WITH REGULAR INCOME

Subchapter I – Officers, Administration, And The Estate

General Note: "Chapter 13 is designed to serve as a flexible vehicle for the repayment of part or all of the allowed Claims of the Debtor." (Senate Report No. 95-989)

§1301: Stay of Action Against Co-Debtor:

(a) Automatic Stay:

    i.   Precluded Actions on Consumer Debt: Upon the filing of a Chapter 13 Order for Relief, an Automatic Stay is placed on the Debtor's estate, preventing the creditor from:

        a.   Taking any action to collect a Consumer Debt from:
            1. The Debtor on a consumer Debt he is individually liable for; OR
            2. A Guarantor or other party who guaranteed the Debtor's Consumer Debt; OR
            3. A Co-Debtor who is jointly liable on a Debt with the Debtor

        b.   Commencing or continuing any civil action to collect a Consumer Debt from:
            1. The Debtor on a consumer Debt he is individually liable for; OR
            2. A Guarantor or other party who guaranteed the Debtor's Consumer Debt. OR
            3. A Co-Debtor who is jointly liable on a Debt with the Debtor

    ii.   Applicability: The holder's Claim must be based on a Consumer Debt of the Chapter 13 Debtor (defined by §101(7) as a Debt incurred by an individual primarily for a personal, family, or household purpose).[64]

    iii. Exceptions to the Automatic Stay:

---

[64] Note: Therefore, the stay does not apply to those business Debts incurred by an individual (a) with regular income (as defined by §101(24)), (b) engaged in business, (c) that is permitted by §109(b) and §1304 to obtain chapter 13 relief).

(1) <u>Business Debts</u>: If the individual became liable on/secured the Debt in the ordinary course of his business; OR

(2) <u>Converted Case</u>: If the case is closed, dismissed, or converted to Chapter 7 or 11; OR

(3) Presentment or Dishonor of a Negotiable Instrument (as per §1301(b), below); OR

(4) <u>Court Grants Relief from Stay</u> (as per §1301(c), below).

(b) Exception to Stay for Negotiable Instruments - A creditor may:
1. Present a Negotiable Instrument
2. Give Notice of Dishonor of a Negotiable Instrument (this is so that he may preserve his substantive rights against the co-Debtor as required by applicable non-bankruptcy law).

(c) Relief From the Automatic Stay:
i. The court must grant relief from the Automatic Stay in the following cases:

(1) <u>Lack of Consideration</u>: To the extent the Debtor did not receive consideration for the Claim by the creditor (i.e. the Debtor is really the "co-Debtor" and the individual protected by the Stay, or the non-Debtor party, actually received the consideration for the creditor's Claim (ex: Ralph, the Debtor in bankruptcy, is named as a co-Debtor on a loan made by Bank to his little sister Victoria. If Ralph did not receive any loan proceeds, the Bank may be relieved from the Stay to proceed against Victoria)); OR

(2) <u>Plan Impairs Creditor</u>: To the extent the Debtor's plan proposes not to pay the Claim; OR

(3) <u>Irreparable Harm to Creditor</u>: To the extent the creditor's interest would be irreparably harmed by continuation of the stay
Ex: (a) If there is reasonable cause to believe that property is about to be disposed of by the co-Debtor which could be used to satisfy his obligation to the creditor, the court should lift the Stay to allow the creditor to perfect his rights against the property; (b) If property is subject to rapid depreciation or decrease in Value the Stay should be lifted to allow the creditor to protect his rights to reach that property; (c) the co-

Debtor filed bankruptcy himself, or threatened to leave the jurisdiction, or lost his job).

  ii. Requirements:
      a. Request of a Party in Interest; AND
      b. Notice and a hearing

(d) Lifting of Stay for Impaired Creditor (under §1300(c)(2)):

  1. The Stay will be lifted for the party making a request (under §1301(c)(2)) <u>20 days</u> after the request is filed.

  2. <u>Exception: Objecting to Relief</u>: The Stay may not be lifted if the Debtor (or a co-Debtor or guarantor):
      a. Files a written objection to the proposed action; AND
      b. Serves it upon the requesting party

§1302: Trustee:

(a) Appointment of Trustee

  1. <u>The Standing Trustee</u>: An individual shall serve as a Trustee if:
      a. The United States trustee appoints her (under 28 U.S.C. §586(b)) to serve as "standing trustee" in Chapter 13 cases. AND
      b. The individual qualifies under §322.
  2. <u>The Disinterested Trustee</u>: The United States trustee must otherwise:
      a. Appoint 1 Disinterested Person to serve as trustee in the case; OR
      b. Elect to serve as a Trustee herself in the case.

(b) Duties of the Trustee[65] - The Trustee must:

  (1) Perform Certain Duties Specified §704:
      a. <u>Accountability</u> - be accountable for all property received by the estate (in accordance with §704(2)); AND

---

[65] Note: The Trustee is no mere disbursing agent of the monies paid to her by the Debtor under the plan (§1322(a)(1)). The duties imposed upon her are similar to certain relevant duties of a liquidation trustee under §704.

b.   Ensure Debtor's Performance - ensure that the Debtor performs his intentions regarding retention or surrender of certain property (pursuant to 521(2)(B)) (in accordance with §704(3)). AND

c.   Investigate Financial Affairs – of the Debtor (in accordance with §704(4); AND

d.   Examine Proofs of Claims – and object to improper Claims (in accordance with §704(5)); AND

e.   Oppose the Discharge of the Debtor – if advisable (in accordance with §704(6); AND

f.   Furnish Information to Parties in Interest – regarding the estate and its administration (in accordance with §704(7)) (unless the court orders otherwise); AND

g.   Prepare Final Report and Accounting – of the estate and its administration to be filed with the court and the U.S. Trustee (in accordance with §704(9); AND

(2) Appear (and be heard) at any hearing that deals with:
(A) The Value of property subject to a Lien; OR
(B) Confirmation of a plan; OR
(C) Modification of the plan after confirmation (provided by §1323-1325).

(3) Dispose of moneys received - or to be received in a case under Chapter 13 of the Bankruptcy Act[66] (under regulations issued by the Director of the Administrative Office of the U.S. Courts); AND

(4) Advise and assist the Debtor in performance under the plan (not on legal matters). AND

(5) Ensure that the Debtor makes timely payments under §1326.

(c) Duties When Debtor is in Business: If the Debtor is engaged in business, then in addition to the duties specified in (b), the Trustee must perform the duties specified in §1106(a)(3) and 1106(a)(4) (Note: These are the investigative and reporting

---

[66] Chapter XIII of act July 1, 1898, ch. 541, as added June 22, 1938, ch. 575, §1, 52 Stat. 930, which was classified to chapter 13 (§1001 et seq.) of former Title 11.

duties normally required of a Chapter 11 Debtor or Trustee by §1106(a)(3) and (4)).

§1303: Rights and Powers of Debtor:

a. The Debtor has, exclusive of the Trustee, the rights and powers of a Trustee with respect to using, selling, or leasing estate property (in accordance with §363(b) 363(d), 363(e), 363(f), and 363(l).[67]

b. This power is subject to any limitations on a Trustee under Chapter 13.

§1304: Debtor "Engaged in Business":

(a) Definition - A Debtor is "Engaged in Business" if:
1. He is self-employed; AND
2. He incurs trade credit in the production of income from his employment.

(b) Permissible Operation by Debtor of Certain Business Activities:
1. Operation of Business - A Debtor engaged in business may operate the business of the Debtor, unless the court orders otherwise.
2. Rights and Powers:
   a. A Debtor Engaged in Business" shall have the exclusive right (exclusive of the Trustee)of the Trustee to:
      i. Sell, use, or lease its property in the Ordinary Course of Business (pursuant to and subject to §363(c)); AND
      ii. Obtain Credit (pursuant to and subject to §364)
   b. This power is subject to any limitations or conditions that the court prescribes

(c) Requirement to File Reports on Operations: A Debtor engaged in business shall perform the duties of the Trustee specified in

---

[67] Note: This does not imply that the Debtor does not also have other powers concurrently with the Trustee. (ex: Although §1323 is not specified in this section, it is intended that the Debtor has the power to sue and be sued).

§704(8) (requiring it to file in court certain financial statements relating to the operation of the business).

§1305: Filing and Allowance of Post-Petition Claims:

(a) Who May File: A proof of Claim may be filed by any Entity holding the following Claims against the Debtor:
   (1) Tax Claims: A Claim for taxes that become payable while the case is pending; OR
   (2) Post-Petition Consumer Debt: A Claim that:
      a. Is a Consumer Debt; AND
      b. Arises after the date of the Chapter 13 Order for Relief; AND
      c. Is for property or services that the Debtor needs under the plan.

(b) Allowance of Claims
   1. Governing Law: 11 U.S.C. §502 governs the allowance of §1305(a) Claims.
   2. The standards of §502 are applied as of the date the Claim is allowed (and not the Petition date) (i.e. The Claims should be allowed under §502(a), §502(b), or §502(c), or disallowed under §502(d) or §502(e), the same as if the Claim had arisen before the Petition date.)

   3. Exception: Certain post-Petition Claims disallowed under §1305(c) (below).

(c) Disallowed Claims: A post-Petition Claim for property or services needed by the Debtor under the plan (filed under (a)(2)) must be disallowed if the Claim holder knew (or should have known) that Trustee did not approve of the Debtor's incurring the obligation (and getting the approval was practicable).

§1306: Property of the Estate:

(a) Definition of "Property": Property of the Estate includes the following:
   (1) All property specified in the §541 that the Debtor gets:
      a. After the commencement of the case; AND

    b.   Before the case is closed, dismissed, or converted to a
         Chapter 7, 11 or 12 case (whichever happens first).
         AND
(2) Earnings from services that the Debtor performed:
    a.   After the commencement of the case; AND
    b.   Before the case is closed, dismissed, or converted to a
         Chapter 7, 11 or 12 case (whichever happens first).

(b) Possession of Property:
    1.   The Debtor shall remain in possession of all of the estate's
        property.
    2.   Exception: If otherwise provided in a confirmed plan or in
        an order confirming a plan.

§1307. Conversion or Dismissal:

(a) Conversion:
    1.   The Debtor may convert a Chapter 13 case to a Chapter 7
        case at any time.
    2.   Any waiver of the right to convert under §1307(a) is
        unenforceable.

(b) Required Dismissal:

    1.   If the Debtor requests that a case be converted under §706,
        §1112, or §1208 (CONVERSION/DISMISSAL PROVISIONS),
        and the case is not converted, the court must dismiss the
        Chapter 13 case.
    2.   Any waiver of the right to dismiss under this subsection is
        unenforceable.
(c) Conversions to a Chapter 7 Case; Dismissal of Case For Cause:

    i.   Grounds to Convert: A court may convert a Chapter 13 case
       to a Chapter 7 case, or may dismiss a Chapter 13 case for
       cause, including:
       (1) Unreasonable delay by the Debtor that is prejudicial to
           creditors
       (2) Nonpayment of any fees and charges (required under 28
           U.S.C. Ch. 123)
       (3) Failure to file a plan timely (under §1321)
       (4) Failure to start making timely payments (under §1326)
       (5) Denial of Confirmed Plan:

        a. Denial of confirmation of a plan (under §1325)
        b. Denial of a request for additional time to file another plan or a modification of a plan
- (6) Material default -by the Debtor with respect to a term of a confirmed plan
- (7) Revocation of Confirmed Plan:
  - a. Revocation of the order of confirmation (under §1330)
  - b. Denial of confirmation of a modified plan (under §1329)
- (8) Termination of a confirmed plan- because a condition specified in the plan (other than finishing payments under the plan) occurred
- (9) Only on Request of the U.S. Trustee - Failure of the Debtor to file information (required by §521(1)) by:
  - a. 15 days after the Petition is filed
  - b. The Court may allow more time
- (10) Only on Request of the U.S. Trustee - Failure to file information (required by §521(2)) on a timely basis.

  ii. Requirements: A case may only be considered for conversion if:
      a. A Party in Interest or the U.S. Trustee requests it; AND
      b. There is a proper notice and a hearing

  iii. Interest of Creditors and Estate: The Court's determination to convert or dismiss a Chapter 13 case must take into Account the best interests of the creditors and the estate.

  iv. Exception: This subsection does not apply when the Debtor is a farmer. (See §1307(e), below).

(d) Conversion to Chapter 11 or 12 Case:
1. The court may convert a Chapter 13 case to a Chapter 11 or 12 case at any time before the confirmation of a plan under §1325.
2. Requirements:
   - a. A Party in Interest or the U.S. Trustee requests it; AND
   - b. There is a proper notice and a hearing
3. Exception: This subsection does not apply when the Debtor is a farmer. (See §1307(e), below).

(e) Conversion when Debtor is a Farmer - The court may not convert a Chapter 13 case to a Chapter 7, 11, or 12 case if the Debtor is a farmer, unless the Debtor requests the conversion.

(f) Conversions to other Chapters: In all cases of conversion under §1307, a case may only be converted to another chapter if the Debtor could be a Debtor under that chapter.

Subchapter II – The Plan

§1321: Filing of Plan:

The Debtor shall file a plan.

§1322: Contents of Plan:

(a) Mandatory Provisions - The plan must contain the following:
    (1) Payment of Debtor's Future Income: The plan must give to the Trustee's supervision and control, whatever portion of the Debtor's future income that is needed to implement the plan.
    (2) Payment of Priority Claims:
        a. The plan must provide for full payment of all §507 priority Claims.
        b. Payment is to be made in deferred cash payments.
        c. Exception: The holder of a particular Claim may agree to a different treatment of his Claim.
    (3) Identical Treatment of Claims: The plan must provide identical treatment for all Claims in a class.

(b) Optional Provisions - Subject to (a) and (c), the plan may contain the following provisions:

    (1) Designation of Classes:
        a. The plan may designate classes of unsecured Claims (as provided in §1122)
        b. The plan may not discriminate unfairly against any class
        c. The plan may treat Claims for a consumer Debt differently than other unsecured Claims if there is a co-Debtor who is liable on the Debt
    (2) Rights of Claim Holders:

a. The plan may modify the rights of both secured and unsecured Claim holders

b. Exception: The rights of a secured Claim holder may not be modified if the Security Interest is in the Debtor's principal residence.

c. The plan may also leave the rights of holders of any class of Claims unaffected.

(3) Defaults: The plan may provide for curing or waiving defaults.

(4) Joint Payment of Claims: The plan may provide that payments on any unsecured Claim are to be made together with payments on other (secured or unsecured) Claims.

(5) Maintaining Payments: The plan may provide (even if it modified the rights of Claim holders in (2), above):

a. That any default be cured within a reasonable time; and

b. That payments be maintained while the case is pending on any Claim (secured or unsecured), where the last payment is scheduled to be due after the final payment under the plan is due.

(6) Payment of Post-Petition Claims: The plan may provide for the payment of any Claim (or a part of a claim) allowed under §1305.

(7) Executory Contracts/Unexpired Leases: The plan may provide that (subject to §365: EXECUTORY CONTRACTS AND UNEXPIRED LEASES) any executory contract or unexpired lease of the Debtor not previously rejected under §365 be assumed, rejected, or assigned.

(8) Payment of Claims: The plan may provide that any Claim (or a part) against the Debtor be paid from the estate's property or from the Debtor's property

(9) Vesting of Property: The plan may provide that Property of the Estate vest in the Debtor (or any other Entity) either when:

a. The plan is confirmed; or

b. At a later time

(10) Other Provisions: The plan may include any other appropriate provision not inconsistent with the Bankruptcy Code.

(c) Special Rules for Debtor's Principal Residence: Notwithstanding (b)(2) and applicable non-bankruptcy law:

(1) Curing Default Causing Lien on Property: A default with respect to, or that gave rise to, a Lien on the Debtor's principal residence may be cured under §1322(b)(3) or §1322(5) until the residence is sold at a legal foreclosure sale.

(2) Modifying Payment Schedule under Mortgage: In a case where the last mortgage payment (on the original payment schedule for the Claim) is due before the final payment under the plan, the plan may provide for the payment of the Claim as modified under §1325(a)(5).

(d) Limit on Pay Period
   1. The pay period under the plan is limited to 3 years.
   2. Exception: The court may approve a 5-year period for cause.

(e) Availability of Funds to Cure Defaults
   1. If it is proposed in a plan to cure a default, the amount necessary to cure the default is determined in accordance with:
      a. The underlying agreement; and
      b. Applicable non-bankruptcy law
   2. This subsection applies regardless of the provisions of subsection (b)(2) and §506(b) and 1325(a)(5) (ALLOWED SECURED CLAIMS).

§1323: Modification of Plan Before Confirmation:

(a) Modification - When Allowed:
   1. The Debtor may modify the plan without approval at any time before confirmation.
   2. The Debtor may not modify the plan if the modified plan does not meet the requirements of §1322 (CONTENTS OF PLAN).

(b) Effect of Modification: After the Debtor files a modification under §1323 (MODIFICATION BEFORE CONFIRMATION), the modified plan becomes the plan.

(c) Effect of Acceptance/Rejection: If a secured Claim holder accepts or rejects a plan, the acceptance or rejection remains binding unless:

1. The modified plan changes the rights of the holder; AND
2. The holder withdraws or alters his earlier acceptance or rejection.

§1324: Confirmation Hearing:

a. A Party in Interest may object to confirmation of the plan (distinguished from merely rejecting a plan).
b. The bankruptcy judge is required to provide notice and an opportunity for hearing objections to confirmation.

§1325: Confirmation of Plan:

(a) Mandatory Confirmation: The Court must confirm a plan (except as provided in (b)) if:

 (1) Satisfaction of Plan Requirements: The plan satisfies the provisions of Chapter 13 and other applicable provisions of the Bankruptcy Code.
 (2) Fees Paid: Any required fees (under 28 U.S.C. Chapter 123 or the plan) have been paid.
 (3) Good Faith Proposal: The plan has been proposed:
   a. In good faith; and
   b. Not by any illegal means
 (4) Distributions at Least as Large as Under Liquidation: The property to be distributed under the plan for each allowed unsecured Claim is equal to or greater than what would be paid on the Claim if the estate were liquidated under chapter 7 on the plan's effective date.
 (5) Secured Claims - For Allowed Secured Claims In the Plan:
   (A) Acceptance by Secured Creditors: The Claim holder has accepted the plan; or
   (B) Creditor's Liens:
     (i) The plan provides that the holder of such Claim retain the Lien securing such Claim; and
     (ii) The property to be distributed under the plan for the Claim is equal to or greater than the allowed amount of the Claim on the plan's effective date; or
   (C) Debtor Surrenders Collateral to Secured Creditor: The Debtor surrenders the collateral to the Claim holder.
 (6) Debtor's Compliance Feasible: The Debtor will be able to:
   a. Make all payments under the plan; and

b.   Comply with the plan

(b) When Court May Not Approve Plan

(1) Objections to Plan:
   a.   The court may not approve the plan if any of the
        following object to its confirmation:
        1.   The Trustee; or
        2.   The holder of an allowed unsecured Claim
   b.   Exception: If either of the following is true as of the
        plan's effective date:
        (A) Value of Property: The property to be distributed
            under the plan for the Claim is equal to or greater
            than the Claim amount; or
        (B) Debtor's Income Is Applied to Payments:
            1.   The plan provides that all of the Debtor's
                 projected disposable income for the plan's first
                 3-years will be applied to make payments
                 under the plan. OR
            2.   The 3-year period begins on the date that the
                 first payment is due under the plan.

(2) "Disposable Income" - In §1325(b) "Disposable Income"
     means income which is:
     1.   Received by the Debtor; AND
     2.   Not reasonably necessary to be spent for any of the
          following:
          (A) The Debtor's (or a dependent's) maintenance or
              support; AND
          (B) If the Debtor is engaged in business - Expenses
              needed to continue, preserve, and operate the
              business.
(c) Payment of Income to Trustee: The court is authorized to order
     any Entity (defined in §101(15)) to pay any income of the
     Debtor to the Trustee (Note: Any Governmental Unit is an
     Entity subject to such an order).

§1326: Payments:

(a) Debtor's Payments Under The Plan:

(1) <u>Time</u>: The Debtor must start making the payments proposed by the plan within <u>30 days</u> after the plan is filed (unless the court may order otherwise).

(2) Payments Made Before Confirmation:

    a. The Trustee must hold all payments made (under §1326(a)) until the plan is either confirmed or denied.

    b. <u>If a plan is confirmed</u>, the Trustee must distribute any payment as soon as practicable.

    c. If a plan is denied:

       i. The Trustee must return any payment to the Debtor

       ii. The Trustee may deduct any unpaid Claim allowed under §503(b) (ADMINISTRATIVE EXPENSES).

(b) Recurring Payments: Before or at the time of each payment to creditors under the plan, the following must be paid:

    (1) <u>Administrative Expenses</u>: Any unpaid Claim for Administrative Expenses (under §507(a)(1)); and

    (2) <u>Trustee's Fee</u>: The Standing Trustee's fixed fee (under 28 U.S.C. §586(e)(1)(B)) if a Standing Trustee (appointed under 28 U.S.C. §586(b)) is serving in the case.

(c) Payments to Creditors

    1. The Trustee must pay the creditors under the plan.

    2. <u>Exceptions</u> – If otherwise provided in:

       a. The plan; or

       b. The order confirming the plan

§1327: Effect of Confirmation:

(a) Binding Effect of Confirmation

    1. The Debtor and each creditor are bound to a confirmed plan.

    2. They are bound regardless of whether:

       a. The creditor's Claim is provided for by the plan; and

       b. The creditor has <u>objected to</u>, <u>accepted</u>, or <u>rejected</u> the plan.

(b) Vesting of Property

    1. The plan's confirmation vests all of the estate's property in the Debtor (free and clear of any Claim or interest of any creditor provided for by the plan, as specified in §1327 (c), below).

    2. Exceptions:

       a. Where the plan itself provides otherwise

       b. Where the order confirming the plan provides otherwise

(c) "Free and Clear"
   1. The property that vests in the Debtor under (b) is free and clear of any Claim or interest of any creditor provided for by the plan.
   2. Exceptions:
      a. Where the plan itself provides otherwise
      b. Where the order confirming the plan provides otherwise

§1328: Discharge:

(a) Discharge of Debts
   i) The court must discharge all of a Debtor's Debts provided for by the plan or disallowed under §502, except:
     (1) Debts provided for under §1322(b)(5); or
     (2) Debts for Alimony, Child Support, Student Loans and Benefits, and Personal Injury Where the Debtor was Intoxicated (see §523(a)(5), (8), or (9)); or
     (3) Debts for restitution (or a criminal fine) included in a criminal sentence of the Debtor.

   ii) Time of Discharge: Discharge occurs as soon as practicable, but after the Debtor makes all payments under the plan

   iii) Exception to Discharge: The court may approve a written waiver of discharge executed by the Debtor after the Chapter 13 Order for Relief

(b) Discharge Where Payments Not Complete: The court may only discharge a Debtor that has not completed payments under the plan if:
   (1) Excusable Circumstance: The Debtor did not complete the payments because of circumstances that the Debtor should not be held responsible for; and
   (2) Payment At Least As Great as Liquidation: The property distributed under the plan for each allowed unsecured Claim is equal to or greater than what would have been paid to the creditor had the estate been liquidated under chapter 7 on the date of the hearing (under §1328); and
   (3) Modification Impracticable: It is not practicable to modify the plan under §1329; and
   (4) The plan has been confirmed; and

(5) There was <u>notice</u> and a <u>hearing</u>.

(c) Discharge From Unsecured Debts
   i) <u>Unsecured Debts Discharged</u>: A discharge under (b) discharges the Debtor from all <u>unsecured</u> Debts that are:
     1. Provided for by the plan; or
     2. Disallowed under §502 (ALLOWANCE OF CLAIMS OR INTERESTS)

   ii) <u>Non-Dischargeable Debts</u>: The following Debts are not discharged:
     (1) A Debt to cure a default (under §1322(b)(5)); or
     (2) A Debt that is excepted from discharge (specified in §523(a))

(d) Post-Petition Claims Not Discharged - In any case, a discharge under §1328 <u>does not</u> discharge the Debtor from a Debt if:
     1. The Debt is based on an allowed post-Petition Claim (filed under §1305(a)(2)); and
     2. Prior trustee approval to incur the Debt was practicable but was not obtained.

(e) Revocation of Discharge
   i. The court may revoke a §1328 discharge if:
     (1) The Debtor obtained the discharge through fraud; and
     (2) The Party in Interest requesting the revocation did not know of the fraud until after the discharge was granted.
   ii. Requirements:
     1. A Party in Interest must request that the discharge be revoked; and
     2. The request is made within <u>1 year</u> after the discharge was granted; and
     3. There is <u>notice</u> and a <u>hearing</u>.

§1329: Modification of Plan After Confirmation:

(a) General Rule Allowing Modification
   i. The plan may be modified any time after confirmation:
   ii. Requirements:

a.   Either the Debtor, the Trustee, or an unsecured Claim
     holder with an allowed Claim must request the
     modification; and
b.   Payments under the plan have not been completed
iii. Modifications Allowed:
     (1) An increase or reduction of the amount of payments on
          Claims of a particular class; or
     (2) An extension or reduction of the time for payments; or
     (3) A change in the amount of the distribution to a creditor
          (but only to the extent needed to take account of any
          payment of the Claim outside of the plan).

(b) Additional Requirements and Results of Modification
     (1) Any modification under (a) must comply with the
          requirements for an original plan (§1322(a), 1322(b), and
          1323(c) and the requirements of §1325(a)).
     (2) The modified plan becomes the plan unless the modification
          is disapproved after notice and a hearing.

(c) Limitation
     1.   A plan modified under §1329 may not provide for payments
          past 3 years from the time the first payment under the
          original plan was due
     2.   Exception: The court may approve a period of up to 5 years
          for cause.

§1330: Revocation of an Order of Confirmation:

(a) Revocation Based on Fraud:
     1.   The court may revoke an Order of Confirmation (under
          §1325) if it was procured by fraud.
     2.   Requirements:
          a.   A Party in Interest must request the revocation of the
               order; and
          b.   Time: The request must be made within 180 days after
               the entry of the order; and
          c.   There was notice and a hearing.

(b) Disposition of Case: The court must dispose of the case under
     §1307 (CONVERSION OR DISMISSAL) if:
     1.   The court revokes an order of confirmation revoked for
          fraud (under (a)) and:

2. Either:
   a) The Debtor does not propose a modification of the plan under §1329 within the time set by the court.
   b) The Debtor proposes the modification but it is not confirmed by the Court within the time set.

Uniform Fraudulent Conveyances Act

§2: Insolvency:

(1) Person: A Person is Insolvent when the Present Market Value of the Person's assets is less that that amount required to pay debts as they become due.

* * *

§3: Fair Consideration:

Fair consideration is deemed to have been given if:
(a) Conveyance of Property/Release of Debt is made in exchange for:
    1. A fair equivalent; and
    2. In good faith
(b) Security Interest: A Security Interest is given:
    1. To secure a present advance or antecedent debt; and
    2. The amount of the claim is not disproportionately small to the Value of the property

§4: Conveyance by an Insolvent:

A Fraudulent Conveyance is deemed to exist (for Creditor of the Conveyor) if:

  a) The Person conveying the property is <u>Insolvent</u>; and
  b) <u>Fair Consideration</u> (under §3) is not given (regardless of actual intent)

§5: Conveyance by a Person in Business:

A Fraudulent Conveyance is deemed to exist (for creditors of the Conveyor and of the transaction) if:
  a) The Person making the conveyance is engaged in a business; and
  b) The Conveyance is made without <u>Fair Consideration</u> (under §3) (regardless of actual intent); and
  c) The "Conveyor" has an unreasonably small capital left after the conveyance.

§6: Conveyance by a Person About to Incur Debts:

A Fraudulent Conveyance is deemed to exist (for present and future creditors) if:

a) The Person conveying the property <u>intends</u> or <u>believes</u> that he is about to incur debts beyond his ability to pay them as they become mature (i.e. he knows he will soon be Insolvent); and

b) <u>Fair Consideration</u> (under §3) is not given (regardless of actual intent).

§7: Conveyance Made With Intent to Defraud:

A Fraudulent Conveyance is deemed to exist if it is made with actual intent to <u>hinder</u>, <u>delay</u>, or <u>defraud</u> Creditors (present or future creditors).

§9: Rights of Creditors Under Fraudulent Conveyance Law:

(1) The Fraudulent Conveyance Rule
  - i) Rights of Creditors
    - (a) <u>Set Aside Conveyance</u> or <u>Annul Obligation</u> to the extent necessary to collect on his claim; or
    - (b) <u>Disregard the Conveyance</u> and Attach or Levy Execution upon the conveyed Property
  - ii) <u>Exception</u>: Creditor may not assert such powers if the property has been sold:
    - a) To a Good Faith Purchaser:
      1) A Purchaser
      2) For Fair Consideration
      3) Without knowledge of the Fraudulent Conveyance Upon purchase; or
    - b) Someone who obtained title from a Good Faith Purchaser

(2) Rights of Non-GFP Innocent Purchaser - A non-Good Faith Purchaser may keep the property as <u>Security for Repayment</u> if:
  a) He is a Purchaser; and
  b) The Purchaser gave less than fair consideration for the property; and
  c) The Purchaser did not have <u>actual fraudulent intent</u>

* * * *Selected Provisions From Article 9 Of The Uniform
Commercial Code

§9-203: Attachment And Enforceability Of Security Interest:

(1) Requirements for Attachment:
  i) A Security Interest Attaches ONLY If:
    (a) The collateral is Secured with either:
      1. Possession: In the Possession of the Secured Party (pursuant to agreement); or
      2. Security Agreement: Debtor has signed a Security Agreement which:
        a. Is in WRITING; and
        b. Describes the Collateral (as per §9-110) (Note: When collateral is crops or timber, a description of the land is required); or
      3. Control of Investment Property - If:
        a. The collateral is INVESTMENT PROPERTY; and
        b. The Secured Party has Control over the Investment Property (as per §9-115(1)(e)); and
        c. The Secured Party is Controlling it pursuant to an agreement; and
    (b) Value has been given; and
    (c) Debtor's Rights: The Debtor has Rights in the collateral
  ii) Requirements are subject to
    a) §4-208 for Security Interests of a Collecting Bank
    b) §9-115 and §9-116 for Security Interests in Investment Property
    c) §9-113 for Security Interests arising under the Article of Sales (Article 2)

(2) Time of Attachment: A Security Interest attaches:
  a) When it becomes enforceable against the Debtor (with respect to the collateral); and
  b) Either:
    i) As soon as the events specified in (1) take place (they Must Coexist); or
    ii) When agreed (if agreement explicitly postpones the time of attachment)

(3)   Rights to Proceeds: Secured Party has the rights to Proceeds under §9-306 (i.e. no need to specify that proceeds will be covered by the S/A, unless otherwise agreed. You usually must specify if you do __not__ want proceeds to be covered by the S/A).

(4)   Transactions subject to this article are also subject to other statutes; those statutes shall supersede this article (ex: small loans, retail installment selling statutes, etc.).

§9-204: After-Acquired Property; Future Advances:

(1)   A S/A may provide for After-Acquired Property to secure the obligations covered by the S/A (except as provided below in (2)).

(2)   Consumer Goods Exception:
    a)   After-Acquired Property will not attach to a S/I if:
        1.   The S/I is in Consumer Goods; and
        2.   The After-Acquired Property is given as additional Security
    b)   Exceptions: After-Acquired Property __will__ attach in Consumer Goods if:
        1.   Debtor acquires rights in the After-Acquired Property within __10 Days__ after the Secured Party gave Value; or
        2.   They are Accessions (see §9-314)

(3)   Future Advances:
    a)   Obligations covered by a S/A may include Future Advances or other Value.
    b)   It is not necessary for the Future Advances to be given pursuant to a commitment (see 9-105(1)).

§9-301: Priority Over Unperfected Security Interests:

(1)   Classes of People who take Priority over an Unperfected Security Interest:
    (a)   A Perfected S/P entitled to priority under §9-312; or
    (b)   A Person who becomes a Lien Creditor before the Security Interest is Perfected (but see (2)); or
    (c)   A Buyer: Requirements to qualify as a "Buyer":
        1)   The Buyer must be either:
            a)   A Buyer __not__ in the Ordinary Course of Business; or
            b)   A Bulk Transferee; or

    c) A Buyer of Farm Products - in the Ordinary Course of Business; and

2) The Buyer cannot be a Secured Party; and

3) The Buyer must:
    a) Have No Knowledge of the S/I; and
    b) Give Value; and
    c) Receive delivery (of collateral) before the S/I is perfected; and

4) The Collateral must either be:
    a) Goods; or
    b) Instruments; or
    c) Documents; or
    d) Chattel Paper

(d) Transferee of Accounts, General Intangibles or Investment Property who:
1) Gives Value before they are perfected; and
2) Is without knowledge of S/I; and
3) Is not a Secured Party

(2) PMSI Exception: A Secured Party takes priority over any Lien Creditor or "Bulk Transferee" (whose rights arise between the time of attachment and filing) if the Secured Party files a PMSI:
a) Before Debtor receives the collateral (i.e. before attachment); or
b) Within 10 Days after Debtor receives Possession of the collateral

(3) A Lien Creditor is
a) A Creditor who obtains a Lien on property involved by attachment, levy, or the like; or
b) An Assignee for the Benefit of Creditors from the time of assignment; or
c) A Trustee in Bankruptcy from the date of the filing of Petition; or
d) A Receiver in Equity from the time of appointment

(4) A Person who becomes a Lien Creditor after a S/I is perfected, takes subject to that S/I only to the extent that it:
a) Secures Future Advances made to Debtor:
    1. Before the Third Party becomes a Lien Creditor; or
    2. Within 45 Days after the Third Party becomes a Lien Creditor; or

b) Is made Without Knowledge of the Lien; or
c) Is made pursuant to a Prior Commitment entered into without knowledge of the Lien

§9-306: Rights In "Proceeds":

(1) "Proceeds"
   a) Proceeds may be obtained from:
     1. Whatever is received upon:
       a. Sale; or
       b. Exchange; or
       c. Collection; or
       d. Other disposition (of collateral or proceeds); or
     2. Insurance payable from the loss/damage of the collateral, unless the insurance check is made payable to a non-party of the Security Agreement (Note: can be endorsed by Third Party to become valid); or
     3. Any payments or distributions made with respect to investment property collateral.

   b) Proceeds may be in the form of:
     1. Cash Proceeds - Money, checks, deposit accounts, etc.; or
     2. Non-Cash Proceeds - all other proceeds

(2) Continuation of the S/I: Unless otherwise provided by the UCC, a S/I in collateral continues in:
   a) Collateral - even if it is sold/disposed of, unless the disposition was authorized by the Secured Party; and
   b) Proceeds - ONLY if the proceeds are IDENTIFIABLE

(3) The Security Interest in Proceeds
   i) A S/I in Proceeds is considered Continuously Perfected if the original collateral was "re-perfected" within 10 Days (of "conversion" to proceeds) (i.e. the date of perfection in the Proceeds relates back to date the original collateral was perfected).
   ii) The Proceeds becomes unperfected 10 Days after the Debtor receives the proceeds - Unless they are "re-perfected" (within the 10 day period).

iii) A S/I in proceeds can only be perfected by the rules spelled out in the UCC, for original collateral of the same type (except as provided in this section).

iv) Perfection can be continuously maintained in Proceeds if:

    (a) AUTOMATIC RE-PERFECTION occurs; Automatic re-perfection occurs if either:

        1. Non-Cash Proceeds: (ex: a car for a car)

           a. The filed Financing Statement covers the original collateral; and

           b. The proceeds are collateral in which a S/I may be perfected by filing (i.e. not cash) in the office where the Financing Statement was filed (even if you don't re-file) (Default Rule: silence means you have a S/I in proceeds); or

        2. Non-Cash Proceeds bought with Cash Proceeds: If the non-cash proceeds on are acquired with cash-proceeds, perfection continues if the Financing Statement indicates the types of property constituting the proceeds (ex: a car for cash, to buy a new car); or

    (b) Proceeds are CASH PROCEEDS (ex: Accounts), AND:

        1. Cash-proceeds are identifiable; and

        2. A filed Financing Statement covers the original collateral; or

    (c) The original collateral was Investment Property and the proceeds are Identifiable Cash proceeds; or

    (d) The S/I in the proceeds is perfected before the 10- Day period expires.

(4) S/I In Proceeds of an Insolvent Debtor - A S/P (with a perfected S/I in proceeds) can only maintain a S/I in:

    (a) Non-Cash Proceeds, which are

        1. Identifiable; and

        2. In a separate deposit account, containing only proceeds; and

    (b) Money Cash-Proceeds, which are

        1. Identifiable; and

        2. In the form of money

        3. Not commingled with other money

        4. Not deposited into a deposit account prior to insolvency; and

    (c) Instrument Cash-Proceeds (i.e. checks, notes), which are

        1. Identifiable; and

2. Not deposited in a deposit account prior to insolvency proceedings; and

(d) Cash-Proceeds in Accounts - In all cash and deposit accounts of the Debtor (in which proceeds have been commingled) perfection may be maintained, yet it will be:

    (i) Subject to any right to set-off; and

    (ii) Limited to:

> An "Amount" (<= any cash-proceeds received by Debtor within 10 days of insolvency)
> less - (I) Payments to S/P on "account of cash proceeds" (within 10 Day period)
> less - (II) Cash Proceeds received by Debtor during 10 Day period

(5) Priorities with Returned/Repossessed Goods

  i) Requirements for Priority:

    a) The Sale of goods must result in an Account or Chattel Paper which is Transferred by the seller to the S/P; and

    b) The goods must be returned or repossessed by the Debtor or the S/P.

  ii) Rules of Priorities for Returned/Repossessed Goods

    (a) RE-PERFECTION: The Original Security Interest re-attaches to the goods, continuing perfection if:

      1. The goods were collateral at the time of the sale; and

      2. The Debt attached to collateral not paid at the sale; and

      3. It was perfected when the goods were sold; and

      4. Either:

        a. If Perfection by Filing: S/P files a new F/S only if the original Filing is not still effective; or

        b. If Non-Filed Perfection: S/P takes possession of goods or file a new F/S

    (b) CHATTEL PAPER:

      1. An unpaid Transferee of the Chattel Paper maintains a S/I in the goods against the Transferor.

      2. If Transferee of Chattel Paper is entitled to priority (pursuant to §9-308), then he takes priority over RE-PERFECTED Secured Parties (see (a)above).

(c) ACCOUNTS:
1. An unpaid Transferee of an account has a S/I in goods against the Transferor.
2. This S/I is subordinate to a re-perfected S/I (see (a) above)

(d) A S/I of an unpaid Transferee (pursuant to (b) and (c)) must be perfected to protect themselves against
1. Creditors of the Transferor; and
2. Purchasers of the returned/repossessed goods

§9-312: Priorities Among Conflicting Security Interests In The Same Collateral:
(Between Perfected S/P's only; for other priority conflicts see §9-301)

(1) Scope: Rules stated in other sections of Part 3, as well as the following other sections of the UCC shall govern when applicable:
a) §4-208 (S/I of Collecting Banks in items being collected, accompanying documents, and proceeds)
b) §9-103 (S/I related to other jurisdictions)
c) §9-114 (Consignments)
d) §9-115 (S/I in Investment Property)
(2) S/I in Crops:
a) A Perfected S/I in crops takes priority over an earlier perfected S/I if:
1. The New Creditor gave Value to enable Debtor to produce the crops during the production season; and
2. The New Creditor gave money within 3 Mos. before the crops become "growing crops" (ex: by planting them); and
3. The Earlier S/I secures obligations due more than 6 Months before crops became "growing crops"
b) It is irrelevant that New Creditor had knowledge of earlier S/I.

(3) PMSI Super-Priority in INVENTORY:
i) A Perfected PMSI in inventory has Priority over a conflicting S/I in the same inventory.
ii) PMSI "Super-Priority" applies Only to:

314

a) The same inventory; and
b) Identifiable cash proceeds received on or before the day
    that Debtor delivers the inventory to a Third Party
    buyer (Okay if proceeds are money, checks, deposit
    accounts; No good if converted to cash proceeds; must
    be direct cash proceeds (ex: car-trade-ins are not good,
    Accounts receivable and Chattel Paper are also no
    good))

iii) Requirements for PMSI Priority
    (a) The PMSI is perfected when Debtor receives
         possession of inventory; and
    (b) The "Purchase Money" Secured Party gives written
         notice to the conflicting Secured Party only if the
         conflicting Secured Party filed a financing statement
         covering the same types of inventory before:
         (i) The "Purchase Money" Secured Party filed (or
              Debtor receives Possession); or
         (ii) The beginning of the 21 Day period (in which a
              PMSI is temporarily perfected without filing or
              possession (as per §9-304(5))); and
    (c) The Conflicting Secured Party received the notification
         within 5 Yrs before the Debtor receives possession of
         the inventory (i.e. since a notice is effective for 5 Yrs,
         S/P can continue making PMSI's without further
         notices within 5 yr. period); and
    (d) The notice states that the Person sending it expects to
         obtain a PMSI in the debtor's Inventory (describing the
         inventory by or type)

(4) A PMSI in Non-Inventory Collateral (ex: Equipment):
    A Purchase-Money-Secured Party has priority over conflicting
    secured parties in collateral or its proceeds if the:
    a. PMSI is perfected at the time Debtor receives possession of
        the collateral; or
    b. PMSI is perfected within 10 Days after Debtor receives
        possession of collateral

(5) First in Time, First in Right: In all other cases (not specified
    above), priority between conflicting S/I's in the same collateral
    shall be determined according to the following rules:
    (a) First to Perfect:
         1. Conflicting S/I's Rank according to priority in Time of
             Filing or Perfection.

2. Priority dates back from the earlier of the first
    Perfection or Filing as long as later there is no period in
    which there is neither filing nor perfection (i.e. it is
    continuous).
(b) The First to Attach the collateral, if all conflicting S/I's
    are unperfected.

(6) The date of Filing/Perfection for collateral is the same date to
     apply to Proceeds of that collateral (for purposes for §9-312(5)).

(7) Future Advances:
     a) A S/P will maintain the SAME PRIORITY (under (5) above
         or §9-115(5)) in Future Advances (as per §9-301(4)) as he
         did in his original advance (loan) if the Future Advances are
         made:
         1) After the original S/I is perfected (by filing or
             possession (or under §9-115 or §9-116 on Investment
             property)); or
         2) Before/while the S/I is perfected

     b) In all other cases, a perfected S/I has priority from the date
         the advance was made (i.e. if you perfect collateral worth
         $10M and initial Lien is for $2M (covering a $2M cash
         advancement), a subsequent advance for $6M will have the
         same priority as the first loan's Lien)

§9-504: Secured Party's Right To Dispose After Default:

(1) Disposition of Collateral:
     i)   Upon default, a S/P may sell, lease, or otherwise dispose of
          collateral, either:
          a. In its present condition; or
          b. Following any commercially reasonable Preparation or
              Processing
     ii) Any sale of goods is subject to the Article on Sales (Article
          2)
     iii) Proceeds of the disposition shall be applied in the order of
          the following:
          (a) Selling Expenses - the reasonable expenses of retaking,
              holding, preparing for sale/lease, and selling/leasing
              (including reasonable attorney/legal expenses involved

(to the extend provided for by S/A (and not prohibited by law)))
- (b) Satisfaction of Debt - under his Security Agreement
- (c) Satisfaction of other Debts - secured by any Subordinate S/I holders if:
    1) Written notice of demand is received before distribution of the proceeds is completed; and
    2) Reasonable proof of S/I is presented (upon S/P's request)

(2) Deficiency and Surplus:
- a) If the S/I secures an Indebtedness, then, unless otherwise agreed:
    1) The Debtor is entitled to surplus of the sale from the S/P; and
    2) The S/P (seller) is entitled to deficiency from the Debtor
- b) If the underlying transaction was a Sale of Accounts or Chattel Paper then, ONLY if the Security Agreement provides:
    1) Debtor is entitled to surplus of the sale from the S/P; and
    2) S/P (seller) is entitled to deficiency from the Debtor

(3) Notice of Disposition:
- a) Disposition may be made by public or private proceedings.
- b) Disposition may be made as a one whole sale, or in separate Transactions (under separate contracts).
- c) Disposition sale must be made under any commercially reasonable terms (including the method, manner, time, and place of the sale)
- d) S/P is not required to sell all collateral to one party.
- e) Secured Party must notify Debtor of time and place of sale unless:
    1) After default, the Debtor agrees not to be notified; or
    2) Collateral is perishable; or
    3) Collateral is very sensitive to market (Value changes quickly); or
    4) Collateral is of a type customarily sold on a recognized market
- f) Notification:
    1) For Consumer Goods, no other notification must be sent

       2) For all other goods, notification must be sent to all other Secured Parties who sent Selling S/P a written notice of claim of an interest in the collateral.

  g) The S/P may purchase the collateral:
     1) At any Public Sale; or
     2) At a Private Sale, if
       a. The collateral is of the type sold in a recognized market; or
       b. The collateral is of a type which is subject to a widely distributed standard price quotation.

(4) Even if the Secured Party files to make a proper sale, a Purchaser takes Free of the S/P's (and any other subordinate's) right/interest in the collateral if:
  (a) Collateral sold public sale:
     1) Collateral is sold at a Public Sale. and
     2) Purchaser has no knowledge of any defects in sale process. and
     3) Purchaser does not buy in collusion with another Secured Party, the Person conducting the sale, or other bidders. and
  (b) The Purchaser acts in Good Faith (in all other sales (i.e. private sale)).

(5) Non-Qualifying Sales or Dispositions:
  a) A Person has rights and duties of a S/P if:
     1) She is liable to a S/P under either a:
       a. Guaranty; or
       b. Indorsement; or
       c. Repurchase Agreement; or
       d. The like; and
     2) She either:
       a. Receives a Transfer of collateral from the S/P; or
       b. Is subrogated to her rights
  b) Such a Transfer of collateral is not considered to be a "Sale or Disposition of Collateral" under Article 9.

§9-505: Disposition Of Collateral:

(1) Compulsory Disposition Of Collateral
   a) A S/P who has taken possession of the collateral must dispose of it under §9-504 within 90 Days after he takes possession if:
      1) The Debtor has paid 60% of either:
         a. The cash price of a Consumer Goods PMSI; or
         b. The loan of any other S/I in Consumer Goods and
      2) The Debtor has not signed a statement after default, renouncing or modifying his rights under this Part
   b) If the S/P does not dispose of the collateral (pursuant to §9-504) within 90 Days, the Debtor may recover on the S/P's liability either
      1) In conversion; or
      2) Under §9-507(1)
(2) Acceptance of Collateral as Discharge of Obligation
   a) In all other cases (not specified in §9-505(1)) the S/P may propose to retain the collateral as Discharge of Debtor's obligation (i.e. Strict Foreclosure)
   b) Notice:
      1) If the Debtor has not signed a statement renouncing or modifying his rights under this subsection, the S/P shall, after default send written notice of his proposal (to keep the collateral in satisfaction of the debt).
      2) Additional Notice:
         a. Consumer Goods: No other notice is required
         b. Other Cases: S/P must send a copy of the notice to all other Secured Parties who:
            1. Have sent the S/P a written notice of their aim to interest in the collateral; and
            2. S/P has received the notice before either:
               i)   The Debtor renounced or modified its rights; or
               ii) S/P sends Debtor notice to accept collateral as discharge.
      3) If anyone entitled to receive notice (including Debtor) objects to the S/P's proposal within 21 Days after notice was sent, S/P must dispose of the collateral (under §9-504).

4)   The S/P may keep the collateral in satisfaction of the Debtor's obligation if he does not receive any written objection (within <u>21 days</u>).

INDEX

ABANDONMENT, §554

ABSTENTION, §305

ADEQUATE PROTECTION, §361
Chapter 12, §1205

ADMINISTRATIVE EXPENSES,
§503

APPEALS
Bankruptcy, §28 U.S.C. 158
District Court, §28 U.S.C.
1291
Interlocutory, §28 U.S.C. 1292

ATTORNEYS
Compensation, §328, §330
Disclosure of Transactions
with Debtor, §329
Employment, §327
Sharing of Compensation,
§504
Priority of expenses and fees,
as administrative, §507

AUTOMATIC STAY, §362
Co-debtors §1201, §1301

AVOIDANCE POWERS OF
TRANSFERS
Disallowance of Secured Claim,
§506
Fraudulent Transfers, §544, §548
Liability of Transferee §551
Limitation on Avoidance, §546
Post-Petition Transfers, §549
Preferences, §547
Preservation for Estate, §550
Recovery from Transferees, §550
Strong Arm Powers, §544

BANK ACCOUNTS, MONEY OF
ESTATE, §345

BIRFURCATION, §506

BUSINESS OPERATIONS,
By Debtor-in-Possession, §1104,
§1204
By Trustee, §721, §1104, §1203
Chapter 13, Sole-Proprietor-
ship, §1304

CASH COLLATERAL, §363

CHILD SUPPORT AND
ALIMONY
Automatic Stay, effect on,
§362
Dischargeability, §524
Lien Avoidance, §522
Preferences, §547
Priority, §507

CLAIMS
Filing requirement, §501
Grounds for Disallowance, §502
Post-Petition claims for
Administrative Expenses, §503
Post-Petition claims
(Chapter 13) §1305
Priority claims, §726

CLOSING OF CASES, §350

CO-DEBTORS
Claims Against Estate, §509
Stay Agreements, §1113

COMMENCEMENT OF CASE,
§301, §303

COMMITTEES OF CREDITORS,
§705, §1102, §1103

COMMUNITY PROPERTY
Claims, §101
Discharge, §524
Property of Estate, §541

CONFIRMATION OF PLAN,
§1128, §1129

INDEX

CONVERSION OF CASES
Chapter 7, §706
Chapter 11, §1112
Chapter 12, §1208
Chapter 13, §1307
Effect of Conversion, §348

"CRAM-DOWN", §1129

CREDIT, OBTAINING POST-
PETITION, §364

CREDITOR COMMITTEES, §705,
§1102, §1103

CUSTODIAN, TURNOVER, §543

DEBT LIMITATIONS, §109
Adjustment by Congress, §104

DEBTOR-IN-POSSESSION, §1101,
§1107, §1203, §1304

DEBTOR'S DUTIES
Meeting of Creditors, §341
Schedules and Papers, §521, 1203

DEFENSES AVAILABLE TO
ESTATE, §558

DEFINITIONS, §101, §102

DISCHARGE
Chapter 7, §727
Chapter 11, §1141
Chapter 12, §.~ 1228
Chapter 13, §1328
Effect of discharge, §524
Exceptions, objections, §523

DISCLOSURE STATEMENT,
§1125

DISMISSAL OF CASE
Chapter 7, §707
Chapter 11, §1112

Chapter 12, §1208
Chapter 13, §1307
Effect of Dismissal, §349

DISTRIBUTION ON CLAIMS,
§727

EQUITABLE SUBORDINATION ,
§510

ESTATE PROPERTY, §541

EXPENSES, ADMNISTRATIVE,
§503

EXCLUSIVITY PERIOD, §1121

EXECUTORY CONTRACTS, §365

EXEMPTIONS, §522

EXEMPTIONS, EXCEPTIONS,
§522

FILING OF PETITION,
REQUIREMENTS FOR §109

FINANCING, POST-PETITION,
§364

FRAUDULENT TRANSFERS,
§544, §548

GUARANTORS, §509

HYPOTHETICAL CREDITOR OR
PURCHASER (see Trustee and
Avoidance Powers)

IMPAIRMENT OF CLAIMS, §1124

INJUNCTIONS, §105

INTELLECTUAL PROPERTY,
CONTRACTS INVOLVING, §365

INDEX

INTERIM TRUSTEE, §701

INVOLUNTARY CASES, §303

JOINT CASES, §302

LEASES AND EXECUTORY
CONTRACTS, §365
Claims for Termination, §502

LIENS,
Definition, §101
Disallowance of Sec. Claim, §506
Fraudulent Transfers, §544, §548
Limitation on Avoidance, §546
Post-Petition Effect of Security
Interest, §552
Preferences, §547
Statutory liens, §724
Strong Arm Powers, §544
Subordination, §510, §724
Tax liens, §724

LIQUIDATION
Distribution of property, §724,
725, §726
Priority claims, §726
Subordination of claims, §510

MEETING OF CREDITORS, §341

MONEY OF ESTATES, §345

NOTICE OF FILING OF CASE, §342

PARTNERSHIPS, TRUSTEE'S
Claim Against Partners, §723

PETITION, FILING OF, §109,
§301, §302

PLANS
Chapter 11
Classification of Claims, §1122
Confirmation Hearing, §1128
Confirmation Requirements,
§1129
Contents of Plan, §1123

Cram-down, §1129
Disclosure Statement, §1125
Filing of Plan, §1121
Modification of Plan, §1127
Revocation of Confirmation
Order, §1144

Chapter 13
Acceptance by Secured
Creditor, §132
Confirmation Hearing, §1324
Confirmation Reqs, §1325
Contents of Plan, §1322
Filing of Plan, §1321
Modification of Plan
After Confirmation, §1329
Before Confirmation, §1323
Payments Under Plan, §1326
Revocation of Confirmation
Order, §1330

-PETITION
Administrative Expenses, §503
Claims for Administrative
Expenses, §503
Chapter 13 claims, §1305
Effect of Security Interest, §552
Financing, §364
Transfers, §549

PREFERENTIAL TRANS, §547

PRIORITY CLAIMS, §507

PROOF OF CLAIM
Allowance, Objections, §502
Filing, §501

PROPERTY OF ESTATE,
Composition, §541
Chapter 12, §1207
Chapter 13, §1306
Content, Scope, §541
Use, Sale or Lease, §363

PUBLIC RECORDS, ACCESS, §107

323

INDEX

REORGANIZATION
Conversion, §348, §1112
Cram-down, §1129
Dischargeability, §523, §524, §1141
Debtor-in-possession, §1101
Plan (see plan)
Secured claims (see Secured Claims)
Trustee (see Trustee)

REAFFIRMATION
AGREEMENTS, §524

RECLAMATION, §546

REDEMPTION OF
COLLATERAL, §554, §722

RELIEF FROM STAY, §362

REPURCHASE CONTRACTS, §549

RESTITUTION
Non-Dischargeable, §1328

SECURED CLAIMS
Determination, Valuation, §506
Post-Petition Effect of Security
Interest, §552

SELF-INCRIMINATION,
IMMUNITY, §344

SETOFF, GENERAL, §553
Defense to Turnover, §542
Secured Claim, §506
Stay, §362

STATUS CONFERENCE, §105

STATUTORY LIENS, §545

STRONG-ARM POWERS, §544

SUBORDINATION OF CLAIMS,
§507, §510

SUBROGATION CLAIMS, §507, §509

SUBSTANTIAL ABUSE, §707

SUPER-PRIORITY
Claims, §726(b), §507
Failure of Adequate Protection, §507
Obtaining Credit, §364

SUPPLEMENTAL INJUNCTIONS, §524

TAXES
Administrative Expense, §503
Automatic Stay Applicability, §362
Liability, Determination of, §505
Liens, Penalties, §724
Priority Claims, §507
Special Provisions, §346, §728, §1146, §1231

TRANSFEREE
Liability of Transferee §551
Recovery from Transferees, §550

TRUSTEE
Appointment in Chapter 11, §1104
Avoidance Powers (see Avoidance)
Compensation, §326, 330, 331
Duties
Chapter 7, §704
Chapter 11, §1104
Chapter 12, §1202
Chapter 13, §1302
Election in Chapter 7, §702
Eligibility to Serve, §321
Interim Trustee, §701
Qualification, §322
Removal, §324
Role and Capacity, §323

INDEX

Successor Trustee, §703
Vacancy, §325

TURNOVER OF PROPERTY OF
ESTATE, §542, §543

UNCLAIMED PROPERTY, §347

UNITED STATES TRUSTEE, §307

UNEXPIRED LEASES, §363, §365

UNSECURED CLAIMS, §506

VOIDABLE TRANSFERS, §547

VOLUNTARY CASE FILING, §301